The Divine and
Human Comedy of
Andrew M. Greeley

The Divine and Human Comedy of Andrew M. Greeley

Allienne R. Becker

Foreword by Andrew M. Greeley

Contributions to the Study of American Literature, Number 7

GREENWOOD PRESS
Westport, Connecticut • London

Library of Congress Cataloging-in-Publication Data

Becker, Allienne R.
    The divine and human comedy of Andrew M. Greeley / by Allienne R. Becker;
foreword by Andrew M. Greeley.
       p. cm.—(Contributions to the study of American literature, ISSN 1092–6356 ; no. 7)
    Includes bibliographical references and index.
    ISBN 0–313–31564–7 (alk. paper)
    1. Greeley, Andrew M., 1928– —Criticism and interpretation. 2. Balzac, Honorâ de,
1799–1850—Influence. 3. Catholic Church—In literature. 4. Catholics in literature. 5.
Christian fiction, American—History and criticism. 6. Christianity and literature—United
States—History—20th century. I. Title. II. Series
PS3557.R358Z55   2000
813′.54—dc21   00–025114

British Library Cataloguing in Publication Data is available.

Library of Congress Catalog Card Number: 00–25114
ISBN: 0–313–31564–7
ISSN: 1092–6356

First published in 2000

Greenwood Press, 88 Post Road West, Westport, CT 06881
An imprint of Greenwood Publishing Group, Inc.
www.greenwood.com

Printed in the United States of America

The paper used in this book complies with the
Permanent Paper Standard issued by the National
Information Standards Organization (Z39.48–1984).

10 9 8 7 6 5 4 3 2 1

To Isidore H. Becker—my husband, my proofreader, and my best friend

Contents

Foreword

An author approaches literary criticism of his work with a certain unease. He understands that (classic) criticism involves reading a book, understanding it, and interpreting it. Will the critic really read what the author has said? Will he understand it? How will she interpret it? If said author is then asked to write a foreword to the critic's book, he must say whether he thinks the critic has read his work generously and understood it sympathetically. Then he must address the question of whether the critic's interpretation seems valid—or to be more precise whether it does not seem invalid.

It is easy for me to say that Professor Becker has been both generous and sympathetic. I believe that anyone who buys a book or at least reads one someone else bought has the right to have an opinion. (Those who have opinions without reading the work are to be dismissed without further consideration.) Often it has seemed to me that some readers are neither generous nor sympathetic because they begin their reading with preconceived notions. That is their privilege. I much prefer, however, critics who are willing to give me the benefit of the doubt, who are willing to dialogue with my work with open minds and even open hearts.

As to the issue of interpretation, I find surprise in Professor Becker's interpretations, but not invalidity. I was not aware when I was writing of many of the themes she discusses—rarely I suspect is an author aware of such matters, so taken up is he (or she) with the telling of the story. But I cannot deny that the themes are there. Perhaps they were lurking in the far reaches (or, to change the metaphor, in the dark subbasements) of my preconscious as I tried to get down on computer screen what the characters were doing and saying.

But what about Professor Becker's Honoré de Balzac's model? At first I admit that I was astonished. I knew he was a famous French novelist, but I had never read him. After I read Professor Becker's first essay, I began, naturally enough, to read him. It is surely the case that like Balzac I am trying to create a whole world with my stories, though, so far, not one with more than six hundred characters! As for the other comparisons Professor Becker makes, I must leave judgment to the readers of this book.

The other matter that surprised me was her suggestion that there was anger in my novels. Graham Greene wrote somewhere that the job of a novelist is to be an angry critic of his society. I smiled at that, because I thought that by such a standard I was not much of a novelist. However, Professor Becker's quotes on this subject leave little doubt in my mind that there is indeed a strain of anger in my stories, although it seems to me that some of the anger is not politically correct. Neither false prophets of reform in the Church who try to impose their ideologies on others nor prosecuting attorneys who abuse their power are fashionable targets.

I do not apologize, however, for my anger at either assault on human dignity and freedom.

I am grateful to Professor Becker for her generosity, her sympathy, and for her challenge that I continue to defend dignity and freedom from those with both church and state who would violate it.

Andrew M. Greeley

1

Introduction

While having lunch with Andrew Greeley once in Boston, I began to notice similarities between him and Honoré de Balzac. As he talked enthusiastically about the main female character, Gabriella Light, in *Angel Fire*, the book he was writing at that time, he spoke of her so realistically that it was as if he were discussing someone whom he knew very well. It was then I recalled how the great novelist Honoré de Balzac spoke the same way about his characters. After he had created some two thousand of them, they were so real to him that he could no longer recall which people, when they came to mind, were real and which ones were his fictional creations. I began to notice certain other similarities between the two novelists Greeley and Balzac; this is the reason for using the French author's title, *The Human Comedy*, in the title of this book.

Both writers have explored many forms of the prose narrative. Balzac never thought of himself as a "novelist," but as a "romancier" or a writer of *romans*, *roman* being the French word for a rather long prose narrative of adventures, the study of customs or of characters, or the analysis of feelings or of passions. The French word *roman* was applied to this kind of fiction because formerly stories of this kind had been written in the Latin language, stories, for example, such as *Amadis of Gaul*. Therefore a story written in the Roman manner was dubbed a *roman* in French and in other languages as well, such as German.

English language literary criticism distinguishes between the novel and the romance with the essential difference being the way in which the author conceives of his characters. The *romancier* creates characters that are stylized and can often be identified with archetypes. The novelist, on the other hand, works with the social order and personality. However, as Northrop Frye observes in *The Anatomy of Criticism*, "Pure examples of either form are never found; there is hardly any modern romance that could not be made out to be a novel, and vice versa" (305). Both Greeley and Balzac have written some stories that can be described as romances, whereas others are more properly called novels. For the most part, their fiction is a blending of the two forms. One could apply the term *romantic novel* to some of their works. Furthermore, both writers have used a blending of the techniques of realism and romanticism in their fiction. Fantasy, mysticism, the paranormal as well as harsh realism are to be found in the writings of each. In referring to both Greeley and Balzac, the term novelist will be applied while recognizing that the term *romancier* or *romancer* would be equally applicable.

Honoré de Balzac (1799–1850) is famous for his monumental work *La comédie humaine (The Human Comedy)*, comprising about ninety novels. At the present time, Greeley has written about forty long novels which on the library shelf take up almost as much space as Balzac's *Comedy*. People inquire of Greeley as they did of Balzac how it is possible to write so much. In a letter to Madame Zulma Carraud, Balzac talks of his writing, giving us some idea of his work habits. "I must tell you I am buried under a mountain of work. My life alternates mechanically: I go to bed at six or seven in the evening, like the fowls; at one in the morning I am awakened, and I work till eight . . . (*Correspondence* I 349). Later writing again to the same woman he says, "I have only a single good quality, it's the persistent energy of rats, who would gnaw through steel if they lived as long as crows" (*Correspondence* II 69). Greeley's schedule resembles Balzac's. He retires at about eight in the evening and begins his writing day about four in the morning and continues working until the rest of the world wakes up and the phone, the fax, and the doorbell demand his attention.

Interestingly many people of Balzac's day considered his fiction to be a collection of erotica. Of course that time is long past. Balzac defended himself against those who held this view of his fiction and other detractors in the introduction of *The Human Comedy*, saying that the time had not yet come for an impartial judgment to be made of his work (I 8–10). The same comment can be made to those blind, unlettered people who can see in Greeley's fiction only "steamy novels." It is the intention of this book to make the impartial judgment of his fiction that is needed. Catholic clerics and the editors and writers for pseudo-intellectual Catholic magazines do not have the proper literary background and training to evaluate his work. They are also probably uncomfortable in reading his works because he holds up a mirror for them in his fiction, just as Balzac does for his contemporaries, in which they can behold themselves and the Church based on the empirical data that he has collected and evaluated as a sociologist. Those who have no desire to change find it easier to denigrate his novels than to accept his challenge to make the corrections and improvements needed. Some also seem to be so preoccupied with sex that they cannot see the broad sociological portrait of society that he draws.

According to Balzac, when people want to destroy an author, they label him immoral if he depicts something evil or abusive in society so that it can be corrected. Balzac is especially incensed that when he depicts the evils of society and of individuals guilty of sexual sin, his critics call him immoral, but they do not comment on the morality of other portions of his work in which he portrays virtuous people as a contrast to the evil ones. He does treat such themes as homosexuality, for example, in the story of Vautrin who is in love with Lucien de Rubempré. He does have scenes of cruelty with much lust, passion, and sexual sin. In *La cousine Bette*, the Baron Hulot is consumed with lust. Often Balzac does depict a dark side to sex which is like the "demonic sex" sometimes in Greeley's fiction. Nevertheless, Balzac insists, and rightly so, that there are more virtuous characters in *The Human Comedy* than evil ones with evil being punished when it does occur. In fact, many of his characters are of irreproachable virtue. Very clearly his characters are punished for breaking society's laws. Yet Balzac demonstrates great sympathy for his characters neither accusing nor excusing them, but accepting them as they are in a nonjudgmental way, leaving it to God to separate the sheep from the goats. As a good realist, actually the father of the realist movement, he does not moralize and neither does Greeley.

Lamenting that his works are not understood or appreciated, Balzac defends them by saying that history depicts life like it is, and therefore so does he; only romances depict a better world than the one in which we live. The same comments can be made about Greeley's fiction. Some people in reading *The Cardinal Sins*, for example, are so taken up with the sexual sins of one priest that they cannot even see the beautiful example of chastity and priestly holiness of the other priest in the novel whose virtues are a perfect contrast to the former one's sins.

Both Greeley and Balzac approach their fiction from a sociological perspective. Greeley, an eminent sociologist and professor of social science at the University of Chicago, portrays society in his writings as only a sociologist with years of collecting and analyzing empirical data can do. Balzac's avowed purpose in writing his *Comedy* is to portray the society of his time, the history of its mores, manners, and morals. His fiction has such a wealth of detailed observation that the people of his day could not believe he wrote from experience. Some saw him as a hunter of documents, a tireless investigator, a "father confessor," who recorded his observations. Others said he wrote from intuition and genius. Balzac explained "I carry a whole society in my head" (Bertault 32). His documentary style of writing came from his going to a place and soaking up its atmosphere so he could write convincingly about it. Balzac believed that ethnic and geographical influences are very strong on people, whom he saw as being a product of the environment in which they live. So precise is he in his portrayal of his age that he can be considered as an historian of the nineteenth century. In fact Anatole France considered him to be the greatest historian of modern France. Others agree that his fiction is enlightening. Friedrich Engels wrote in a letter to Margaret Harkness in 1888, "I have learned more [from Balzac] than from all the professional historians, economists, and statisticians put together" (Marx and Engels 43).

Since Balzac believes that man is a function of his environment and the environment is a function of man, he writes exhaustively describing the details of the milieu in which his characters live. Architecture, furniture, clothing, all play an important part in his fiction. Similarly Greeley carefully describes the clothing of his characters and their milieu.

Balzac's original idea in writing *The Human Comedy* was to compare humanity and animality. The French naturalist, Georges Louis Leclerc, Comte de Buffon (1707–88), had written a book describing the animal species which shows that animals take their form from the environment in which they develop. Society also changes people and molds them according the conditions in which they live. Frequently it is to be noted Balzac actually uses animal imagery to describe a character. The character will be consistently described in terms that identify him or her with a particular animal. This technique can also be found in Greeley's fiction. For example, feline imagery is used to describe Finnabair in *The Magic Cup*.

Andrew Greeley portrays the society of America, as he has experienced it, and from the knowledge and empirical data he has compiled as a sociologist. Ethnicity is very important in both the works of Balzac and those of Greeley. As Paris is the city which is at the heart of Balzac's fiction, Chicago is at the center of Greeley's. Both depict the Catholic society of their age and country—Balzac nineteenth-century French, Greeley twentieth-century Irish American. Both are Catholic writers. Balzac, seen as the initiator of the novel of ideas, or apologetic novel, stands at the head of a long tradition of writers that includes Bourget, Bazin, Péguy, Mauriac, Bernanos, Green, and finally Greeley.

During his career Balzac went from hostility toward Catholicism to embracing it and praising it in his fiction. On March 13, 1850, on the occasion of his marriage to Madame Hanska, he went to confession and received communion. The day of his death August 16, 1850, he received the Sacrament of Extreme Unction and died in the embrace of the faith. There are many comments in support of the Catholic faith in his fiction. For example, in *La vieille fille* he speaks of "la sublime religion catholique" (IV 260), the sublime Catholic religion, and in *Le médecin de campagne* he writes of "la sublime et divine idée de la communion catholique," the sublime and divine idea of the Catholic communion (VIII 438). There are many priests—confessors and spiritual directors—in his fiction. Some are very holy men. One recalls the beautiful death of César Birotteau in the presence of his confessor, l'abbé Loraux whose face had been made sublime by the practice of Catholic virtues and emitted a celestial radiance (V 455, 591). His priests are by and large, like most of his characters, driven by a desire for power, but suffer when they sin. Similarly some of Greeley's priests are hungry for personal power and gain and commit gross sexual sins, whereas others are outstanding examples of priestly holiness.

Believing that Catholicism created modern societies and will preserve them, Balzac writes in the *L'avant propos*, the introduction to *The Human Comedy*, that Christianity, specifically Catholicism, is the most powerful element of social order and is a complete system for the repression of the depraved tendencies of man (I 8). A writer, in his opinion, should try to lead his country back to religion. He finds that Catholicism offers the hope of forgiveness which can make the sinner sublime. Heaven is at stake in the battles that his characters wage, as it is in the skirmishes of the people in Greeley's fiction. Most of Balzac's sympathetic characters are practicing Catholics.

Radiant rays of faith and hope and glorious transformations of souls illuminate the fiction of Balzac which takes its beginning in earthly sorrows and leads to heaven. In selecting *The Human Comedy* as the title of his great opus, Balzac borrowed from the title *The Divine Comedy* by Alighieri Dante (1265–1321). However Dante's comedy begins, not on earth as does Balzac's, but in hell and ends in paradise. In the two novels that Balzac considered his best work, *Louis Lambert* and *Seraphita*, the lead characters have a deep longing for heaven and the presence of God. In *Les proscrits* we read that it is a question of giving man wings to penetrate the sanctuary where God hides himself from our sight (X 335). Interestingly Dante Alighieri is a character in this story. Similarly Andrew Greeley also tries to penetrate the sanctuary of God who he says is the main character in all his novels.

Popular success came to Balzac with the publication of *Physiologie du mariage*, which was considered to contain some spicy stories and salacious remarks and especially excited the curiosity of his women readers. This work in which Balzac discusses many aspects of marriage can be compared, to a certain extent, with Greeley's *Love and Play* and *Sexual Intimacy*. In April 1830 two new novelettes written especially for women completely won them over. The so-called scandal caused by his fiction served only to increase his popularity with his women readers, both middle class and aristocratic, who considered him to be *their* novelist and who wrote him thousands of letters and brought him tremendous popular success. Women loved him; they confided in him and he in turn consoled them. Andrew Greeley's experience parallels Balzac's also in his popularity with women who compose the largest segment of his readers and who keep his mail box filled with their letters.

Balzac's popularity incensed Catholic critics, described by Philippe Bertault, as "pen-pushers without intelligence," who reproached him "with a kind of vicious ill-temper" (191). Greeley also, because he is popular, has his detractors who are equally vicious and lacking in ability to appreciate the depth of his fiction and the sociological and religious truths it contains.

Popularity has always been the bane and the blessing of novelists. Popular fiction is regarded with disdain by the literary establishment. However one can be a popular novelist without writing popular fiction. Popular fiction is a particular kind of writing which is different from the fiction of Balzac and Greeley. According to Northrop Frye, one of the outstanding literary critics of the twentieth century, popular literature is fiction that is written for the sole purpose of entertaining and amusing its readers (*The Secular Scripture* 21). Since both Greeley and Balzac have avowed serious purposes in writing their fiction, they cannot be described as writers of popular fiction. In addition to the sociological portrayals of society that one finds in the fiction of both these writers, Greeley states that he writes not to educate people but to illumine them—to give them light; Balzac says that an author should be a tutor to his readers. Therefore the fiction of Balzac and Greeley belong to what is called "serious literature" by the literary establishment, because they portray something of the life of their times, human nature, ethnicity, and religion, among other things. Examples of popular fiction in the contemporary United States are the writings of Stephen King, Anne Rice, Louis L'Amour, and others who write only to entertain their readers and whose fiction makes no attempt to do more than that.

This brings us to one more way in which we can distinguish the novel from the romance. The romance is told primarily for the sake of the story and it is written as a commercial product. According to Frye, the author of the romance has compromised himself by the writing of popular literature (*Anatomy* 41). The novelist, on the other hand, has moral dignity, because of the serious content that he puts in his story. Nevertheless some popular writers create what the literary establishment considers "classics." For example, Nathaniel Hawthorne, Edgar Allan Poe, Washington Irving, to list but a few American authors, are writers of popular fiction—they wrote only to entertain—but are now considered to be part of the literary élite.

A hundred years from now, if someone wants to get a good picture of the Catholic Church and Catholic society in twentieth-century America, he will be able to find it in the fiction of Andrew Greeley who has the courage to portray Catholic life the way it is, and not the way the hierarchy would like it to be idealized. His commitment to truth is very evident in everything he writes as a scholar, a priest, and a teller of tales.

One technique employed by Greeley and invented by Balzac deserves special mention. It is that of having characters appear in more than one novel, giving them an added dimension of reality and making it possible for the author to create a society. Characters who do not know one another might, for example, have the same doctor or lawyer and thus be linked together. Often a character who was the protagonist in one novel will reappear in later novels as a minor figure, but since the reader knows him or her from previous fiction, the character enters the new novels as a well-developed character instead of a flat one, as minor figures usually are. The reader learns that since the previous encounter with the person in an earlier novel, the character has experienced many things and the reader is eager to know what has happened. This gives Greeley's fiction and Balzac's a richness that would not otherwise be possible in that they both portray not just individuals but an entire society.

Although Balzac uses the word *comedy* in the sense that Dante uses it, signifying a happy ending, there is comedy in his fiction in the usual sense of the word, meaning humor. Often, however, Balzac's humor is grim and ironic with a sense of the incongruous and the absurd. His characters, nevertheless, are usually better off at the end of the novel that they were at the beginning. Balzac does not display the sparkling wit and lively humor that Greeley does as we shall see when we explore his novels in depth.

When we compare Balzac and Greeley from the point of style, Greeley is by far the superior stylist. Many people have said that Balzac's style of writing is not good. Although he displays force, vitality, and variety, at times his prose is stilted, pedantic, or clumsy and even in poor taste or bogged down by his own personal observations on sociology or psychology. His phrases are often overloaded and exaggerated, awkward, monotonous, theatrical, but also colorful, picturesque, exact, and rich. A tendency to sensationalism and melodrama are to be found in his works. His long descriptions, often using a technical vocabulary, become tedious and boring as do his philosophical disquisitions. By contrast Greeley's style is clear-cut, to the point, witty, without personal observations and comments.

Some of Balzac's characters are bigger than life—they are romantic. Sometimes these grand romantic characters are placed in trivial circumstance. His realistic characters tend to be mediocre people. Being interested in sociology, Balzac represents many social classes. He often refers to people as "the banker," "the policeman," "the lawyer." We find this also in the fiction of Greeley who, for example, refers to his characters as "Mike the Cop" or "George the Bean Counter." A broad range of characters from top-level Vatican dignitaries to Chicago Mafia types appear in Greeley's pages, since he too depicts the society of his world. Both authors write extensively about crime and justice. In Balzac's world the courts back the criminals more often than they do the victims. Greeley also points out the failings of the legal system. Both authors write much about money, which always plays a significant part in realistic fiction. The members of the stock exchange, bankers, and accountants figure in their works. To both authors love, marriage, and integration into society are important.

Another stylistic device that is common to both Balzac and Greeley is the mentioning of real people and places in their fiction and even having them take part in the action of the plot. Kings of France Louis XVIII and Charles X appear in Balzac's fiction, as do actual members of the nobility; in Greeley's novels we find the Kennedys, Vatican officials, and other real people as characters. In the fiction of both, environments are very significant with characters behaving differently in different settings.

A documentary style is found in the fiction of both Balzac and Greeley. Both use actual documents to develop plots and to give necessary exposition. Letters, newspaper clippings, and the like are commonly found in the novels of both.

Since Balzac borrowed from Dante in choosing the title for *The Human Comedy* and since we too have borrowed from Dante's title in naming this book *The Divine and Human Comedy of Andrew Greeley*, it is necessary to say a few words about Dante and his *Comedy*. In his letter to Can Grande Della Scala, his friend and patron in Verona, Dante wrote that he had taken the word *comedy* and broadened its meaning so that it was no longer limited to the amusing or farcical. Old Greek Comedy, as exemplified by Aristophanes, contained very little humor and was replete with the ridiculous designed to make people laugh at something unnatural or obscene. Characters would do something childish or absurd and out of keeping with their true character. Ridicule became so intense that the government finally forbade the mention of names and details of incidents. The so-called New Greek Comedy strove to express the ethos of people, or character.

Dante conceives of comedy as a work with a happy ending written in "lax and humble" language (Dante, *Eleven Letters* 188).

Furthermore, Dante rejects the idea of the ancients that comedy must deal only with humble people. This view is embraced by both Balzac and Greeley who do not restrict their fiction to depicting people of humble station in life and who use language which corresponds to that used by people of the class represented. For example, Balzac uses the jargon of thieves in their conversations and Greeley uses the slang of teenagers when they converse. Greeley's language is more lax than Balzac's because he uses the speech of contemporary America which tends of be rather colorful, direct, and even scatological.

Since for Dante the world was full of symbolic meaning, his writings are symbolic. In *Il convivio*, Dante explains that his writings are polysemous and to be understood in four ways—literally, allegorically, morally, and anagogically. Truth is hidden in the literal interpretation and one should find profit in reading his fiction. Furthermore, in the anagogic interpretation, he "gives intimation of higher matters belonging to the eternal glory" (*Il convivio* 187). Balzac, of course, loves to philosophize and in his fiction and in Greeley's also are found "intimations of higher matters."

Both Greeley and Balzac conceive of comedy as the depiction of the ethos of people and of character. In their sociological approach to fiction they are similar. While Greeley the sociologist resembles Balzac, Greeley the priest is more like Dante. In agreement with Dante, Greeley considers everything as sacrament and symbolizing reality. In his view "all is grace." Both Dante and Greeley are immersed in the Love that moves the sun and the other stars. Both are in love with Lady Wisdom, called "Beatrice" by Dante. When one finds her, one finds beatitude, in Greeley's fiction and in Dante's. God is the main character in all of Greeley's novels, the writing of which he considers to be his most priestly work.

Because of the points of similarity among Greeley, Balzac, and Dante, the title of this book, *The Divine and Human Comedy of Andrew Greeley*, is most appropriate. This book will show the following: Greeley writes novels of ideas in the Balzacian tradition, works that have as their avowed purpose the illumination of the reader and therefore cannot be classified as popular fiction, which is written solely to entertain and amuse. His fiction, while focusing on the Chicago Irish, depicts the manners, ideas, and conflicts of contemporary society in general and those of the Catholic Church in particular. As a sociologist, Greeley has an extensive knowledge of popular culture and displays it in every story. When he depicts the sins and failings of both secular society and members of the Church, it is in hope of reforming them and making the world a better place. His satire can be blistering and biting as he portrays the sin, weakness, inadequacy, ineptitude, and incompetence that he observes in the world around him. Some of the aspects of society that he satirizes are the media, academia, the legal system and law enforcement, the Mafia, militant feminism, and the Catholic Church. Only an experienced priest who is skilled in working with people could create fiction in which the human soul is so well analyzed and depicted. It is his unique blending of sociology and religion that makes his fiction timeless and universal. All his fiction is a mixture of comedy and tragedy. Sometimes violence overtakes his characters, even snuffing out their lives. However in Greeley's divine comedy, God is the great comedian and life always triumphs over death in what he calls "the great cosmic joke" and brings about a glorious ending. Greeley uses as one of his main themes the metaphor of human love, including sexual love, to illustrate what the love of God is like. The search for the Holy Grail, the search for love, is a theme that occurs frequently. Another theme is that of having a person in middle life, usually disillusioned, returning to his hometown, where he will find a second chance for happiness. Greeley's fiction always shows that people can have a second chance, and even a third or fourth or more, to find happiness. For this reason, Christmas and Easter themes abound in Greeley's stories as his characters are renewed and become "resurrection people" who have arisen from the ashes of the past to live in newness of life. Greeley is equally adept in many genres—legends, myths, romances, novels, science fiction, fantasy, and *le roman fleuve*, among others. In fact, he has created a new literary genre, the sociological apocalyptic novel. His speculative fiction, which he also uses to illumine his readers, is unlike that of most speculative fiction, which is written solely to entertain and in which the characters remain flat and undeveloped. Greeley's characters in all his fiction grow and are not the same at the end of the story as they were at the beginning. His prose is rich; his language is colorful and humorous. Accomplished in the art of caricature, Greeley can create memorable characters with just a few words. Since his characters tend to reappear in novel after novel, he creates an entire society as did Balzac in *La comédie humaine.*

Greeley achieved fame as a novelist in 1981 with the publication of *The Cardinal Sins. Time* magazine brought the news of this event to its readers in a detailed article. This was, however, not Greeley's first book for he was already world-renowned for his work in sociology, having authored scores of scholarly books in that field. It was not even his first full-length fiction, for in 1979 he had published *The Magic Cup* followed by *Death in April* (1980). However, with *The Cardinal Sins*, which has sold over three million copies, it became obvious that a serious new novelist had arrived.

Why does an eminent sociologist, scholar, university professor,and priest of the Roman Catholic Church become a novelist? The answer to the question is as multifaceted as is Andrew Greeley himself. Shortly after his ordination to the priesthood in May of 1954, Greeley was assigned to Christ the King parish in Beverly in the Chicago area. About a year and a half after his arrival at Christ the King, Providence knocked on his rectory door in the person of a certain Henriette Macklin who asked him if he would write for the high school magazine *Hightime* on a regular basis. The two short stories he wrote for Ms. Macklin and *Hightime* were his first fiction. Soon thereafter the editor of *Today* magazine for teens asked him to write stories for them. Bowing to the clerical idea that priests do not write fiction, Greeley at first wrote under the pen name of Lawrence Moran. When in the summer of 1958, he wrote an article which he presented at the Catholic Social

Action Conference held that year in Chicago, Ralph Gorman, editor for *Sign* magazine, asked him to rewrite the material he had presented for publication. Having decided that his opinions were worth consideration, he decided to begin publishing under his own name.

Impressed by the articles in *Sign*, Philip Scharper, editor at Sheed and Ward, asked Greeley to write a book on the same subject as the articles. At first he declined, but later decided that someone needed to write about the changes taking place in the Church. "Since nobody else seemed ready to do it, then I'd do it myself," Greeley decided (*Confessions* 174). The same kind of reasoning led him to write novels later on. His first book *The Church in the Suburbs* was published with the permission of Cardinal Strich. Later Cardinal Meyer read what Greeley had written, thought it was excellent, and urged him to continue writing with his complete and total support. The imprimatur for his first book was granted June 8, 1959, launching a new author who has been making lot of waves ever since.

In hopes of serving the Church with his skills in sociology, in 1960 Greeley entered graduate school at the University of Chicago with the Cardinal's blessing. For his Master's degree, he made a comprehensive study on "the peaceful self-segregation of Catholics and Protestants in an affluent quasi-suburban community like Beverly" (*Confessions* 204). In the spring of 1961 he passed his preliminary examinations for the doctorate. His doctoral dissertation, proving his thesis that being Catholic is no longer an obstacle to an academic career or intellectual excellence, was published in 1963 as *Religion and Career*. In only twenty months he had completed his Ph D. in sociology. After finishing a postdoctoral, he was invited to remain permanently at the University of Chicago and is still there engaged in research as professor of social science in the university's National Opinion Research Center.

The academic education of this priest of the Chicago archdiocese has resulted in an unending series of books. *Life for the Wanderer* (1969), *The Friendship Game* (1970), *The Jesus Myth* (1971), *The Sinai Myth* (1972), *Unsecular Man* (1972), *Sexual Intimacy* (1973), *Ethnicity of the United States* (1974), *Love and Play* (1975), *The Sociology of the Paranormal* (1975), *The American Catholic* (1976), *Neighborhood* (1977), *The Mary Myth* (1977), *The Religious Imagination* (1976), *Religion a Secular Theory* (1976), *The Making of the Popes* (1978), *Confessions of a Parish Priest: An Autobiography* (1986), *The Catholic Myth: The Behavior and Beliefs of American Catholics* (1990), *Faithful Attraction: Discovering Intimacy, Love, and Fidelity in American Marriage* (1991), *Religion as Poetry* (1995), *Sex: The Catholic Experience* (1995), and *The Catholic Imagination* (2000) are but a few of approximately 140 titles. In his opinion his most significant contribution as a sociologist is the work he has done on the religious imagination. He considers his work on Mary as the sacrament of the womanliness of God to be his most significant contribution to religious thought.

For sixteen years, Greeley also wrote a very successful column in the Catholic press and for nine of those years, three columns a week for the secular press, all of which brought him large quantities of mail. Because of clerical opposition, he stopped writing the column in 1983, but later resumed it in 1986 in the *Chicago Sun-Times* for which he still writes today.

Interestingly, this extremely versatile author published a children's story with the title *Nora Maeve and Seby* in 1976. He has also written a lot of poetry some of which was published under the title *The Sense of Love* (1992).

But why novels and romances? Why after spending twenty-five years in scholarly analysis and piercing commentary on the American Catholic Church during the transitional years since Vatican II does he begin writing fiction while still continuing his unrelenting pace of writing scholarly works in sociology and religion? Fiction began to interest him when he was fourteen years old and read his first adult novel, *The Robe,* by Lloyd C. Douglas. Since the book had been denounced in the Catholic press, young Greeley felt some guilt about reading it. Despite slight fears that he was going against his Catholic heritage, he read the book, unable to put it aside until it was finished. This was the beginning of a long intellectual and imaginative process that led to fiction writing about forty years later. Reading *The Robe* made him reflect on the relationship between fiction and the religious imagination. Experiencing for the first time the power of a novelist to create a world that would stir his religious imagination—for Douglas made the people he had learned about in religion classes in school come alive—he imagined that Douglas's Diana looked like a girl in his neighborhood, a girl whom he depicted forty years later in his own *Ascent into Hell.* Reading *The Robe* was a very strong religious experience for Greeley. As he explains, "Jesus and his friends became real to me those late evenings in the quiet of my room in a way they had never been before. It was a turning point in my life" (*Confessions* 87).

He began to wonder why more people did not write stories like *The Robe.* Later he read *The Nazarene* and *The Apostle* by Sholem Asch and *Quo Vadis* by Henry Sienckiwicz. He asked himself why the Church did not use fiction to transmit its heritage. Still later he found the answer to this question. "Religious leaders, trained in dry, propositional theology distrust story; they demand that the story be edifying (which the parables of Jesus were not), that the characters be saints, not sinners in need of salvation (as all the readers are), and that the storyteller offend not even the most timid of the 'faithful,' a demand which would have put Jesus himself on the Index of Forbidden Storytellers" (*Confessions* 87).

Eventually it was sociology that forced Greeley to become a storyteller. In the seminary he had been taught to view religion from the perspective of dogma and theology. In parish work, he had learned to view religion from the point of view of human problems and the responses that people make to religion. Sociology taught him to perceive religion "from the empirical experience of the sacred to the articulations, imaginative and propositional, by which we try to share our experiences with others and to represent them to ourselves" (*Confessions* 222). He began to realize that religion is storytelling before it is dogma and theology and that religion in America mostly takes place in ethnic contexts.

Viewing religion as a set of symbols that attempt to explain reality, he decided that one should try to analyze its symbols and determine what they are attempting to convey. This idea led him to synthesize sociology and theology into new ways of theological thinking. Three authors especially influenced his thought on symbols—Mircea Eliade, Michael Polyani, and William James. From Eliade he learned that there are certain basic elements of religious experience that are almost universal. It was from Eliade's *Patterns of Comparative Religion* that he got his first ideas about Mary's reflecting the womanliness of God. He embraced Eliade's thought that the rites of religion relate our lives to ultimate realities. Coming to the realization that men of science work with symbols, myths, patterns, and stories in ways similar to those of religion, he agreed with Polyani that human knowledge did not follow the pattern of the so-called scientific method. From James he learned that the quest for truth is "an exercise in model fitting" (*Confessions* 224). As he explains, "We fit our explanation schemes (models, narratives, symbols, culture system, whatever we choose to call them) to the reality we experience and then modify the explanations to make them fit reality better. Knowledge is an empirical, pragmatic exploration through mystery" (*Confessions* 225). Science has no monopoly on the ways of knowing.

By 1970 Greeley had the elements of his paradigm of religion—experience, symbol (image), story, and community. Having learned from Eliade, that myth is a story that tries to explain reality, and not a legend to amuse its readers, Greeley employed his sociology of religion for the first time to convey truth instead of facts and as a result wrote *The Jesus Myth*, a series of reflections on the religious symbolism of Jesus. As Greeley explains in the introductory note to this book: "The word myth is used in the title of this volume in a specific and definite sense. A myth is a symbolic story which demonstrates, in Alan Watt's words, 'the inner meaning of the universe and of human life.' To say that Jesus is a myth is not to say that he is legend but that his life and message are an attempt to demonstrate 'the inner meaning of the universe and of human life' " (*Myths of Religion* 13).

Commenting on *The Jesus Myth, The Sinai Myth*, and *The Mary Myth*, which followed—all three have been published together in *The Myths of Religion* (1989)— Greeley remarks, "Autobiographically, these books are the story of a parish priest on his way to becoming a novelist" (*Myths* 2). In researching and writing these three books Andrew Greeley came to the belief that poetry, fiction, and metaphor are superior to expository prose and that they precede intellectualized religion. The imagination provides the raw material of religion.

In *The Jesus Myth*, Greeley concludes, "The poetic image is never an exaggeration of reality, it is an understatement of it" (*Myths* 170). *The Sinai Myth* is, according to Greeley, "an exercise in sociology" (*Myths* 175). This book raises the question: What do the religious symbols of the Hebrew people really signify? The answer he gives is this: the Sinai revelation shows that God passionately loves people. Love is at the heart of the universe (*Myths* 338).

Although his Marian piety was nonexistent when he began writing *The Mary Myth*, in this book he reevaluates Mary from his point of view as a social scientist, showing how God is revealed through her, envisioning Mary as the "feminine component of the deity" (*Myths* 356). The word myth as used in this book signifies a story that is a "*mysterion*," a "*sacramentum*," "a revelation of a "Great Secret" (*Myths* 356). However, all Jewish and Christian myths must be based on historical events to have any value.

Deriving his idea of religion and religious symbolism from the writings of Clifford Geertz and Thomas Luckmann, Greeley's approach to the Mary myth is based on sociology, the history of religion, and what he calls "language" theology. Mircea Eliade contributed to his thinking on the history of religions, as did Erich Neumann, to a lesser degree. The theological foundation is based on the work of Langdon Gilkey, Paul Ricoeur, Peter Berger, Nathan Scott, Thomas Fawcett, Ian Ramsey, and especially David Tracy.

Taking a four-faceted model representing the various aspects of the Mary myth—Madonna, Sponsa, Virgo, and Pieta—as a paradigm for examining reality, Greeley, as a social scientist, organizes his data into these four categories hoping to provide new insights and perspectives (*Myths* 363). The study is both a sociological and a religious one. To Greeley the whole of reality is sacramental. By "sacrament" he means "a thing become symbol which reveals to us its graciousness and the graciousness of Being in which it is rooted and from which it has been thrust into a being of its own" (*Myths* 386). As Greeley often remarks, all is grace. The entire material world can reveal the graciousness of God, including sexual differentiation. While all things have the potentiality of becoming sacrament, sexual differentiation among other things has special sacramental efficacy (*Myths* 387). God is neither male or female, but God may be regarded as both male and female. To express this concept Greeley speaks of the androgyny of God. Mary is the Catholic religious symbol that reveals to us that Reality is androgynous (*Myths* 536), revealing that God loves us with strengths we attribute to women as well as the traditional masculine ones. God loves us with a Madonna/Virgo/Sponsa/Pieta love. Greeley concludes that if we see Mary as a sacrament of God, then every woman should also be viewed as a sacrament of God's love.

Considering his work on Mary as the sacrament of the womanliness of God to be his most significant contribution to religious thought, Greeley states that "God loves us with a power and force and strength that makes human sexual arousal look mild and moderate by comparison" (*Myths* 488).

Continuing to develop his eventual "experience/symbol/story/community paradigm"as a sociological model of religion, Greeley learned story theology from John Shea, who showed him that religion is image and story before it is theology. People need the stories of their tradition which explain life and its complexities to them.

In *Religion: A Secular Theory*, Greeley develops the hypothesis that religion arises from the experiences of life which renew hope in us and that these experiences are expressed in images or symbols which we receive from our religious tradition. Religious experiences are told as stories that are shared by our community which embraces the same symbols and stories. Religion therefore is the collection of stories which one uses to interpret the basic thrust of his life. Stories are the very heart of religion. Jesus used stories or parables to convey to his disciples his experiences of the Father. Although this method of teaching had not been used in the Hebrew tradition for two hundred years, Jesus chose it as the best way to communicate what God is like.

Greeley's paradigm of religion has four components: (1) the hope-renewal experiences which can be called "grace"; (2) the memory of the experiences which is made into symbols or sacraments that convey meaning and reveal order and purpose to us; (3) the stories of our hope-renewal experiences which we tell others in order to stimulate in them similar memories; and (4) the community or people who share our imagery and symbology and who in turn can foster more hope-renewal experiences in us. Seen in this frame of reference, a story is a pattern by which we take the experiences of life and try to shape them and guide our experience in the future. The stories produced by Catholic experience will be comedies, stories with happy endings. There is no tragedy for Christianity whose hope is in God. As Greeley says:

The Catholic story is comic because it believes in the basic goodness of the world and the basic goodness of humankind (both sacramental), both analogical, that is to say both revealing of and metaphors for God. The Catholic instinct has always been to emphasize the basic and fundamental capacity of the world and its institutions and people for salvation—that is to believe in fresh starts, new beginnings and happy endings which are new beginnings. The Christmas story is the happy-ending story par excellence, and while the Catholic, in the midst of Christmas festivities, does not deny that the child who is born will die, it does nonetheless insist that it is the *birth* of a child which is what the story is about and not the death, because even the child who eventually dies on the cross only dies for a time and will be born again, as all of us are born again. (*Confessions* 436)

By now it should be easy to understand why Greeley refers to his novels as "comedies of grace."

At the beginning of his career as a novelist, Greeley took the writings of the Catholic novelists as models for his fiction. From reading Green, Waugh, Marshall, Mauriac, Bernanos, Undset, Bloy, and Claudel, he learned that the novelist writes for a mature audience, not being concerned that a young reader would find the story shocking. These novelists wrote about sin not from their experience of it but from their imaginations.

Another important milestone for Greeley on the way to becoming a novelist was the learning of age-regression techniques from Erika Fromm, causing memories of his distant past to surface, the most prominent of which was that of Twin Lakes where he spent the summers during his childhood and adolescence. Commenting on this Greeley says, "The sheer raw vividness and power of the memories constrained me to turn to fiction writing. What until then had been a pipe dream became an obligation, a necessity. In most of my novels the experience of summer and summer resorts while growing up is important not merely as background against which the stories unfold, but as integral parts of the novel's structure"

(*Confessions* 15). Writing fiction became a way for him to clarify his thoughts and memories.

Deciding that the ideas he had been expressing in his nonfiction scholarly research could be put into stories, he began writing novels so that he would find a much larger reading public than he had with the nonfiction. And rightly so. Large numbers of people who never have heard of Greeley the sociologist and priest, read his novels, completely unaware of his sociological and religious writings. Equipped from the years of sociological research with what he describes as a "freight-train load of empirical data," he turned to writing "stories of God," "comedies of grace"and sold twelve million copies in the first four years and twenty million copies to date.

As Jesus told of the love of the Heavenly Father in stories, parables, Greeley writes stories of God's love and forgiveness, "stories of grace" "parables of divine love" (*Confessions* 283). All his stories are epiphanies depicting God breaking into the ordinary happenings of everyday life. God is the main character in all his fiction. Although he does not moralize in his fiction, nor try to persuade people to ethical conduct, he does not write to entertain people either; his stories are, in his words, "deadly serious." To open people to the presence of God breaking into human life is why he writes so that they will know that God loves us all.

The most often used motif in Greeley's novels is that of God's passion for us compared to human passion. This sexual metaphor, which is essential to his fiction, is found in the Jewish and Christian scriptures and in the Catholic liturgy. Specifically The Song of Songs in the Old Testament scripture employs human erotic love as a metaphor for Divine love. Saints like John of the Cross and Teresa of Avila, both Doctors of the Church, compare union with God to marriage. Ecstasy of the spirit, the experience of the mystics, can only be compared to ecstasy of the body, which is just a tiny reflection of the spiritual reality. There is nothing else in human experience that can be likened unto it. The one experience takes place in the body, the other in the spirit. The one is physical; the other is spiritual. Although the spiritual experience is far greater in intensity than the physical experience, both of them will be surpassed by the infinite love of God which the beatified soul will experience in heaven. This being true, Greeley sees no reason why the metaphor of one kissing the loins of a lover cannot be a proper symbol for God's passion and love for us. It is this metaphor, the image of human love as a sacrament of Divine love, that gives his fiction the religious impact and effectiveness that it has.

Believing that God has called him to write fiction, he explained his position when someone accused him of writing novels that would shock the laity:

I argued vigorously that in an era when a fifth of the priests in the country leave to get married, when Cardinals die in whorehouses, when bishops are arrested for solicitation, when priests are convicted of pederasty, when the Vatican Bank wastes billions, when 80 per cent of the laity reject the Church's teaching on birth control and premarital sex, when there are financial scandals all over the American Church (including Chicago), it was a little hard to think my novels were going to shock anyone. (*Confessions* 476–477)

Greeley's female readers are certainly not shocked by what they read. In him they have found a priest who understands them and the great injustices they have suffered. Approximately three-fourths of all readers of Greeley's fiction are women, and women account for about two-thirds of all his stories purchased. A self-avowed feminist, Greeley relates to women with his deep understanding of their problems and mental attitudes. In his nonfiction works, such as *Angry Catholic Women* written with Mary Durkin, his sister, he shows a sensitivity to the issues that women encounter in their relationships with American society and the Catholic Church in the United States. In his fiction he employs his vast knowledge as a sociologist to portray the life of women in their relationships with their husbands, fathers, brothers, and priests. His sociological research provides the foundation of his fiction which depicts reality as it is experienced in the American Church today. When women discover Andrew Greeley the novelist, they feel that they have at last found a priest who understands them, is sympathetic to their problems, and tells them the truth. They realize that they have finally found a priest who has a high regard for women.

Because of his reputation for speaking the truth plainly and boldly without hedging, Greeley's opinion is much sought after by the media. Appearing frequently on television, he has become a well-recognized and well-trusted authority on the Church today. Because his opinions and his fiction are based on the empirical data that he has amassed as a social scientist at one of America's most prestigious institutions, the University of Chicago, his credibility with the American Catholic is enormous. Millions of people read his novels to experience the truth they find there. Scholars read his nonfiction knowing that his scholarship is above reproach and what he says is accurate and true.

We shall now proceed directly to Greeley's fiction. First, however, it is necessary to establish the boundaries of our study. It is limited to the mainline, fantasy, and short fiction of the author; excluded are the detective stories of Blackie Ryan and the mystery stories of Nuala Anne McGrail, which merit a volume in themselves.

WORKS CITED

Balzac, Honoré de. *La comédie humaine.* Paris: Gallimard, 1952.

———.*Correspondence of Honoré de Balzac.* Trans. C. Lamb Kenney. 2 vols. London: Richard Bentley, 1878.

Bertault, Philippe. *Balzac and the Human Comedy.* Trans. Richard Monges. New York: New York UP, 1963.

Dante, Alighieri. *Dante's Convivio.* Trans. William Walrond Jackson. Oxford: Clarendon, 1909.

———. *A Translation of Dante's Eleven Letters.* C. S. Latham. London: Riverside,1891.

Frye, Northrop. *Anatomy of Criticism: Four Essays.* Princeton: Princeton UP, 1957.

———. *The Secular Scripture: A Study of the Structure of Romance*. Cambridge: Harvard UP, 1976.

Greeley, Andrew M. *Confessions of a Parish Priest: An Autobiography*. New York: Simon and Schuster, 1986.

———. *The Myths of Religion*. New York: Warner, 1989.

Marx, Karl and Friedrich Engels, *Literature and Art: Selections from Their Writings*. New York, 1947.

2

The Quest for the Holy Grail

Andrew Greeley began his literary career with a trilogy of romances based on the Irish version of the legend of the Holy Grail in which a quester finds a magic cup and a magic princess. The first story, *The Magic Cup*, is set in sixth-century Ireland; *Death in April* in the contemporary world of Paris and Chicago; and *The Final Planet* in the distant future on the planet Zylong. The hero in each is named O'Neill, the name of the ancient Irish kings. All three stories are steeped in Celtic tradition and Catholic sacramentality.

Rejecting the grail legend as it has come down to us with its negative sexuality, Greeley goes back to the ancient Celtic sources of the legend to write "life-affirming, flesh-affirming comedies of grace" (*Confessions* 381). He does, however, actually have one of his characters in *The Magic Cup*, Flan the Teller of Tales, recount the old Irish version of the legend by using what the French literary critic, Jean Bellemin-Noël describes as the *mis en abîme* technique, common to fantasy fiction, whereby an embedded story parallels and mirrors the main action of the story. It is the story of how Art MacConn, known as Arthur in the British version, finds and rescues his magic princess, his grail, Delvcaem, returning with her victorious to Tara where, as king, he rules a prosperous Ireland with his new bride.

Basically this is the story of the quest for the holy grail in the Irish tradition. However, there are many variations and differences in the literary versions of Celtic mythology. Moreover, Greeley himself adapts and changes the grail legend to suit his purposes, as he explains in the note at the end of *The Magic Cup*. In the three novels under discussion, *The Magic Cup*, *Death in April*, and *The Final Planet*, the story is based on the grail theme, but each story is unique and has its own distinctive tone, atmosphere, and individual plot differences. The characters in each story bear resemblances to those in the other two volumes of the trilogy, but at the same time have their differences. For example Cormac, the hero of *The Magic Cup*, is in his mid-twenties, much more mature than the pubescent Brigid who becomes his princess; Jim in *Death in April* is forty years old, bored with life, and plays the gallant knight to the forty-year-old widowed Lynnie; the twenty-five-year-old Seamus in *The Final Planet* resembles an adolescent male with his breast fixation and his prurient curiosity as he pursues his Princess Marjetta, a mature woman who is an officer in the military on her planet. All three women are strong and self-willed and serve to bring about the transformations in the men they love turning them from their macho self-interest to having a tender loving regard for others. In each story the hero who is pursuing his magic princess discovers that she is also pursuing him. The women characters also develop with their individual psychological dispositions. Nevertheless, each story is essentially the search for the holy grail.

A product of generations of Irish, Welsh, and Breton storytellers and the inter-twining of myth, fable, and legend, the legend of the grail, first developed in prehistoric Celtic mythology in tales of an old maimed king whose realm is laid waste because of his union with an evil queen and of a young prince's search for a magic cup and/or a magic princess which will restore fertility to the land. Interestingly, in the Irish versions of the legend the grail is not a chalice, but a cup or a woman or both. According to the renowned Celtic scholar Jean Markdale in his monumental work *Celtic Civilization* (268), the grail is a symbol of femininity and represents the solar mother-goddess; the quester is identified with the moon. The quester's return is seen as a *regressus ad uterum* (271). The son returns with his moisture to the mother who is withering in the fire.

Breton *conteurs* who related ancient Celtic legends to musical accompaniment on a harp or on the *rote*, a medieval stringed instrument, spread the stories of the grail throughout France. The first literary version of the legend was written by Chrétien de Troyes in his famous *Perceval, or Le conte du graal.* At that time the word *graal* meant a dish or a platter such as one would find in the homes of the wealthy. Chrétien describes the grail as a holy thing; only one wafer from it sustains the life of the dying, old king. He relates that Perceval, a fatherless Welsh boy reared by his mother, journeys to King Arthur's court and then to the Grail Castle. Since Chrétien did not live to finish the writing of the story, it was continued by three other authors: Wauchier de Denain, Manessier, and Gerbert de Montreuil. Interestingly, to Wauchier the grail is rich, not holy, and has properties that are connected with the reproductive and vegetative powers of nature.

Near the end of the twelfth century Robert de Boron identified the grail with the cup of the Last Supper in his *Joseph d'Arimathie* or the *Roman de l'estoire du graal*, which relates how Joseph of Arimathea brought the chalice to Britain. Finally, about 1220 there appeared the grail-Lancelot cycle in which the chaste Galahad replaces Perceval as the grail hero. One part of the cycle, the *Queste del saint graal*, influenced by the body-hating Manichaeism of medieval France, became a prose classic, but it deprived the legend of its original Celtic, life-affirming, positive sexuality. In fact, in some of the older versions the quester had been notorious for his love conquests as was Gawain. A German writer, Wolfram von Eschenbach took Chrétien's version of the legend and remodeled it using an unknown version by one Kiot. The version of the story that has come down to us makes salvation in the quest of the grail come through denial of the flesh and sexuality.

Greeley adapts the earlier versions and emphasizes positive sexual values so that salvation comes through the sexual union of the knight with his magic princess, for in Greeley's versions of the legend, the grail and the girl are identified with each other. Furthermore, the girl who takes a very active part in seeking the quester is depicted by Greeley as being a sacrament of God's love, a source of renewal of life and hope, revealing the life-giving, nurturing, healing tenderness of God. What Greeley is saying is that God is like a woman, only better. According to Greeley, "The girl is the Grail and the Grail is the girl and both are God in the Celtic version of the legend" (*Confessions* 22).

In all Greeley's fiction, woman is depicted as a sacrament of God, bringing grace and salvation. As Greeley explains, "Choose another paradigm if you wish. But if Mary be a sacrament of God, so is every woman, and therefore the fear and hatred of women which has obsessed Catholicism since it emerged in the neo-Platonic world is blasphemy" (*Confessions* 374). By extension, all life to Greeley is like the quester legend. "Life, if it is anything at all, is a quest for a Grail, an end of a rainbow, a leprechaun with a pot of gold, a Bali Ha'i in the South Pacific" (*Confessions* 21). The quest is always for gentle love, for the "warm and cherishing" God, for the "cherishing self," and the gentle lover in oneself (*Confessions* 22, 23). In each of the three novels under discussion, *The Magic Cup, Death in April*, and *The Final Planet* the hero finds the love that he seeks and is transformed by it.

The Celtic spirit of the ancient grail legend lives on in Greeley's fiction. At the very onset of his career as a novelist, Greeley identified himself as an Irish American author. His heroes and heroines are Irish. The men are at times fumbling comic heroes overwhelmed by the women they love who are always strong-willed and determined. Viewed as sacraments of God, the women characters are treated with special distinction as they have always been held in high regard in Celtic culture. In the very first chapter of *The Magic Cup*, the reader is introduced to Lady Ann who speaks out angrily in the conversation between her husband and Cormac (18), showing that Irish women are not to be pushed around by their men and are known to speak their minds.

In depicting woman as a metaphor for God and emphasizing a positive life-affirming sexuality in *The Magic Cup,* Greeley is portraying the traditional attitude of the masses of Catholic people who believe that sex is good and holy. In his book *Religion as Poetry* (1994), Greeley maintains that there have always been two traditions in the Church in regard to sexuality—the high church tradition with its horror of sex and the popular tradition of the masses that affirms the goodness and sanctity of sex. Greeley shows that the Church's negative ideas on sexuality reflect the high church tradition, or what he refers to as the "prose tradition" of the Church (49). Coexisting with the negative sexual attitudes of the high church tradition of erudite scholars and ecclesiastics, the popular tradition, or "poetic tradition,"of the people has constantly maintained the goodness of sex. These two traditions have coexisted in the Church since the beginning. However, according the Greeley, it was not until the twentieth century with its universal education and literacy that the Church has made a serious attempt to imposed the high church tradition upon the Catholic people in the pews. The popular tradition with its belief that married love is good and holy is the one that has prevailed down through the ages even in the medieval Church and is the one that Greeley emphasizes in his fiction from his first work, *The Magic Cup,* to the present.

In *The Magic Cup*, the reader encounters the Church's two traditions of sexuality. The high church tradition is represented by the Holy Abbot Colum of Iona and other monastics who appear in the book—Kevin of Cashel, Kiernan of Clonmacnoise, and Kathleen of Glendalough. Typical of the high church tradition, Abbot Colum disapproves of married priests and even more of married bishops. Interestingly, there is in the book a married bishop and even some married monks whose families are attached to the monasteries (108). The attitudes of the hero Cormac and his Princess Brigid reflect those of the popular tradition that sex is wonderful and holy.

The Magic Cup is a delightful retelling of the ancient grail legend in which Andrew Greeley introduces his readers to some of the basic themes that recur in his subsequent fiction. Chief among them are woman is a sacrament of God's love; the love that exists between a man and a woman is an analogy of the love that God has for each one of us; the Love that is pursued is even more ardently pursuing the quester. Repeatedly in all his novels Greeley uses sexual union as a metaphor for the soul's union with God, which is in keeping with the teaching of those great Doctors of the Church St. John of the Cross and St. Teresa of Avila as expressed emphatically in their writings.

The characters of *The Magic Cup,* such as Cormac and Brigid, are prototypes of the heroes and heroines whom we will find again and again in the author's subsequent fiction. The women Brigid and Lady Ann, wife of the Bishop of Enda, are types of the Celtic woman that will continue in his fiction through many stories.

As the story of *The Magic Cup* opens in Ireland of the sixth century, Lady Ann is entertaining a visitor, Cormac, "a fierce young man" with "huge eyebrows of flaming red," as she waits in her home on the Hill of Slaine for her husband, Bishop Enda, to return with the Holy Abbot Colum from their visit to King Dermot MacFergus. Sexual overtones pervade the chapter. Immediately the reader recognizes that the author is not writing in the high church tradition. Here is a sexually active woman who in her thoughts expresses her ever-increasing desire for her husband's body, while the good Bishop assures her that it is not in the least sinful as they enjoy a very passionate sexual life together. In this the very first chapter of his very first novel, Greeley befuddles those who are advocates of the high tradition and delights the followers of the popular tradition who rejoice that finally a priest can speak convincingly and appreciatively of married love. At this point, celibates of the old school throw down the book in horror, especially when they read that the bishop is "a pitiless and determined lover thirsting for a conquest" (23) and that if guests had not arrived, he would have dragged his wife "off to bed in the middle of the day even though she was five months pregnant" (79). This flies in the face of the ancient tradition that considered it sinful for husbands and wives to have sex once the wife had conceived. The popular tradition that married sex is good and reflects God's love is maintained by Bishop Enda and later Cormac when he marries his magic princess. It is the tradition that is upheld in all Greeley's fiction in which much of the comedy has strong sexual overtones.

Delightful comedy is found in the author's first novel. The charming nymphet Brigid baits Cormac, whose bondwoman she is, by drawing water for his bath, while indicating that she fully expects to bathe him. Always able to trounce him as they spar with words, she irritates him so much that on a later occasion he dunks her in a tub of water and then rips her clothing from her tiny budding body. As lust overwhelms him, he wants to possess her, but he resists and turns instead to comic gallantry (51–52).

One of the highlights of comedy in this book occurs when the beautiful Finnabair, Cormac's father's mistress, comes to Cormac's quarters intent on seducing him. Just when Cormac's passion for her pounds for release and he is savagely kissing the alluring courtesan, the nymphet Brigid enters his bed chamber with a bit of warm milk "to ease his sleep." It is a very humorous scene.

When Finnabair puts a *geis* on Cormac forcing to leave Ireland, the little pagan girl, Biddy, as Cormac affectionately calls her, follows him and has a powerful impact on him. The tough, often brutal and aggressive man becomes protective. Like his counterparts in the other two stories of the trilogy, Cormac is a writer who uses his talent in the pursuit of his princess. Cormac, the bard, composes love poetry about his magic princess and her beautiful breasts and sings them to Biddy. Because of his love for Brigid, Cormac turns from being a rough, brooding, rather self-centered person into a compassionate, tender, and loving one by the end of the story.

Brigid is also transformed. With the passing of time her tongue gets sharper and she always gets the best of Cormac as they spar with words. Her banter is high spirited, witty, and at times caustic, but mostly it is a defense mechanism to hide the true emotions of her heart. Always a strong person, she becomes stronger, more determined as she grows in her relationship with Cormac. While he is at times portrayed as a fumbling hero—on one occasion he ran into a tree and stunned himself—she saves his life several times. At the end of the book and after her marriage to Cormac, Brigid is happy, playful, peaceful, trusting, and Christian. Her happiness is so great that "sometimes when he was about to enter her the joy was so great she felt she would die" (229). She symbolizes the old pagan Ireland and the new Christian one that is beginning to emerge.

After the kingship is decided by personal combat between Cormac and Aed MacSweeney who impales himself on Cormac's sword, Biddy who has become a mature woman sexually heals her husband of his impotence. Similarly Lynnie heals Jim O'Neill in *Death in April*.

The love story of Cormac and Brigid has the tone and atmosphere of a medieval romance, recalling such love stories as the French *Aucassin et Nicolette*. The whole world seems new and magical with everything giving rise to wonder and delight, making the readers feel as though they were experiencing life afresh with the eyes of youth. Greeley's fiction always has a youthful quality about it. The very idea that a magic cup and a magic princess can exist gives rise to hope. When the hero finds both of them in the little girl he had known for years, more or less like "the girl next door," readers also feel that perhaps they can also find happiness near at hand. As Biddy explains, "You will only find the magic princess and her magic cup when you search for her inside yourself" (71). And this is what Greeley is saying to his reader. Happiness *is* to be found; it even pursues us more ardently than we pursue it, just as Biddy pursues Cormac who is searching for her.

The fantasy sequence in which Biddy encounters the Tuatha de Danann is especially delightful and the quintessence of the story, illustrating as it clearly does the pagan-Christian conflict in Biddy and in Ireland (125 ff). Deep in the forest at night, dancing wildly to the beat of the drums and the pipes, these mysterious, people wearing transparent clothing, welcome her into their group headed by Lug and Erihu, the king and queen of the fairies. After they strip her of her garments so she can dance freely, they marvel at her beauty. This scene shows Brigid and Ireland, by extension, torn between pagan and Christian ways. As she dances furiously with Lug she sees a woman in white at the edge of the meadow. It is the same woman who had appeared in her childhood dreams telling her that she would be Queen of Ireland. This woman with the black hair and brown skin has a troubled expression as she sees Brigid dancing with the pagan Lug (127). This same unnamed woman also appears in *Death in April* in the dreams of Jim O'Neill who says he knows who she is but doesn't believe in her. What Greeley is depicting here is Mary and the feminine characteristics of a God who watches over us like a mother. As a constant reminder of this dimension of God's love Greeley makes frequent use of Jungian symbolism to enrich the narrative. Water, the feminine archetype, is found in almost every scene in this book and in the other two books of the trilogy.

Not only is the symbolism of the romance rich, the language of the story is always interesting. Greeley is a talented writer who has more than a nodding acquaintance with the Blarney Stone of his ancestral heritage. There are many interesting and well-turned phrases and picturesque speech. For example, on one occasion Biddy "points her tiny finger at Cormac like an abbess accusing a postulant of fornication."

In the frequent water descriptions we find some interesting and noteworthy similes. One such is "The moonlight splashed the waters of the river as though someone had spilled a pitcher of milk" (117). Again we read in another place that the waves on the water "glittered brightly in the chill sunlight like jewels on the stem of a chalice" (97). Such descriptive expressions tend to make *The Magic Cup* a true treasure, and it is easy to see why this delightful story of human and divine love was made into an opera which has been performed in Chicago.

Although the book is complete in itself, to understand it fully one should read the other two stories of the trilogy and compare them, for the stories help to illuminate and complement one another like three paintings in a triptych.   In *Death in April* the redheaded Irish American James McCormac O'Neill finds his magic princess in the girl Lynnie whom he had known in his youth. Instead of a story of young love like *The Magic Cup* and *The Final Planet*, this is the story of a second chance, a theme that Greeley has dealt with in other books like *Summer at the Lake*. It resembles *The Magic Cup* in that the princess in both is rather like the girl next door . However, the atmosphere and the tone of this romance are completely different from those of *The Magic Cup* and also from those of *The Final Planet*. The prince, whose middle name McCormac recalls the hero of the first romance, is no longer young. He is a bored, wealthy, forty-year-old, ex-expatriated American author living in Paris. World-weary, disillusioned, and filled with sad memories, he does not have much in common with Cormac or even Seamus of *The Final Planet*. His princess, Lynnie, is a forty-year-old widow with five children. She is identified with Brigid of the first story by also having the name of Brigid; Jim O'Neill's princess is Evelina Brigid Conroy Slattery aka Lynnie with the violet eyes and golden hair.

Jim shares with Cormac of *The Magic Cup* and Seamus of *The Final Planet* anxiety over women. With a series of women and already two marriages in his past, he both hates and fears women but is unable to live without them. His good friend, the Parisian psychotherapist Monique, describes him accurately as "the last of the knights of the Round Table, a red-haired Lancelot forever seeking his grail, his sacred vessel." According to her informed opinion, he equates women with death and flirts with both (13).

A tired middle-aged man, who fears he is washed up as a writer, Jim suffers from impotency despite his frequent sexual fantasies. He also has a lot of guilt and worries that he is a bad parent to his teenaged daughter who is trying to get him to return to the Church.

Forceful like Cormac, Jim can even be brutal and rough at times, a man of violent passion. According to Monique, he has to prove his manhood by winning his woman by defeating a dangerous enemy. When he gets her in his power, she does not want a knight in armor but a man she can love back; he then becomes terrified and flees. None of the women in his past have been "brave enough" to run after him and drag him back. His magic princess Lynnie will be the exception.

In a series of flash backs, his relationship with Lynnie is depicted. The two have been close friends since they were toddlers, but when she begins to mature sexually he becomes afraid of her and is guilt ridden if they embrace. Uncomfortable with his body and with sex, Jim, when Lynnie's father tries to turn him into a lawyer—a partner in his firm—and a son-in-law, bolts and does not return for twenty years.

Lynnie does not have the sexual hangups that plague Jim, but accepts her body and her sexuality with a warmth and earthiness that is attributed to her Italian heritage since she has an Italian mother. Later we will encounter a full-blown "Italian Madonna" in the character Maria in *Ascent into Hell*, whom Lynnie may be said to foreshadow.

The lake where they live plays an important part in their lives. With the use of Jungian symbolism and archetype continuing as encountered in *The Magic Cup*, the lake becomes almost a character in the *Death in April*, being a constant correlative for the feminine aspects of God. We read: "The waters of the lake were mirror smooth. The sun was a huge rose dipping beneath the dark clouds poised in the western sky" (33). To those versed in symbolism, water is the eternal feminine and the sun is God. In this passage the sun is seen as a rose, the flower that represents Mary, who reflects the feminine qualities of God's love. The mirror smoothness of the lake indicates the peace that God's love brings. All in all, it is a beautiful and skillful use of metaphor.

When Jim returns home after twenty years absence, one of the first things he sees is the lake. The lake now reflects Jim's present attitudes toward God and women, and the reader sees that his negativity toward both have intensified with time: "The lake looked sinister under the quiet April sky. Although it was not very large and had no tricky currents, hardly a year had gone by without at least one drowning. The lake is evil, he thought to himself, shuddering involuntarily . . . Lynnie and the lake. The girl is the lake is the grail is God . . . symbols fit poorly so pedestrian a place as this obsolescent summer resort" (56).

What happens when the two meet again are some very funny scenes in which Greeley is revealed as a master of comedy, witty dialogue, and sparkling repartee. Jim literally collides with Lynnie as she leaves a store carrying packages. When Lynnie invites him to dinner and tries to seduce him, the story becomes at times hilarious. When she greets him at the door wearing only a low-cut nightgown, he is just plain scared. The dialogue is funny, even farcical. Despite his fears, he and Lynnie culminate their physical union, something he had not been able to do when he was young. With Lynnie he is not impotent as he had been with women in Paris. However, he awakens in the night terrified about what he has done.

Another comic scene follows later when Jim has dinner with Lynnie and her five children, because the house is a mess, dinner late, and the children pretend he does not exist. Overwhelmed by the children and two large dogs, "he finally escaped with his life" (90).

As one would expect from a sociologist, Greeley delves into the society of Jim O'Neill's world and satirizes the legal system and the Church in the portraits he draws of lawyers, judges, and clerics. Jim's first encounter with the postconciliar church comes when Lynnie takes him to mass with her after a night of lovemaking. He is astounded to hear a young priest expounding on Divine Love, say, "God loves us with a passion that makes human love look weak by comparison." He is even more astonished to see Lynnie receive communion and in the hand. He reminds her that they had been engaged in what they use to call "fornication" the night before.

She laughs at his bewilderment, especially when he refers to himself as "a notorious sinner and apostate." What is being shown here is the attitude that many Catholics have toward sex, since surveys show that they no longer pay attention to the high church traditions of negative sexuality. The reader must realize that Greeley is not advocating sex outside of marriage, but merely depicting things the way they are. Just as God does not sanction all the actions of his creatures, an author does not necessarily approve or disapprove of the deeds of his characters. To know what Andrew Greeley believes about sex outside of marriage, one must read his nonfiction books and not draw conclusions from his fiction. One must remember that in his fiction he is an author and a sociologist who is depicting people and events as he sees them.

As Jim continues to explore the "new" Church, some great comedy unfolds. When he visits the rectory trying to get help from the Church for Lynnie who is in legal difficulties, he decides that the modern furnishings made the rectory office look more like that of an "expensive dentist or the antechamber in a high-class bordello." The priest, called "Uncle Mike" by some people including Lynnie, freely admits that his archbishop is a bastard who is "too damn mean to help Lynnie," "a bastard capable of anything"(128).

Uncle Mike helps Jim out by making an appointment for him to see Archbishop Daniel Fogarty, an unscrupulous man who bought his ecclesiastical office by giving expensive gifts to the right people. The satiric humor in the sequence that follows is rich. After making him wait for forty minutes, Archbishop Daniel Fogarty appears looking like "the scarecrow from *The Wizard of Oz*" (151). Although he has some papers in his files that would help Lynnie, he refuses to provide them. Losing his temper, Jim bluffs the bishop with threats, forcing him to come up with the documents Lynnie needs. The scene is a highly satiric, caustic, and humorous portrayal of some of the hierarchy in the Church today.

The descriptions of the archbishop are colorful. One phrase stands out: "He [the archbishop] swept out of the room like a head waiter with a big tip" (152).

The Mafia, the legal system, the media, and academia all share in the satire of Greeley's wit and humor. In an attempt to get help for Lynnie in her legal battle, Jim meets with Greg, one of Lynnie's Italian cousins, who is described as "a Mafioso." So that Jim will be able to identify him in the restaurant where they agree to meet, the man comes to the meeting dressed in his "Godfather duds." In an excellent display of the art of portraying human nature, Greeley makes Greg a psychologically well-motivated individual character and not a type as one usually finds in such stories. Much of the humor comes from the incongruities in the behavior and way of life of Greg who speaks with a thick Jersey accent and looks like "a Sicilian lover from a Mastrioanni movie" (181). Despite his education—he is a graduate of Notre Dame with a M.B.A. from the University of Chicago— he imitates the speech of a gangster. As Jim talks with him he thinks that he himself is beginning to sound like a character from *The Godfather*. In an hilarious scene, Greg keeps punching Jim on the arm and Jim punches him back. When Greg asks Jim why he does not put out a contract on the U. S. attorney, Jim almost chokes on his calamari and chianti *classico reservato*. Greg explains that since he is a writer he could use his writing talents to get rid of Ted Masterman, the man in question, who has been trying to indict Lynnie on criminal charges.

After considering Greg's suggestion, Jim begins writing a novel, which is really an exposé of the U. S. Attorney Ted Masterman and the corrupt legal system with its "functional justice." "The story was the magic sword by which the magic princess would be freed" (190). With novel in hand, Jim goes to meet Masterman "with the *High Noon* theme echoing in the back of his head"(210), obviously envisioning the encounter as a shoot-out. Jim is the knight who is going to slay the dragon so that the princess will be free. When he succeeds in blackmailing Masterman with his novel by agreeing not to publish it if Lynnie goes free, he no longer wants the princess. This is a well-written, humorous, and satiric scene with good descriptive detail and dialogue.

Probably the high point of comedy is reached with chapter eleven in which Jim and Lynnie have dinner at the home of Emil Stern, a Jewish lawyer, who might be able to help extricate Lynnie from her legal dilemma. The well-delineated descriptions of the various characters and a dialog which is brisk, witty, and sparkling make the dinner party come alive for the reader.

Ironically Jim does not want to marry his archduchess or princess after he frees her from the legal brouhaha. Although he sees himself as a knight slaying the dragon to help the poor damsel in distress, he is not the typical romantic hero. He feels trapped and strikes her brutally as they quarrel. In this he is quite different from Cormac and even Seamus, because one cannot ever imagine them striking the women that love them.

Despite his shabby treatment of her, Lynnie, who symbolizes God's love and grace, pursues him, telling him that she is grace for him. She also insists that he is grace for her, that God sent him to her when she needed grace. In the end, grace and love triumph as they always do in Greeley's divine and human comedy. Chicago is Camelot, Lynnie is Guinevere, and Jim her knight in shining armor. Because of her love, Jim is transformed into the tender lover she always knew he really was. The title of the story *Death in April* reveals that Jim dies to the self that he was and becomes a new person.

The atmosphere and tone of this second story of the trilogy are quite different from that of the other two stories. Since it is a story of a second chance being given to two forty-year-old lovers in a sophisticated city in the twentieth century, it lacks the pastoral charm and joy of *The Magic Cup* and does not have the exuberant good spirits of *The Final Planet*. It definitely contains more humor and satire than *The Magic Cup*. *The Final Planet*, however, as we shall see is equally comedic and satirical. All three of the stories contain elements of fantasy. The fantasy in *Death in April* is limited to the dream that Jim has of the dark brown woman dressed in white who is always by the lake of his childhood. She recalls the woman of Cormac's dreams. Jim knows who she is and that she is not Irish, despite the Irish brogue she always affects. Although he never remembers these dreams and does not believe in her, Mary touches his forehead in benediction and drifts away in the blue sky. Obviously she symbolizes those qualities in God that can be described as feminine, for although God is neither male nor female both feminine and masculine qualities are attributed to him.

The Final Planet, the third story of the trilogy, is an hilarious romp through the planet Zylong in the far distant future. It is a fantastic science-fiction story in which Seamus O'Neill—Seamus is Gaelic for James—is a glib-tongued Irishman with a colossal breast fixation who seeks and finds his magic princess and sacred vessel Marjetta, a mature and more sophisticated version of Cormac's Brigid. Under the pose of being a wandering minstrel, the space knight acts as a spy for the Lady Deirdre Fitzgerald, countess of Cook, archbishop of Chicago Nova, fleet commodore of Tara, captain abbess of the pilgrim ship *Iona*, and cardinal priest of the Holy Roman Church of Saint Clement.

A lady cardinal? A magnificent lady cardinal! Extremely impressive and imperious, she rules from her throne in regal robes of Celtic blue and red and wearing her blue Brigid's cross, reigning over the five hundred pilgrims from Tara, another planet colonized by Earth, onboard the ion-hyperspace exploration vessel, the *Iona*, which is powered by matter-antimatter conversion generators. With typical Greeley realism, the clothes of the lady cardinal are described in detail down to the brown swimsuit with red fringe to denote her ecclesiastical position. With her gifts of mental telepathy, she flashes her commands to her recalcitrant sheep, like Seamus, who are pilgrims aboard the *Iona* and members of the Holy Order of St. Brigid and St. Brendan, descendants of the Irish who originally settled the planet Tara. She is most awesome when she uses astral projection. With the help of a fowl-mouthed computer named Podraig, the same name as O'Neill's dog in *The Magic Cup* she keeps informed.

Since their spaceship is almost worn out and can only survive one more landing, the cardinal sends Seamus Finnbar Diarmuid Brendan Tomas O'Neill in the guise of a wandering minstrel to spy on the native Zylongis and to prepare the way for them to land, because the rules of their holy order insist that they must not be invaders of a planet but can only enter as invited guests. The twenty-five-year-old Seamus, a giant with a bright red beard, has really only one thing on his mind—sex and finding what he describes as a "proper" woman. Seamus frolics through the planet with much rollicking good humor as Greeley unfolds, with the special acumen of a social scientist, a dystopian society on the verge of collapse. In this fantastic social satire, there are some points of comparison with our own society. The history of Zylong reads much like that of Earth—terror, near genocide, oppression, and slaughter. The Zylongis practice racial exploitation and have had serious problems with discrimination against women. They are the descendants of people who had left earth to escape the corruption there, but as Cardinal Deirdre says corruption comes with the genes, and their now pagan society is disintegrating, much as was the pagan society in *the Magic Cup* and much as our own society is today. When Seamus O'Neill unites with his princess who converts to his religion, as Biddy did to Cormac's, they become the rulers of the new Zylong and a reborn society.

Witty dialogue and repartee and much verbal sparring between Seamus and his "proper woman"characterize the story. O'Neill has much of the country bumpkin about him at the beginning of the narrative, but he does not remain that way, for Greeley develops his characters; they are not the same at the end the story as they were at the beginning. In most science-fiction stories, romances, and popular fiction, the characters are not developed, they do not change.

To see how Greeley develops his characters, let us consider Seamus. In the beginning he is "a twenty-five- year-old bachelor with a wild imagination and a horny body" who has nothing but sex on his mind, but despite his prurient curiosity is really terrified of women. He is "the last great playboy of the western world—indeed, the whole western quadrant of the frigging galaxy" (169). As it turns out, he is good at talking about sex, but in practice he is unskilled and inexperienced. His fear of women is well illustrated in his anxiety about caves and climbing down into "a long hole into a dark, sea scoured cave." As he expresses it, "*You're never sure whether you can get out of these cave things*" (168).

Putting on a macho act like Cormac and Jim O'Neill, he picks up one woman and throws her around like a child in his "spin-the-dolly-in-the-air-routine" (107). He kills two men in less than half a minute, when they try to kill him. After a big fight resembling one of Cormac's bashes, five men lay dead. When his magic princess Marjetta is captured by the enemy in a scene paralleling Brigid's capture by pirates, he goes to the rescue. When he saves her from the hordi, a strange race of mutants that lives on the fringes of Zylongi life, just as they make plans to eat her, he roughly threatens to give her "the back of his hand" (140). Later he admits that she has a lovely ass and "Sure there's a lot better things to do with it than spank it. The threat will be enough" (150).

During the course of the story he comes to regard himself as a latter day Finn MacCool, searching for the holy grail—in this case some tranquilizers to give the Zylongis to protect them from the frenzy of their autumn festival.

Through his union with Marjetta and his experiences with her, Seamus is transformed from a fumbling sex-hungry bumpkin who is only interested in chasing women into a wise, mature man and ruler of the planet Zylong who has learned that love is tender and more important than passion.

The character of Lieutenant Marjetta of the Zylong army, the magic princess, develops even more than that of Seamus. She is a strong woman and, like Brigid in *The Magic Cup*, saves his life on several occasions. Although she is strong and determined from the beginning, she grows even stronger and more determined as the story progresses. In her relationship with Seamus, Marjetta suffers from culture shock. At one point, noting the changes that are taking place within herself, she even asks if she is losing her mind.

It is comical how Seamus tries to convince himself to take the willing Marjetta. After arguing to himself that it would be a mortal sin to do so, he reasons that even the lady cardinal had said if no clergyperson was available for a long time two people could make commitments to each other and contract a valid marriage. Although he had often fantasized about being alone with a naked woman, he was afraid of her, even thinking her to a be "trap" the same way that Cormac and Jim regarded their princesses before succumbing to their charm. Ironically, when she is available and willing, he does not want her as his emotions parallel those of Jim in *Death in April*. Finally when she begs him to take her, his hunger for her overcomes his fear and he learns that she also is afraid of him. Nevertheless they pledge eternal love and devotion to each other. Their honeymoon was idyllic, celebrated in nature with waterfalls and pools of water. Water symbolism is frequent in this book as it was in the other two of the trilogy, reflecting the archetypal feminine qualities.

Sex for the Zylongi was a brief and brutal act. But love has transformed Marjetta and made Seamus tender and gentle. Playfully and aggressively she throws him to the ground, pins him down and strips off his clothing and plays with him, obviously freed from her cultural restraints for on Zylong sex was permitted only during the planting and harvest seasons.

Most significantly Marjetta learns what real love is from Seamus who tells her that God is love. He explains that when we know how to love and be loved in return, we know what God is like. The story illustrates one of Greeley's most important themes—sex is a metaphor of the love of God.

Sex also bonds Seamus and Marjetta together. Once when they split up, she returns and begs to be taken back like a slave to a master, thoughts also expressed by Brigid in *The Magic Cup*. He will have nothing to do with a master-slave relationship, but wants her as an equal partner. Her hunger for him is insatiable and even on Christmas, when she is pregnant, no less, he is expecting to have a long night with her. Having sex with a pregnant woman is enough to rock the old high church tradition of sexuality, but to do it on Christmas Day would have given a medieval Christian for a penance a long fast on bread and water and no sex at all for a long, long time.

There is much good comedy in the book. When Seamus falls into the hands of Samaritha, the Zylongi female doctor, who takes his clothes off to inspect his "biology," the reader chuckles. The episode becomes funnier when he insists to her that in his culture patients and doctors kiss each other so many times each day.

Much of the humor in the book comes from its light and breezy tone as it is told from the perspective of Seamus. His Irish brogue and way of expressing himself are quite amusing with his conversation being sprinkled with words like "gombeen," "idjit," "frigging lardass," "poteen, "onchak" "amadon," and "the creature." When he is engaged in personal combat with Narth, the chief of the enemy, he insults him with ritual insults, comparing him when he swings his axe to a "drunken grandmother with her piss pot" (281). Often his thoughts, which resemble the "asides" of comic actors on the stage, are very funny, especially the ones he relays to the lady cardinal whom he knows to be monitoring him with mental telepathy. The bawdy ballad he writes about how Marjetta lost her virginity and which he sings to her is very much in the comic vein.

When asked by the Zylongi men about his sex life Seamus remarks with a straight face "I can make love only a hundred forty times in twenty-four hours, so you can see my romantic life is quite undistinguished" (90). This was said to men whose laws permitted them to have sexual intercourse only during the planting and harvest seasons in their strictly regulated society, which Greeley the social scientist describes in detail. They fail to recognize the importance of sex for bonding between man and wife as the Catholic Church has done down through the centuries. They do not realize that sex helps to ease married people over the rough spots of their life together.

Death and drugs are conspicuous in this society, which is on the verge of anarchy and collapse. To relax their mounting tensions they sip an hallucinogenic drug during a communion service in a ceremony that has vague elements that seem to have been derived from Church liturgy. But their ceremony actually has little in common with it, since they have been on Zylong for over one thousand years and have changed very much with the passing of time.

In the dystopian society of Zylong with its share of dishonest, crooked, and distrustful people, there is very little friendship or love. One can visualize some of the major emerging problems of our own planet as Greeley the satirist portrays what might happen if current trends continue to develop. Euthanasia is practiced on the elderly and on those that are not considered fit to live. Euphemistically it is said "They go to the god" (79). They become one with Zylong in the public square at festival time. Humanely they are tranquilized before being thrown into a pit. Furthermore, capital punishment is carried out upon those who are not "politically correct" and are socially disruptive; they are not treated as kindly as the elderly but are tossed into vats of acid. Those who have too much clout to be put to death are exiled, expelled from society into the desert where there are hairy mutant creatures that are the result of gene manipulation by Zylongi scientists. Of course these are the sores festering in our own society: assisted suicide, euthanasia, capital punishment, getting rid of those who are not wanted—the weak, the unborn, the elderly—amoral science that creates more problems and human suffering than it alleviates. Greeley the moralist points out the foibles of Zylongi society and by extension of our own. He is a moralist, but he never moralizes; that is, he never preaches. Readers are left to make their own comparisons and conclusions.

So carefully controlled is Zylongi society that even social conduct at dinner parties and sporting events is highly regulated. Although everything is prescribed, yet nothing seems to work right. The entire society is falling apart at the seams, while the people languish in darkness and unhappiness. Even Marjetta says that when she first met Seamus she was overcome with despair and did not want to live. But all that changes for her and for the rest of Zylong when Seamus gets involved in their politics and becomes the leader of their revolution.

When the enemy appears about ready to finish Seamus off, he is saved by a real coup de théâtre. Using astral projection, the lady cardinal appears like a deus ex machina hurling psychic lightening bolts and imaginary thunder at them as she holds high the cross on her crozier, making a dashing figure in her dazzling red robes. They flee in terror. In a grand finale some of the Celtic troops from the spaceship *Iona* come to Seamus's aid playing the bagpipes. Using psychic powers they stop the wind, keeping the pollen, which causes the autumnal frenzy, from blowing in the air. When Seamus conquers the planet and becomes its ruler, he renames it Tyrone, in honor of his Celtic heritage. Marjetta converts to Christianity and takes the name of Pegeen. As the book ends the pilgrims of the *Iona* are settling into their new home and Christmas is being celebrated on Zylong. The final planet has been reborn to newness of life and hope.

Some of the language of the story is worthy of note, for Greeley is a master at creating striking ways of expression. One such is as follows: "The Central Plaza was . . . as dark as a Cardinal's heart" (75). In another place we read: "We are going to redeploy instantly. Which means run like hell" (178). These are typical of Greeley's cutting wit and humor.

In conclusion, *The Magic Cup*, *Death in April*, and *The Final Planet* are a trilogy of stories based on the grail theme, and are steeped in Catholic sacramentality and Celtic tradition. They reveal the author as a humorist, moralist, satirist, and story teller. It is especially interesting to see how he takes the same basic story and adapts it to different times and places. Parallel incidents take place in all three. For example, Crede of the original legend is found in *The Magic Cup* in the person of the girl that Cormac stays with for a while when he thinks Brigid is dead. In *Death in April* she appears as Nancy Corsello who obviouslythrows herself at Jim. We find her again in Samaritha, the friendly doctor of Zylong, who without success begs Jim to make love to her. All the heroines of the stories are strong determined women, metaphors of God, who pursue their knights who are questing for them. In all three stories the metaphor of human love as representing divine love is poignantly depicted and delineated. The male protagonists all learn to love and find the tender God dwelling within their hearts. As a result peace and fertility come to their lands. With very skillful use of language Greeley paints pictures that linger in the mind. With suitable symbolism he frequently enriches his prose. His sparkling and vivacious humor, which is found on almost every page, reveals him as a master of comedy.[1]

NOTE

1. For further commentary on *The Final Planet*, see Allienne R. Becker, *The Lost Worlds Romance from Dawn till Dusk.* (Westport: Greenwood, 1992).

WORKS CITED

Greeley, Andrew M. *Confessions of a Parish Priest: An Autobiography.* New York: Simon and Schuster, 1986.

———. *Death in April.* New York: McGraw-Hill, 1980.

———. *The Final Planet.* New York: Warner, 1987.

———. *The Magic Cup: An Irish Legend.* New York: McGraw-Hill, 1979.

————. *Religion as Poetry*. New Brunswick: Transaction Publishers, 1996.
Markdale, Jean. *Celtic Civilization*. London: Gordon and Cremonesi, 1978.

3

Rumors of Angels

Greeley's fiction, like his nonfiction, may be said to be a sociological study of the Catholic Church and its priesthood since the Second Vatican Council. A social scientist, he uses the information he has gathered in years of study and research to portray the society in which he lives in all his writings, with the fictional works mirroring, and sometimes even paralleling, the nonfictional. For example, one of the four novels considered in this chapter, *The Cardinal Virtues* may even be said to be the fictional version of *The Catholic Myth*, both of which were published in 1990. The other three novels under consideration in this chapter are *The Cardinal Sins* (1981), *An Occasion of Sin* (1991), and *Fall from Grace* (1992). They have been grouped together here because of similarities in them and because they all have main characters who are priests. Some of the author's other novels might fit into this chapter but since he has grouped them into trilogies or in other ways, they will therefore be considered subsequently.

Andrew Greeley's novels of the Catholic Church and its priesthood are serious studies that only someone with his background in sociology could make. He is not an author painting a sensational picture but rather a social scientist describing what actually is taking place in the Church in the latter half of the twentieth century. He depicts the human comedy with all its weaknesses, failings, misdeeds, and mishaps and the divine comedy with all its grace, joy, triumphs, and glorious happy endings. God, who is the main character in all his novels, always has the last laugh.

With *The Cardinal Sins*, which sold over three million copies the first year and went through ten printings, Greeley's social criticism becomes very incisive and penetrating. Although there were satiric elements in the Grail trilogy, his comedy now turns more decisively to satire and social criticism. Using his "freight train load of empirical data" Greeley the social scientist draws a portrait of the society he knows best, the priesthood of the Roman Catholic Church. As he reflects on the manners, ideas, and conflicts of the turbulent and violent times since Vatican II, his comedy now especially resembles Balzac's. With clear-sighted vision, a passion for truth-telling, and trenchant psychological observation, he probes the secret recesses of the sacerdotal soul as it exists from the highest echelons of the Vatican down to the ranks of the seminarians. What he describes is often disquieting, especially to the hierarchy and other priests who desire that the faults, blemishes, and sins of the clergy be kept concealed. Because he has exposed these weaknesses, faults and sins, Greeley has taken a lot of heat and is still taking it. In response to those who say he should not write social criticism of the Church, Greeley replies, "Those who want me to be silent about the weaknesses of Church leaders should take up matters . . . with the authors of the New Testament, who were quite devastating in their descriptions of early Church leaders " (*Piece of My Mind* 134).

It is precisely his love for the Church that motivates Greeley to write critically about her members, in hopes, that in so doing, he may promote change and reform. He is a satirist and it is the nature of satire to criticize human frailty with the prime purpose of correcting what is amiss. At times Greeley's satire is Horatian in that it is genial, urbane, smiling and attempts to correct by gentle and mostly sympathetic laughter. At other times, perhaps most often, it is Juvenalian in its severity. It then indicates with moral indignation and contempt the evil and corruption he finds. With biting gibes and cutting rebukes, contemptuous, sarcastic, and taunting language, he vents his anger at the incompetency, weakness, and bungling of the hierarchy and lower clergy, as it is depicted in his fiction. Irony, wit, witty subtlety, caricature, and humor are some of the techniques he uses in creating his satire, which is always distinguished by its good taste and urbane sophistication.

With characteristic blunt honesty, Greeley in the four novels under discussion, satirizes the priesthood of Catholic Church as it really is from the activities of the humblest inner city parish to the secret dealings of the curia behind Vatican walls. Homosexuality, pedophilia, sexual liaisons with women, financial scandals, administrative incompetence—in short, all the ills that plague the Catholic Church, as reported in the media today, are depicted without any whitewash.

In *The Cardinal Sins,* the satire largely resides in the contrast between Kevin Brennan and other priests, especially Patrick Donahue, who are corrupt, dishonest, or depraved. With Kevin, the reader experiences life in the seminary, where they turn out priests "like sausages," where shallow men with sleek facades and glib tongues are favored over those who are serious, intellectual, reserved, and profound. The seminary is shown to be an institution where obedience, not charity or zeal for souls, is the most important virtue to a faculty whose teaching skills are below average. With Kevin, we observe Patrick Donahue, a man who "cannot keep his pants zipped"and has both homosexual and heterosexual affairs, advance in the Church to the high offices of archbishop and cardinal, while Kevin, who is ever faithful to his commitment to celibacy and is more capable intellectually and has greater influence with people, is kept always on the fringes of the ecclesiastical establishment. Through Kevin's eyes, we also view Church leaders like the lunatic Cardinal O'Brien, Archbishop Raffaelo Crespi, the self-serving apostolic delegate, or the sexually active homosexual Monsignor Martinelli, and a Church leadership that corrupts the process of papal elections.

With a good sense of contrasts and clear-sighted vision, Greeley places Kevin Brennan against this backdrop of sin and corruption and lets him exemplify the splendor of the priesthood. Not that he is by any means perfect. Far from it. Rather Kevin is proud, ruthless, competitive, and a "hard-eyed fighter." But he is faithful, and he reflects Greeley's profound love and dedication to the celibate priesthood and all it represents. Despite his evident failings, Kevin is to be perceived as a sacrament of a world that transcends ours. To Greeley: "The celibate priest is a sign of transcendence, a rumor of angels, a man who points to the world beyond this one . . ." (*The Catholic Myth* 199–200). A celibate priest represents the "God who lurks" in our world even if he does not always exercise his office very well.

That there are many priests today who do not exercise the office of the priest-hood well is obvious to anyone who reads the newspapers or listens to the tele-vision. The priesthood is experiencing many problems. The numerical decline of the clergy, decreased financial contributions from the laity, and a loss of respect for church leaders are but a few of the problems. The Catholic Church Extension Society estimates that by the year 2005 there will be only twenty-one thousand parish priests in the United States, reflecting a loss of 40 per cent since 1966. According to Greeley, the priesthood is in "terrible disarray. The morale of the priests is awfully, awfully low. They're battered, they're hurting, they don't have much hope for the future, and they're not terribly interested in recruiting young men to follow them. . ." (*Conversations* 195). As for the hierarchy: "With a few notable exceptions, the hierarchial leadership exists as a spectrum running from mediocre to psychopathic" (*Reader* 32). Greeley expresses his dissatisfaction with this state of affairs both in his nonfiction and in his novels, beginning with *The Cardinal Sins.*

The Cardinal Sins is a fast-paced novel, with psychologically well-motivated and fully developed characters who hold the reader's interest from the first page until the very end. With brilliance and power, the author displays a constant play of laughing intelligence, swiftness, adroitness, smoothness, graceful wit, and at times bold, even harsh, realism. The language is always colorful, sometimes scato-logical, but consistently urbane and sophisticated. Although the tone of the novel is basically serious, there are many comic episodes and characters, for the satire is usually blended with humor and wit.

The Cardinal Sins is the story of Pat, Kevin, Maureen, and Ellen who grow up together and whose lives are intertwined. The principal theme of the novel is that God's love pursues the four main characters through their human loves for one another. Patrick Donahue and Kevin Brennan enter the priesthood. Eventually Pat becomes a Cardinal, Maureen a painter, Ellen a psychiatric nurse and an author, and Kevin a Ph.D. in psychology and an author. The story is told largely from the point of view of Kevin. Ellen's and Maureen's points of view are presented through the letters they write to each other. When the story switches to Pat's view point, the text is in italics to inform the reader of the switch. Since Pat is the priest who keeps yielding to the sins of the flesh, some people, unfamiliar with literary devices, have ridiculously accused Greeley of putting the so-called purple passages in italics to call attention to them. Actually, however, Pat's cardinal sin, his dominant fault, is not lust but covetousness; Kevin's is pride; Ellen's is anger with occasional gluttony; and Maureen's is sloth. All are plagued by envy and lust. As Greeley points out with dry ironic humor in the introductory note to the novel, "Cardinal sins have nothing to do, of course, with the members of the Sacred College [the Cardinals], who, as we all know, commit hardly any sins."

In the summer of 1948 shortly before Kevin is due to enter the seminary, there occurs a very tender, magical, and mysterious interlude in which he discovers the sexual beauty of Ellen as they swim nude, but chastely, in a pond on a hot, humid Sunday afternoon. Throughout his years in the seminary and the priesthood, this memory of Ellen and what he feels for her at this time, which is "infinitely beyond physical desire," sustains him. Always when tempted, this image of Ellen keeps him faithful to his commitment to the celibate priesthood.

Unable to marry Kevin, Ellen settles for Tim Curran. After having four babies in five years and losing her husband to an embolism, she becomes a victim of self-pity. Angry with Kevin, because he will not leave the priesthood and marry her, and angry at God and the Church since she feels they are to blame for what has happened to her, she abandons the faith, stops going to mass, and becomes embittered. Because he is a celibate priest, Kevin is able to minister to her and help her to build a new life for herself. In time, she becomes a psychiatric nurse, a writer, and eventually marries a Jewish psychiatrist, Herb Strauss. The high point of the book is when Ellen, now very happy and successful, comes to Kevin and asks him to hear her confession. After listening to her relate ten years of sins, he says she did not confess the one thing, the only sin, that matters—that she was mad at God and the Church and pretended for a long time she could get away from both. Finally, after she makes her confession that she blamed God and the Church for things that were within her, Kevin says that the Church had never let her go. No matter how far people try to run, they cannot outdistance the love and forgiveness of God whose love is stronger than death and pursues people in all their loves and never lets them go. As Andrew Greeley says: "Our flawed and errant humanity cannot block God's overwhelming love" *(Bible and Us* 97).

The love that Kevin and Ellen have for each other continues to grow, especially after the reconciliation scene, described above. Later when Kevin has been a priest for about twenty years and is a successful psychologist with a national reputation as an author, he confesses to himself that he is still just as much in love with Ellen as he had been twenty-four years before. Ellen, too, admits she loves Kevin.

Eventually, when Ellen offers to make love to Kevin without it's changing their commitments to her husband and the Church, Kevin declines, much to her relief, saying that it would destroy the love they have for each other. Kevin firmly believes in celibacy for priests, but he suggests that perhaps it should be optional.

Ironically, the priests in Cardinal Patrick Donahue's archdiocese believe that he is a staunch advocate of celibacy, while he actually carries on an intimate relationship with Maureen Cunningham for many years. The tumultuous affair between Pat and Maureen is set in contradistinction to the chaste relationship of Kevin and Ellen.

Pat is, to be sure, filled with self-loathing and guilt because of his sexual relationship with Maureen. Surely one of the most interesting and complex characters that Greeley has created, Patrick Donahue is a man for whom sex is demonic and torturous. The first indication that sex is a problem for him comes when, as a new high school graduate, he explores Maureen's body, planning to have intercourse with her despite her resistance, but suddenly stops making love to her, when his passion turns to fear and revulsion after she has yielded to him.

Donahue, the son of a garbage man, hopes to get a scholarship to attend Notre Dame. When the assistant coach from South Bend comes to observe him playing basketball, Pat freezes up, but Kevin comes to his rescue. They win the ball game and the city championship only because Kevin tips a rebound to Pat from one of Pat's missed shots, permitting him to sink it in the basket as the final buzzer sounds. This is the beginning of a pattern of behavior that will last the rest of their lives in which Kevin repeatedly "tips rebounds" for Pat.

Since his main interest at the time is chasing girls, Kevin is surprised to hear that Pat wants to enter the seminary with him. In Kevin's frequently expressed opinion, Pat has no business being a seminarian, priest, bishop, archbishop, and finally cardinal, as he eventually becomes.

Pat's "call" to the priesthood comes about under strange circumstances after an episode that further reveals his sexual problems. He has an experience in which a "strange light" rises up from the waters of the lake and envelops him, causing him to experience joy, happiness, cleansing, and renewal. All the women in the world were in the light—nursing, healing, and loving him. They merge into one woman, whom he believes to be the mother of Jesus. He becomes convinced that she wants him to become a priest and that he must do so to be "free of the damnation" that is fighting for his soul. Kevin is equally convinced that Pat does not belong in the seminary or the priesthood, yet loyalty to his friend makes Kevin continue tipping rebounds for Pat throughout his career, making it possible for Pat to remain in the seminary and later in his priestly office.

Pat is unable to live the celibate life. Not only does he have trouble leaving women alone, he also has homosexual affairs and is described as being a "switch hitter." In the seminary, he has a sexual relationship with another seminarian. Later we learn that when Pat has sex with a male, he does not have the feelings of guilt and remorse that he experiences with women. Interestingly, when he goes to Rome to study he chooses as his mentor the homosexual Monsignor Martinelli.

His sexual relationships with women continue to be a problem. On one occasion, he forces himself on Georgina Carrey and more or less rapes her, conceiving a child. Remorse and contrition consume him immediately. Later, after he becomes a cardinal, he tries again to rape Ellen one night after a dinner at which she was a guest in the cardinal's mansion, but suddenly filled with anxiety and sorrow, he stops and apologizes. He first mentions the word *homosexual* in connection with himself, when he admits to Ellen that he loves Kevin more than everyone else. Finally, at the end of the book, he tells Kevin, in a scene filled with pathos, that he loves him. When Maureen dies near the end of the story, there comes the following startling revelation at her deathbed that Pat had done everything in his life to please Kevin.

Kevin cannot help but be affected by the various loves of his life and God pursues him through them all. At the end of the book, he experiences a kind of rebirth having been humanized by his sufferings and those of his friends. He is not as proud or ruthless as he had been and he is becoming more open to the love others offer him. The book ends with Kevin reciting in Latin, "so God could understand," the psalm for the dead which ends "For with the Lord is kindness and with him is plenteous redemption: And he will redeem Israel from all their iniquities" (307).

There is much humor in the book; the satire of seminary life has its share. Discipline is so strict that a seminarian is not permitted to walk by himself on the grounds of the seminary. With biting sarcasm Kevin remarks: "You weren't supposed to walk by yourself—I suppose because you might have dirty thoughts while you walked, or maybe just because you might have thoughts, something the seminary seemed to frown upon" (46). The stern discipline and isolation from society of the seminary definitely does not prepare priests for life in a twentieth-century parish. With typical Greeley wit, Kevin jests that the "rector was one of the best minds of the eighteenth century" (42). What *does* Kevin learn in the seminary? Cynicism.

There is more satire when Kevin is assigned, after his ordination, as curate to Monsignor Rafferty, where cynicism is an attitude that is essential to success. As a character, the monsignor is a type; he is easily recognized by anyone who ever knew a monsignor of the old school. As Greeley draws him, he is exaggerated to the point of becoming a caricature in order to emphasize the satiric nature of the narration. To those readers who have known a person like Monsignor Rafferty, the portrait is mordant sarcasm. This monsignor, for whom the money counting room is the most important in the rectory, treats Kevin like a child and a servant. When Kevin discovers and reveals that the head usher has been stealing from the Sunday collections, the monsignor is more concerned about keeping it a secret so as to maintain his reputation as a good administrator than he is in recovering the money.

While the monsignor drives a Cadillac and enjoys his booze, Kevin, not permitted to own a car or drink any alcoholic beverage until he has been a priest for five years, must make communion calls on foot and avoid social drinking. So strict is Monsignor Rafferty's discipline that Kevin is not even allowed to have Saturday off to officiate at the weddings of friends.

The satire of the novel also deals with the homosexual affairs of the clergy very deftly and even bluntly. In a great scene demonstrating Greeley's adeptness with situation comedy, Greeley depicts the homosexual Monsignor Antonio Martinelli, Pat's Roman patron, who makes a rather humorous attempt to seduce Pat, when he is at the family villa working on some Church business with him. This is rich comedy, such as one might find in the plays of the great French writer of comedy Molière.

Greeley has tremendous talent in sketching memorable characters like Antonio Martinelli with a few well-chosen and well-turned phrases. *The Cardinal Sins* has it share of such characters like, for example, Archbishop Raffaelo Crespi, the apostolic delegate to the United States, who has a "squat figure, dark skin, and a low forehead" and looks like "the stereotype of a Mob hit man." He is also a type; he is illustrative of the career priest who is more interested in his personal advancement than in the Church and hopes to gain a cardinal's red hat.

One of the most memorable characters in the novel is Daniel Cardinal O'Neill. The satire involving him is especially vitriolic. The sequence in which he appears is highly satiric comedy while at the same time being almost tragic, depending on one's point of view. Great comedy can border on the tragic as such works as *Le Misanthrope* or *Tartuffe* by Molière, one of the greatest writers of comedy of all time, attest. Greeley pictures life as he sees it with its inconsistencies and cross purposes. With a few deft strokes, Greeley describes O'Neill as "a tall, thin scarecrow of a man with a fringe of brown hair around a gaunt head" (159). "He bursts into the room like a cyclone coming in off the plains" (167). "He was a hurricane of words, swirling, pounding, reeling, spinning, utterly unpredictable save in one respect: the subject was almost invariably himself" (167). A psychopathic liar who makes up fanciful stories in which he is the inevitable hero, he cannot tell reality from the lies he invents. Financially incompetent, he moves from one diocese to another, only one step ahead of the bailiff. To buy favor in Rome he sends mass stipends of one thousand dollars to Rome to influential people. Unlike most psychopaths he has a woman, who falsely claims to be his cousin, and with whom he has been allied for twenty-five years. After spending every evening with her, he comes home drunk about eleven o'clock. Although the "hand-wringing pope," whom Kevin describes as a "disaster," will not remove him from his office, Cardinal O'Neill finally drives his Cadillac into the lake while he is drunk and drowns.

The satire is even more caustic when Kevin has a face off with his new cardinal, his old friend, Patrick Donahue. When Pat orders Kevin to give up his work at the university and come to work for the archdiocese, he refuses. Inwardly furious but outwardly calm, Kevin threatens to reveal Pat's sexual indiscretions to the Vatican, if Pat insists on pursuing the matter. The scene is an excellent example of satiric comedy.

In addition to satiric comedy there is also much comedy of situation in the book. An example of situation comedy occurs when Kevin has to make a quick trip to Rome and stays at Maureen's home. He awakens to hear Maureen closing his bedroom windows when a thunderstorm strikes. When she sits down on the bed and asks if they can talk, he wishes he had brought his pajamas with him. The reader pictures him holding the bedclothes tightly around himself, knowing that he is naked under them.

One of the high points of comedy comes when Georgina Carrey summons Kevin by announcing to him on the phone that she intends "to get" Pat—he is the father of her daughter Patsy—and to expose his affair with Maureen. As he waits nervously for Georgina to appear he fixes himself a large drink of Jameson's on the rocks, followed by a second and a third. When he is halfway through his third drink, she appears wearing nothing but a purple towel around her waist. Here we have comedy of both situation and dialogue.

"Remarkable what they can do with cosmetic surgery these days," Kevin taunts her as he pretends to appraise Georgina's body. Swaying provocatively toward Kevin, she demands that either he make love to her or she will have the story of Pat and Maureen in the newspapers the next day. Undaunted, Kevin calls her "a cheap old whore" and leaves. The scene ends with Kevin firing a parting shot from the door, "Mind you, Gina, surgery or not, your tits really look good for someone your age" (193). This is a classic example of Greeley's ability to handle both comedy of situation and dialogue.

All the changes in the Church since the Second Vatican Council are reflected in the story as Kevin experiences them. He reads John Noonan's book *Contraception* and joins the ranks of priests who are changing their minds about birth control. Schools close, priests and nuns abandon their vocations in droves, the hierarchy moves toward a new policy on annulments, mass attendance drops to half what it was, and financial scandals haunt the bishops. Not only is the Church the subject of Greeley's scrutiny and satire. He takes a few good solid swats at yellow journalism in the novel. First there is Sister Rogeria, "a plain young woman with a dagger face and disorderly brown hair," who misrepresents herself and interviews Kevin and publishes a series of sensational articles in which she deliberately misquotes him. Then there is a reporter for an important U. S. publication who cooperates with Antonio Martinelli in blackmailing Patrick Donahue. Shocked that this happens, Kevin comments, "Investigative reporting' covers a multitude of sins . . ." (290). Nevertheless, Greeley is not unsympathetic to all journalists. The girl Monica Kelly, who tries to get at the truth concerning the financial corruption in the Archdiocese of Chicago, is depicted as someone doing an admirable job.

The Cardinal Sins has the happy ending that all comedy must have. There is hope and renewal for the Church. Patrick Donahue is removed from his office as cardinal archbishop of Chicago and sent to work in the curia in Rome. The Church is liberated from the massive weight of the tradition of the Italian papacy with the election of the new Polish pope, John Paul II, who is described as "a sun rising brilliantly above the fog and haze" (300).

In conclusion, *The Cardinal Sins* is a rich, satiric novel that demands reform and renewal in the Church. It is an excellent example of Greeley's divine and human comedy that depicts the people of God as saints and sinners who always have hope with love triumphing over hatred and life prevailing over death.

Published in 1990, nine years after *The Cardinal Sins*, *The Cardinal Virtues*, is the story of Father Lar, short for Laurence O'Toole McAuliffe, the pastor of St. Finian's in suburban Chicago—old, worn-out, angry, disillusioned, and quite cynical—and his pastoral associate, the brand-new priest, Father James Stephen Michael Finbar Keenan, an idealistic young man who claims he can fix anything and sets out to prove it. What results is great comedy—a very satiric and frequently very humorous account of the priesthood at the beginning of the 1990s. The satire in this novel hits at inept Church leaders in the chancery office, showing that the parish is the real church, not the hierarchy. The fighting that Father Lar engages in with the chancery office provides much of the human comedy in the book. The divine comedy is the work of the Holy Spirit in the love that the people have for each other, but especially in the love, sometimes heroic, that Father Lar shows to everyone through his priestly ministry, by opening their minds and hearts to the love of God. Despite his language, which is very human and at times quite earthy, but always effective and to the point, he reflects the splendor of the priesthood.

Father Lar is very different from Kevin Brennan in *The Cardinal Sins*. Although he does have a doctorate and is a good fighter like Kevin, he is very human, filled with compassion, extremely witty, and has a great sense of humor. His main foil is Joe Simon, the vicar general of the diocese, whom Lar describes as "Good second in command and occasional hit man for a Mob boss" (3).

According to Lar, it is even problematic whether Joe Simon believes in God. Ambitious, servile to authority, pushy with those under him, and obsessed with the niceties of clerical protocol, power is the force he uses in dealing with the clergy. Quickly the reader learns that Lar is just the opposite of Joe Simon, for he is disdainful of clerical protocol, indifferent to those in power, and disrespectful to authority when it impinges negatively on his parish. The sparring with words that takes place between them is humorous, but it is also satirizes ecclesiastical leaders who are blind guides, straining out gnats and swallowing camels. Simon who is always threatening Lar, that he is going "to get him" eventually, thinks he finally has him when he accuses Jamie Keenan, the new priest, of pederasty. Actually this time Joe has swallowed a camel. He has underestimated both Lar and his new priest Jamie Keenan, as we shall see when we discuss the climactic comic scene in which Lar "gets" Joe Simon.

Father Lar has been a priest for twenty-eight years and at St. Finian's for six. He is, in his own words "a worn-out, angry, disillusioned Old Priest" (2). He is cynical and he is tired. When he first became a priest, he had wanted to save the world, but now his world has shrunk to being his parish. He is afraid that he will even lose the dream of saving the parish, for as he explains "it is hard to sustain a spiritual dream when so much of your time is devoted to fixing busted machinery" (2).

When Joe Simon calls and asks him to take a new priest at St. Finian's, Lar immediately declines. The three previous new priests that had been assigned to him had disillusioned Father Lar. One of them had carried on at least three love affairs and made passes at all the women on the staff and half of the women of the parish before leaving the priesthood, the second had suffered a nervous break-down, and the third one did nothing but watch television all day long.

Finally the cardinal himself visits St. Finian's to persuade Lar to take a new priest. Lar's description of the cardinal is comical. "The Cardinal's public person is that of a shy vulnerable man, almost like a hobo asking for a quarter to buy a cup of coffee" (5). "Dressed in old black trousers, a worn black sweater, and a collarless shirt with a stud in it (his version of sport clothes), he soft-soaped me while drinking a diet Pepsi" (6). Then Lar adds: "How can anyone turn down someone who looks like a bushy-haired French farmer in a 1940 film and drives a dirty, four-year-old gray Pontiac?" (6).

The basic problem with the cardinal is that he lacks the cardinal virtues of justice, temperance, fortitude, and perhaps prudence. Although he does spend a lot of time praying, Lar believes if he prays for all the people and things he says he does, he would be on his knees all night. To make matters worse, the cardinal surrounds himself with clergy in the chancery who seem unable to grasp the problems of the parish.

In a satiric scene that foreshadows the false accusations of pederasty leveled at Father Jamie, Father Tom "Turk" Nelligan explains how pederasty cases are handled in the diocese. The vicar for the clergy shows up in the middle of the night with another priest and they take the accused man to a rectory on the other side of town, tell him they have hired a good lawyer for him and try to send him off to one of the "funny farms for clergy that are so busy these days" (19).

The sad state into which the priesthood has fallen, as shown in this conver-sation, is depressing to Father Lar. His comments about the Church, often sar-castic, ironic, and humorous, further serve to satirize Catholic society of the 1990s. He summarizes his deepest feelings in prayer.

But Father Lar is not one to give up. In contrast with the cardinal and his staff, Father Lar has an abundance of the cardinal virtues and the theological ones too. To everyone at St. Finian's, where he works with an odd assortment of characters, some of whom are quite comical, he is a great priest. Compassionately, he has taken into the rectory a priest who has had problems with alcohol. The story of Father Mike Quinlan contributes to the satire of the Church in the 1990s, for it is typical of many priests who have become discouraged, overworked and burned out and sought relief in a bottle. Although he is "one of the most brilliant and gifted priests of the archdiocese—tall, handsome white haired, eloquent,"Mike Quinlan, who has now been sober for three years, broke under the strain he experienced as a pastor and became an alcoholic.

Also at St. Finian's is Jeanne Flavin—forty years and old and still unmarried. She serves as director of religious education and is involved in a number of comic scenes. During the course of the story, it is learned that she is an incest victim. Through the patient and sympathetic ministry of Father Lar, she is able to forget

the past and marry. A type of the liberated woman with strong Marxist inclinat-
ions, she is not above yelling at the pastor things like, "You're a male bastard like
all the others" (7).

Typical of the comedy of the novel are the scenes dealing with the teenagers'
attempts to find a suitable date and a mate for Jeanne in what Father Lar refers to
as "raffling off Jeanne Flavin" (231). When Jeanne learns that they have "raffled
her off" to Don Lyons, Father Lar has to mediate the fight between Jeanne and
Jamie, who furnished the kids with the tickets to the Chicago Symphony Orchestra
for the date.

Another interesting and comic character is the rectory cook, a young Irish
woman, whom government agents try to deport as an illegal alien. Because she is
so attractive, George Wholey, one of the right-wing followers of Father Louis
Almaviva, the local superior of the Corpus Christi Institute, wants Father Lar to
fire her and get her out of the rectory. Instead he increases her pay, well aware that
the Church has continually given inferior wages to its employees.

The descriptions of Wholey are concise and particularly well drawn.

George Wholey was the kind of person who would announce proudly with his wife present:
We never once used birth control. We went the abstinence way with the Church. It wasn't
hard on Jill—women don't need it—but it was tough on me."

For all his rigidities and ignorances, George had a certain hangdog charm about him.
he'd become popular with the locker-room gin-rummy set at the club. You could like
George until you discovered, that deliberately or not, he was a mean son of a bitch. (74)

George is the puppet that Father Louis Almaviva manipulates in an attempt
to take over St. Finian's. Father Louis, satirizing the right-wing crazies that have
been trying to undo all the good that the Vatican Council accomplished, is in his
early forties, a "smooth, elegant, aristocratic, charming—a somewhat sawed-off
Mediterranean-lover type." The short description of him is quite good. Father
Louis, a caricature of the sophisticated Latin cleric, is hungry for power and wants
to take over the Church and return it to its pre–Vatican II days. A modern-day
Torquemada type, whose theory of dealing with women reveals the kind of person
he is, instructs his followers that women "appreciate being chastised by their
husbands because it reminds them of their proper place" (225). According to him,
the marriage bed is "an altar of sacrifice" (109).

Father Louis is not the only priest who has harmed the people of St. Finian's.
Lar brings people back into the Church people who were driven out by priests like
"dippy Mickey Scott," "one of the all-time great assholes of our galaxy," who
made up his canon law as he went along and made it a policy to "always to make
life as tough as possible for those unfortunate enough to walk into his rectory"
(257). During prayer Lar wonders about the "idiots" in the priesthood who are
messing up peoples lives. " Why the hell," I demanded of God that night, "do we
have to spend so much time undoing the hurt that the assholes have caused?"
(259).

As the book progresses, the reader becomes aware that although the cardinal and his colleagues in the chancery office do not possess the cardinal virtues, Father Lar has them all to an heroic degree. This can be observed in his dealings with the various and sometimes quite comical people that cross his path. People like Jackie, the teenaged portress of the rectory, Parti O'Hara, a young girl who wants to become a priest, Sister Cunnegunda, who thinks it is 1935, or Martina Condon, "a woman who needed periodic fixes of hate the way a vampire needs blood" (26). Then too there is Tom "Turk" Nelligan, a priest at St. Finian's, "a lean little man with a tuft of brown hair around the edge and an eternal frown etched on his narrow face." "He is profoundly cynical about the ecclesiastical institution and has been running on empty . . . for at least a decade" (20).

Other characters satirized by Greeley are plentiful. Kenny McGuire, D.D., the auxiliary bishop, is in Lar's opinion, "one of the great pompous assholes of the free world," a distinction that was earned, not honorary as is his doctorate of divinity. Linda Meehan, the youth minister, is an "intense, stringy generous young woman in her middle twenties." "She would have been an intense, stringy young nun thirty years ago. In these days, dedicated young people calculate, reasonably enough, that the Church can lay valid claim to only part of their lives" (27).

In a humorous and satiric scene, Lar meets with the typical liberated woman, in the person of Maria Sullivan who comes to the rectory, announces she wants a divorce, and is upset when Father Lar does not try to talk her out of it. When she, "a woman of the eighties, at last in full charge of her life," strides briskly out of the rectory, she slips with her high heels in the fresh snow and clumsily falls into a snow bank (291).

Comedy and satire are also provided by Blaise and Sheila Ferrigan Mc Kittrick, stereotypes of liberal ex-priests and nuns, who criticize everything that happens at St. Finian's. These people, who are left-wing caricatures that try to look like the prophet Jeremiah could not relinquish their fixation on the ecclesiastical institution. Although Father and Sister are "playing house" together, the parish is still their obsession" (175). The author uses these small envious characters not only to satirize people like them, but also to take another swat at yellow journalism when Ted McPhaul [read McFoul], another ex-priest and former classmate of Lar's, gets information from Blaise and Sheila Ferrigan McKittrick to write an article for the *National Catholic Observer*.

In an item titled "Ex-Radical Relaxes in Plush Parish," the Ferrigan-McKittricks and McPhaul charge that Lar is "a lazy do-nothing priest living high off the hog in a rich parish" (281). This provides an opportunity for the Irish cook to unleash her repertory of comical scatological expletives on them, describing them as "pissant blatherskites" and "frigging shitehawks." When Jeanne the director of religious education or DRE says, "They didn't check their frigging facts," caustically Lar replies, "They never do" (282). Yellow journalists and their associates are a frequent foil for Greeley in his novels.

One of the especially nice characters at St. Finian's is Patrick McNally—a teenaged boy who wants to be a priest because he admires Father Lar. His father, however, causes quite a wrangle, which is not without its comic elements, when he shows up at the rectory furious that his son would consider being anything but a doctor and blaming Father Jamie for the boy's decision. Actually however the boy wants to be a priest because he admires Father Lar, who cannot understand "why any kid in his right mind would want to be a priest," since "the priesthood is such a mess these days."

One of the best comic scenes in the book takes place in the chancery office as a result of the machinations of George Wholey, who has his son Anthony accuse Father Jamie of sexually molesting him in an attempt to destroy both Father Jamie and Lar, and whose plans backfire. Wholey is backed by the Corpus Christi Institute whose membership is "notably to the right of Pope Innocent III" and "right of Caesar Augustus." They are "trying to repeal the Second Vatican Council and restore the glorious Church of the thirteenth century" (4).

When Lar is brought into the "star chamber" to deal with the accusations of pederasty leveled at Father Jamie some of the best comedic satire of the story unfolds with the raillery of the novel reaching a pinnacle with the unveiling of the chicanery of the chancery. As Lar confronts the cardinal and the chancery staff, the derision and ridicule are mordant. Comparing the cardinal to a renaissance Lord summoning his vassals to pay homage to him, Lar concludes that their "ecclesiastical power game" is "far from Jerusalem" (345–346).

During his "friendly chat with the judges of the star chamber," Lar is made to sit opposite the cardinal who is seated at his ten-thousand-dollar desk. When Lar refers to the chair offered him as "the prisoners dock," the young auxiliary bishop is embarrassed for "no one ever told him that being a bishop's auxiliary demanded such dirty work" (353).

Upbraiding them for the dreadful waste of time of people supposed to be preaching God's love, he says to the cardinal: "The priesthood is a shambles. Morale is in the lower depths. You should be encouraging and reassuring your priests. Instead you hassle them" (358). And to Joe Simon: "You may well be the greatest asshole in the history of the priesthood" (359).

The grand finale of the comedy comes when Father Jamie, his parents, Father Lar, George Wholey, Father Louis Almaviva, and Joe Simon, and sycophants deal with the accusations of pederasty leveled at Father Jamie. Wholey and Father Louis, whom Lar refers to ludicrously as "Father Aquavelvet," want the diocese to pay "a token payment of a hundred thousand dollars to the Wholey family" to cover medical treatment for Anthony, whom they claim was sexually abused by Father Jamie. They further demand that Jamie be transferred to another diocese after a time of reflection in one of the "funny farms" designated for handling child molesters. They also want Father Lar removed from his parish. Joe Simon, who is the inquisitor in charge, tries his usual tactic of raw naked power to intimidate Jamie and Lar.

In a grandstand performance, Lar responds to those who accuse Jamie by demanding that all charges against him be dropped, with George Wholey making a payment of two hundred fifty thousand dollars to the Archdiocesan Inner City

School fund in return for which the Keenan's (Father Jamie and his parents) will drop their suit against him. With tongue in cheek, Lar quips: "I will at least forsake all claims on Father Simon's job when the cardinal finds out how badly he bungled this matter" (432). All charges are dropped against Jamie, when Mrs. Wholey admits that her husband coerced their son into making false accusations against Father Jamie who is totally innocent.

The human comedy plays itself out. Jamie tries to help the Wholeys restructure their marriage and family. Ms. Sullivan, the liberated woman who had talked so much of freedom, comes to the rectory and asks for Father Lar to hear her confession. She is also reconciling with her husband and children.

The divine comedy ends with Father Lar presiding at the Easter Vigil, which proclaims God's great salvific act of love, hope, and redemption. Most of the principal characters of the novel are there united with him in faith—the Ferrigan-McKittricks, the Sullivans, the newlywed Lyons couple, and all the rest. Even the drunk that phones Lar frequently in the night has begun to hope his life can be changed and has joined Alcoholics Anonymous. The story ends with Father Lar realizing that he has been caught up "in a hot flood tide of grace" since the day Jamie arrived and wonders what else God, who is really the main character of all Greeley's novels, has in store for them all. Hope and renewal have come to St. Finian's. The reader closes the book knowing, that with a few priests like Father Lar and Jamie who possess and exercise the cardinal virtues, the Church will survive the incompetent chicanery and bungling of the chancery.

As a priest Father Lar represents the God who lurks in this world. As a "sacramental person," he points beyond himself to a reality that surmounts our own, to the transcendent God who is always immanent, nearer than breathing, closer than hands and feet.

To realize what a rich and admirable character Greeley has created in the person of Father Lawrence O'Toole, one has only to listen to him speak or probe his most inmost thoughts which are given like asides in a stage play. A very caring and sensitive person, he prays for many people, hugs their kids, and bounces their babies. Actually his virtue seems heroic, but of course he would be the last person to think of himself as saintly. The contrast between him and the priests of the chancery makes the satire all the more powerful.

Much humor comes from the comical remarks that Father Lar makes. For example: "I was tempted to jealousy, an experience not unlike rolling in cow dung. Well, I never rolled in cow dung. I imagine that jealousy is almost as vile as envy" (104). Other remarks Father Lar makes are strikingly expressive. When there is a brouhaha brewing in the parish, he remarks colorfully, "The hate meter was turning as purple as the Advent vestments" (285). He describes a late October afternoon "with gray clouds racing across the sky, and the bare trees standing in mourning for summer like relatives at a wake" (145). Winter is a "cruel old grandparent who refused to die" (417). These are typical of the well-turned phrases that grace Greeley's pages.

Finally, in *The Cardinal Virtues* Greeley has written a very comical satire of the Catholic Church and its priesthood in the early 1990s. Although he especially holds up to ridicule the administrators in the chancery office, many other people are also lampooned in portraits which give the characteristic details of each person. In the characters Father Lar and Father Jamie, he has portrayed the splendor of the priesthood and holds out hope to the Church for a brighter future.

Contentious, but charming, witty and outspoken Father Laurence McAuliffe, continues his struggles with the Church in *An Occasion of Sin*, a shining example of Andrew Greeley's satiric mode in which the divine comedy resoundingly prevails over the faults, foibles, and sins of the human comedy. Lar, as he prefers to be called, is given the assignment by his archbishop of investigating the character of his martyred predecessor John Cardinal McGlynn in the hopes of finding the evidence that will squelch a popular attempt to proclaim him a saint. Until the cardinal convinces him that he really wants to learn the truth about his predecessor, Lar refuses the assignment. Reconsidering he decides, "If there was a real saint in this office, maybe we still have a future"(20).

"Jumping Johnny," as he is called by the priests who knew him, because of the way he jumped up through the ranks of the hierarchy, is one of the least likely people to be considered for canonization. His mother used her vast wealth to advance her son's ecclesiastical career. It was suggested that he smuggled money from the Vatican Bank to Poland to fund Solidarity. There were even rumors that he took money from the Catholic Cemeteries office to bail out his brother at the Board of Trade. Furthermore, it was well known that he had a life-long relationship with a woman, Mary Elizabeth Reilly Quinlan, in whose arms he died, when he was shot, some say by mistake, in Latin America.

Since it is very embarrassing to the Church—the present cardinal of Chicago, Cardinal Ratzinger in the Vatican, and their staffs—that "Jumping Johnny" is said to be working miracles, they want to do everything they can to put an end to the affair at once. Knowing that Lar never liked Johnny, and also fully aware that he never hesitates to speak the truth as he knows it, the archbishop gives him the task of investigating John McGlynn's life to find the evidence that will squelch attempts to start a canonization process.

What follows, as Lar searches for the real Johnny McGlynn, is a story such as one has come to expect of Andrew Greeley—a comedy in all its multiple dimensions. With his usual piquancy, he satirizes the sins and failings of the Church and its clergy and at the same time shows the splendor of the priesthood, as it resides in the poor earthen vessels God has chosen to represent him.

Chapter 10 is especially revelatory. In it Lar discusses with his associate pastor, Father James Keenan, canonization and the possibility of Johnny McGlynn's sanctity. Although Lar does not believe in canonization, he does, however, believe in saints as stories of God's love and human response to it. He definitely does not believe, until the end of the book, that John McGlynn is saint. As for the canonization process itself, Lar says: "Jamie, it's all weird. Like trying to put grace in a measuring cup."

When Lar asks, referring to John McGlynn, "How can a son of a bitch be a saint?" Jamie observes that the Apostle Peter would never have made it through the Roman process for canonization.

He was an ambitious, loudmouth, cowardly braggart who ran out on Jesus and tried to compromise on letting gentiles into the Church. I'm sure there were times when Paul spoke of him the way you do about Cardinal McGlynn, even if he didn't have such expressive Anglo-Saxon words in his vocabulary. Besides, he was a married man, and we have no evidence that he stopped sleeping with his wife after Jesus made him the boss of his crowd. Think about it. The first Pope fondling and engaging in intercourse with a woman. No way would they get a positive vote on him." (80)

Since Jamie, fresh from the seminary, is up on the latest procedures of the canonization process, Lar asks him about the "relators and consulters." Jamie replies with his typically mild sarcasm, which always sounds so innocent coming from him, that they are "competent and honest" and would "lie only for the good of the Church" (83).

To find out if Johnny is really working miracles, Lar sets out to discover as much as he can by visiting the people that knew Johnny. He has the task of listening to each of them and trying to sort out the truth, for all of the characters are not reliable narrators. For example, John's sister Kate tries to defame the memory of her brother, while Mary Elizabeth Reilly Quinlan endeavors to enhance his memory, especially by not revealing that she is the mother of John McGlynn's illegitimate daughter. Other people, in turn, have reasons why they do not want the truth told about him. Eventually, Lar arrives at the truth and advises the Pope in a private audience that he now thinks that Johnny, if he had lived longer, would have been one of the "very greatest" archbishops (314). At the end of the book, Lar even acknowledges in an official letter to the cardinal that he considers John McGlynn to be a saint.

As always in Greeley's fiction, God has the last laugh, and, in this particular story, makes the point that grace can turn the life of a man like Johnny around and even make a saint of him.

As Lar peels away the layers of Johnny's character like removing the leaves from a head of cabbage until one comes to the heart, he encounters a fascinating group of people. Some are good, others bad, still others indifferent, but all well described and delineated with a few well chosen phrases and sparking dialogue that is sometimes very comical and often brimming with caustic satire.

John's sister Kate is a hateful and envious woman whose life is filled with bitterness because her father raped her when she was sixteen. Greeley uses this character to satirize the way the Church has been treating incest victims. When Kate tries to tell her mother what happened to her, Delia McGlynn slaps her hard across the face. "You must have been dreaming," she said. "Nasty, dirty dreams, because you're a nasty, dirty girl!" (105). When she tries to tell her brother Johnny, he is not willing to face what happened. Trying to relate this unhappy occurrence to a priest in confession causes the priest to get angry and insist that it was all her fault. Contemptuously, Kate refers to this treatment as the "Church's enlightened view on child abuse" (105). This incident parallels one in *The Cardinal Virtues*, but in that novel Jeanne Flavin is able to overcome the evil that was done to her, through the patient and considerate ministry of Father Lar. Unfortunately, Kate did not find a kindly priest to help her and consequently she is filled with hatred and bitterness.

From Kate, Lar obtains copies of the correspondence between Johnny and his mother Cordelia McGlynn. In it, Lar learns of the way in which Delia tries to buy Johnny's advancement in the Church. John never explains to her that she cannot buy Church offices, but answers her nicely and respectfully, as a loving son. When John is admitted to the College of Noble Ecclesiastics, Kate advises him to continue using the money she sends him to buy influential friends in the Church. One of Kate' letters is especially ironic and funny. She advises her son, "Don't spend too much time working with them Pollacks either. Nothing good ever came out of trying to deal with them" (115).

In the early 1970s when John is working for Giovanni Benelli, she instructs him "never to trust Italians especially the short ones with greasy smiles." She also promises to buy him an archbishopric if he will find out how much they want for it (116). When she sends money to Rome to buy Denver, Lar, totally embarrassed, has to explain that his mother "was round the bend" (250). Ironically, before she realizes her ambitions for John have been fulfilled and that he has, in fact, become cardinal archbishop of Chicago, she dies in a fire caused by the senility of her Alzheimer's disease.

Delia's letters and the conversation with Kate reveal what kind of mother and father John had and enough of their family life to show that it was not the kind of background from which one expects a saint to come.

John's brother, James, is no better than his sister Kate, as one might well expect. Still angry at John, because he removed him from the floor of the Board of Trade, when he bailed him out of financial problems, he shows his hatred by saying he is glad that his brother is dead. According to him, John was as "randy" as their father," who was a "cocksman," while his mother was an alcoholic and "a ball breaker" (131). Amazing that God took a member of that family and turned him into a saint! No one could believe it was possible, but that is exactly what happened and therein lies the divine comedy of the story.

Especially believing that it is impossible for John McGlynn to be a saint is Bishop Louis Kilmartin "Killer" Kane, the prototype of the envious career ecclesiastic. With a few bold strokes, Greeley draws an accurate, well-defined, comical portrait of this type priest. "Louis Kane was prim, prissy, proper, and pompous, an aging kewpie doll with thin silver hair, petulant eyes, and a face shaped by permanent self-pity" (145). He was a "fussy, stupid little man" (146). When Lar meets with Louis Kane, the bishop of Alton, only because the cardinal insists that he do so, Kane arranges his desk in his hotel room in such a way that Lar must sit on the other side of it similar to the way a suppliant priest would have to do in the bishop's own chancery. Frequently tugging at his enormous French cuffs, Kane, who is miffed that Steve was chosen as cardinal to succeed Johnny instead of himself, announces to Lar that once he has heard his testimony he will not need anything else to prevent Johnny's canonization. He informs him that he is certain that John Arthur McGlynn was not a celibate in his days in Rome (146). Because of his hatred for John, Lar realizes that Kane is not a reliable witness.

In continuing his satire of the clergy, Lar's cardinal is a foil for the novels's attack on the hierarchy. According to Lar, his cardinal has not "uttered a candid statement for at least twenty years. When he purports to be candid, he is being more devious than usual" (11). "His coat of arms was emblazoned, it seemed on every flat surface. I often alleged that it could even be found on the toilet paper in his private bathroom, though in true candor, I've never checked" (12). The last comment is certainly true to character for Lawrence O'Toole who always likes to burst bubbles of pride and ostentation wherever he finds them.

The satire of the clergy reaches its zenith in the comical scene that transpires in the chancery around the cardinal's coffee table when they discuss with Monsignor Franno Albergeti of the Nunciature what to do about the turmoil that is being caused in the diocese and in Rome by Johnny McGlynn's miracles.

Albergeti, "a sleek little Sicilian criminal type with an even larger nose (not a Mafia hit man, but the guy who phones the hit man at the Godfather's instructions)" is there because Cardinal Ratzinger is upset and wants the matter brought to an end. Also present is Jim Lane, an auxiliary bishop that the Vatican imposed on Johnny when he was Cardinal. With typical Greeley economy of words and clarity of expression which hit the mark, Lane is described by Lar as a "big good-looking Irishman with white hair, red face, and a booming voice. He is also as phony as a three headed nickel, and beneath his noisy good cheer, he's as mean and nasty and dishonest a man as it has ever been my displeasure to listen to at a clerical gathering" (195). In Lar's characteristic blunt opinion, he thinks Steve, the Cardinal, should "toss Jimmy Lane out on his fat ass" (196).

When Lar reports that he is investigating the miracle that happened the previous night and that medical research seems to indicate that the cure was by natural causes, Albergeti inquires if the paralysis might return to the person who was supposedly cured. When Lar replies that it might not, Albergeti callously responds, "How unfortunate." To which Lar, a caring priest, comments with sarcasm, "The young man might not think so" (197).

When Albergeti, addressing Lar as Monsignor McAuliffe, asks Lar if he is the one responsible for "ending this unfortunate affair," Lar immediately denies that he is a monsignor, for, although he does not say so, "monsignor" is in his view a dirty word. Explaining that his only job is to make a discreet and informal investigation of the late cardinal to see if there are any positive reasons to exclude future canonization, he states, "That's all I'm supposed to do, so I don't see why I had to be here for this meeting, with all due respect for the Red Baron over in the Holy Office." This is Lar's comical way of referring to Cardinal Ratzinger and the Congregation for the Doctrine of the Faith, which is the current title of the infamous Holy Office of the Inquisition. Of course the title Red Baron refers to the red hat of this prelate and to his manner of behavior.

The comedy builds as Dolph Santini, the archdiocesan vicar for liturgy, spirituality and art, suggests that they hold a study day to consider sanctity. His response to all the problems in the diocese is always to hold a study day. The authoritarian Jim Lane calls for closing the seminary grounds to the public so that people will not be able to visit John McGlynn's grave. Another member of the staff, Don Price, suggests the cardinal draft a pastoral letter on the matter, to which Lar exclaims, "You guys don't understand. . . . It's a popular cult. You can no more stop that than you can stop the Chicago River from freezing in the winter" (197).

Dolph Santini who believes that education can solve all problems suggests ludicrously: "An archdiocesan program of instruction on the real nature of the Church perhaps. Something like the Rite of Christian Initiation of Adults." Those who have read *The Cardinal Virtues* know what Lar's opinion of this rite is.

Jim Lane, the Vatican's man in Chicago, suggests, "Maybe a personal plea from the Holy Father" (198), to which Lar retorts, "If they won't obey him when he says they can't practice birth control, why will they obey him when he tells them they can't pray to Johnny McGlynn?" (198)

In this one brief scene, Greeley has created a satiric tableau which takes a good solid swat at many of the failings of the ecclesiastical establishment since Vatican II. What he describes is a "long way from Jerusalem," to use one of Father Lar's favorite expressions. Perhaps the most serious indictment is that they are trying to set limits to God's grace; they are trying to force God into doing things that will fit neatly into their ideas of how the Church should be. The miracles of John McGlynn are of great embarrassment to them.

Determined to get at the truth about John, Lar visits his grave. In a very comic scene he prays: "Look, you SOB, I don't believe that you're a saint. I think these poor people are being taken in. But maybe God has made you a saint. If he did, I don't want to get in his way. But if your really working wonders, you're going to have to pull off something pretty spectacular to convince me. Understand?" (122).

As further investigation reveals, John McGlynn was a genuinely spectacular person. Bravely he risked his life to carry Israeli funds into Poland, at the request of the Vatican, to help finance the organization which became Solidarity, and helped to bring down the Iron Curtain. Many other questions about his conduct were similarly resolved. He did not use Church money to bail his brother out of financial difficulties, but rather family funds at his disposal. Moreover, he was greatly embarrassed by his mother's attempts to buy him advancement. He did have a brief sexual affair with Mary Elizabeth Reilly Quinlan, after he became cardinal archbishop of Chicago, and he did father a child, but after the birth of the child, a dramatic change took place in his life, leading him to become concerned with peace and justice, to such a degree that he died a martyr's death in Latin America trying to promote both.

When Marbeth, as Mrs. Quinlan is called, relates to Lar the story of how she seduced John McGlynn, she tells him that she was an occasion of sin for the cardinal. With divine comic irony the occasion of sin became the occasion of grace in the life of John McGlynn, who did not know that he had conceived a child until the day he saved the life of Marbeth's daughter Caroline. When he looked at the child's face, he saw the face of his mother Delia and suddenly knew that he was her father. This event triggered in him a moving mystical experience in which he fell utterly in love with God who transformed his life. The splendor of the priesthood began to shine through him. All the money his father had left him, he secretly gave to Catholic charities. The traditional French cuffs gave way to black wash-and-wear clerical shirts like the parish clergy wear. Although his mother no longer recognized him because of Alzheimer's disease, he visited her daily. Finally he died a martyr to his commitment to peace and justice. As he approached death, he realized that God had been pursuing him through all the loves of his life until he had fallen in love with him. As the book ends the reader knows that John McGlynn's life had come to a glorious happy ending. Here we see depicted one of Greeley's major themes—God pursues us through all the loves of our life until we finally come to love him as he desires we should and we experience the glorious happy ending that he has planned for us.

In conclusion, the novel is a hard-hitting and comic satire that attempts to purify members of the Church by holding a mirror up to their blemishes. To those who still do not understand the need for satires about the Church Greeley has this to say: "We wash our dirty linen in public because that is the only way to get it clean (*Making of Popes* 9).

The washing of dirty linen continues in *The Fall from Grace*, which deals with the subject of pedophilia and ephebophilia and their impact on the Church. The novel is a satire that calls for changes in the Church, chief among which are the establishing of lay review boards in the dioceses to investigate charges of sexual abuse against the clergy, with the power to prevent offenders from returning to parish work; an end to cover-ups of sexual abuse cases with large payments of money being paid to silence the victims; a refusal of the Church to employ adversarial hardball legal procedures against the alleged victims and their families; recognition that it is not because of the ordination of homosexuals to the priesthood that the Church is having to deal with pedophilia, but rather the ordination of immature men who cannot keep their commitments; acknowledgment that pedophilia is a special kind of kinkiness that cannot be treated with the techniques used to treat alcoholism, as the Church has been trying to do. The novel also satirizes a corrupt legal system and Mafia types who cut deals to prevent justice from being executed. As a concomitant feature of the story, there is an excellent portrait of the battered wife syndrome as it exists in our society today. Furthermore, the book also take a swipe at corrupt laymen on the chancery staff who accept kickbacks from non union contractors they employ.

The story centers around a prominent Chicago family and the passion and violence that ensue when Brien Donahue's male lover phones Kathleen Donahue, Brien's wife of eighteen years, and detonates the explosive information that he has been having an affair with her husband. With the unfolding of this well-crafted novel, as it is related by the various characters, there emerges a strange and disquieting story.

Although the reader does not know it until the end of the book, Kathleen's brother, James Leary, seduced young Brien when they were adolescents and they were homosexual lovers for a time. The affair ceased before James was ordained to the priesthood and before Brien married Kathleen. Because James wanted to keep Brien as part of his life, he manipulated his sister's relationship with the man she loved, Kieran O'Kerrigan, so that the latter left town under the accusation that he had stolen a large sum of money, which James himself had taken and replaced in Kieran's name. Once Kieran was no longer a suitor for his sister, he encouraged Brien to marry her and continues to try to orchestrate their lives, for he still loves Brien "passionately." Although the marriage is never sexually fulfilling for either of them, Kathleen is confounded to learn that her husband, who has beaten her savagely on more than one occasion, has a homosexual lover. Her brother is even more shocked to learn from Kathleen of the savage beatings and Brien's homosexual involvement. James Leary, now vicar general for the archdiocese, is a committed celibate and has been since his ordination.

To make matters worse, Brien's male lover is a priest of the archdiocese, Gerry Greene, who in addition to being an active homosexual is a pedophile, an ephebophile, and a sadomasochistic drug addict involved in satanic ritual. Because Brien refuses to give him his youngest daughter to be the victim of one of his mad rites, he phones Brien's wife, Kathleen, telling her of his homosexual relationship with her husband

Although Greene has been charged with pedophilia in the past, nothing ever came of the charges, because he seems to be a zealous and dedicated priest, kind and sympathetic to the elderly and conscientious about his visits to the sick. After one of his "escapades," the archdiocese sent him to a rest home and six months later when he was pronounced cured, reassigned him to parish work.

Since Gerry Greene's record as a pastoral administrator is excellent, James Leary, vicar general, refuses to believe that Greene is guilty, believing instead that he is "utterly harmless, a good priest assaulted by calumny for many years"(283). Now that he is accused of sexually assaulting the boy Jack O'Malley, son of Kevin and Helen O'Malley, Greene, with his attorneys paid by the Church, is suing the father of the child for libel and threatening to sue a police officer who testified against him. The chief counsel for the Church Ignatius O'Keefe, who refers to the O'Malleys as "the enemy," is costing the archdiocese a fortune as he stonewalls, intimidates, and ridicules the O'Malleys during the depositions, in an attempt to get them to settle out of court for a small amount of money. Not interested in monetary recompense, but insisting that the Archdiocese set up a lay review board to handle such cases, so that in future no one like Greene will be reassigned to parish work, the O'Malleys continue to fight, although going deeply in debt to do so. No one in the Church will even listen to the O'Malleys, until Father Brendan McNulty, associate pastor at St. Praxides, who also is an attorney practicing law in a major law firm in Chicago, decides to champion the O'Malleys against the

Church. Since the archdiocesan psychiatric consultants affirm that Greene is not a pedophile, the Church takes the position that the boys own father assaulted him. Half the priests in the archdiocese, because of a whispering campaign, believe that the father is an alcoholic and a drug addict.

Father Brendan and Kieran, who is now a doctor of medicine and a psychiatrist in practice in Chicago, visit the O'Malleys. They learn that Greene had beaten their son and frightened him into believing he would kill his family if he told them that he had been sexually molested. When Greene demanded that he bring him another boy and a little girl whom he wished to assault, the child reported the unsavory details to his parents, who are now determined to fight to see that the Church changes its policies toward priest sexual offenders.

With great detail, the novel satirizes the treatment the O'Malleys receive from the Church and its lawyers. The female lawyers who take Helen O'Malley's deposition are "three wicked witches," who subject her to fifty hours of badgering with offensive and outrageous questions. When one of the women attorneys asks Helen a question, the other two "deride Helen's answer with their giggles." Typical questions are these: "How often do you engage in intercourse?" or "Has your son ever accidentally seen you and your husband engage in sexual inter-course?"or speaking of the child "How often did you manipulate his sexual organs when you bathed him?" Throughout the proceedings, the archdiocese, showing no regard for the O'Malleys, is "concerned only with drawing out the process of harassing its 'enemies' (the families of pedophile victims) till they break under the strain" (91). Since the archdiocese, considered by its lawyers to be a "cash cow," has never lost a case, their invincibility makes their attorneys recklessly arrogant.

The satire becomes quite acrimonious when the archdiocese's attorneys suc-ceed in turning one of the witnesses for the O'Malleys over to their side. Mizi Collins, a lawyer for the archdiocese, leads Ned Kelly, a janitor who had testified that he had seen Greene rape boys, through a refutation of his deposition. Ned is "a little old man on the wrong side of seventy, a couple of front teeth missing, a red nose and shabby clothes, and the bemused state of the chronic drinker of a bottle of rye a day" (261). One is led to believe that the pastor of the parish, where Ned is janitor and lives in the basement, and Gerry Greene put pressure on Ned to change his testimony, by threatening that he would be put out on the street if he did not. Now in his second deposition, he says he never saw Greene molest any boys and that he had testified that he had in order to obtain the twenty thousand dollars that they paid him.

Ignatius O'Keefe, the chief attorney for the Archdiocese, resembles a character such as one might find in Balzac's *Human Comedy*. He is a "tall handsome man with wavy silver hair and piercing blue eyes," with the reputation of being the best lawyer in Chicago. Although his father drove a garbage truck for the city, he affects a "patrician style" wearing handmade shoes, razor-cut hair, fifteen-hundred-dollar suits, three rings on one hand, and speaks with an affected a New England accent (165–166). Nonchalantly, he offers the O'Malley attorneys a million dollars of the money of the Catholic people of Chicago to settle their case against the archdiocese out of court.

The reader is permitted to get a good look at the infamous Gerry Greene, when the psychiatrist Kieran O'Kerrigan visits his parish on a Sunday morning to check him out at Father Brendan's request. Greene is " a wimpy little guy," who is still pastor at St. Sixtus because "the Church does not want a prominent and respected priest to be disgraced" (118).

A skilled writer and knowledgeable psychologist, Greeley depicts Greene as a mixture of good and evil. To James Leary, the vicar general of the archdiocese, Greene, who was one of his classmates in the seminary, had an excellent record as a pastoral administrator. In Leary's opinion, "he was utterly harmless, a good priest assaulted by calumny for many years" (283). Ironically the parishioners at St. Sixtus find him to be a better pastor than his predecessor, as Kieran learns from a university colleague and a doctor, whom he spots in the crowd after the Sunday mass at St. Sixtus. Ted, the doctor, uncovers many disturbing facts about Greene. Although he had propositioned his classmates in the seminary, he was ordained because of the shortage of priests. Only three doors down from the rectory, he has a house of his own where kids in their late teens are observed drifting in and out. He has been known to hand out six-packs of beer to teens going out on dates.

To complete Kieran's understanding of the problems of the archdiocese in dealing with pedophiles, Brendan asks Kieran to visit a celibate gay priest, John Creaghan. The author uses this character to provide further information about homosexuality and the priesthood. Creaghan tells him that there are several homosexuals in the chancery itself who either refuse to acknowledge their homosexuality or who are so repressed, they honestly don't realize their sexual orientation.

Creaghan, who has known that he is homosexual since childhood, feels that, as a celibate homosexual priest, he is able to "bring a special sensitivity and concern to the priesthood" than he otherwise would and believes that the problem is not the ordination of gay men, but rather the ordination of those who will not keep their commitment to celibacy. He blames the Church for ordaining practicing homosexuals.

Creaghan, an example of a good homosexual priest, who grieves that the priesthood is declining, explains that the diocese is harder on celibate homosexual priests than it is on gays like Greene who are interested only in their own pleasure, and is hardest on straight priests who have affairs with women.

In a discussion on the priesthood, Brendan, a persona for the author and the prototype of the ideal heterosexual priest, is in favor of continuing the celibate priesthood. The cause of the problem, he maintains, is not celibacy, but immaturity. Since marriage is not a cure for immaturity, he reasons, the priests who cannot keep their commitments to Christ and His Church would not be able to be faithful to their wives either.

Brendan with the help of the psychiatrist Kieran O'Kerrigan battles bravely to have Gerry Greene removed from parish work and to get the archdiocese to set up a lay review board to prevent all sexual abusers from being reassigned to parishes. His legal work does not keep him from doing his parish work at St. Praxides where he is the pastoral associate for "Misery" Casey who spends most of his time on vacation or playing gin rummy at the Beverly Country Club. In his absence, Brendan effectively runs the parish doing the work of three priests. An ideal priest, a man who lets the splendor of the priesthood shine through his life, Brendan refuses all monetary compensation and benefits from the archdiocese, so that he can be free to practice law, pursuing sexual abuse cases against the archdiocese, in an attempt to correct injustices. Although he realizes the severe problems that the Church faces, he neither yields to discouragement nor closes his eyes to the evils that plague it.

Some of the most comical satire in the book occurs when Kieran meets with the Mafia boss who is upset because Kathleen has uncovered a letter from her deceased father which could convict him of a serious crime. In an attempt to frighten Kathleen and Kieran, the "outfit," as they are called, has wrecked Kathleen's car and injured her. Kieran demands to have a "sit down" with "Tony the Angel," the mob name of one Mr. Anthony Angelini. The Angel does in fact agree to meet with Kieran at a dark restaurant, which smells of Parmesan cheese and red peppers where they are seated in a very dark alcove in a corner. The Angel is "a little round old man with thick glasses, a benign smile, and the parchment skin which suggested inoperable cancer, a kind of a beardless, dying Italian Santa Claus" (308). Seated beside him one on each side, are two thugs, Joey and Alfie, "two chaplains to an aging cardinal" (308). The scene proceeds like a humorous lampoon of a crime movie. As they lunch on pasta and wine, Kieran, with his hands sweaty from fear, imitates a Mob boss as he tries to reason with Angelini. The situation is resolved after much comedy by Tony the Angel agreeing to phone Kieran if he has any more problems. This episode concludes when Kieran discusses his meeting with James Leary who remarks that Kieran sounds like Humphry Bogart. To which Kieran replies, "You do me an injustice, James. I see myself as more the Robert De Niro type" (312). Comedy of manners, situation, and dialogue are all here blended into sophisticated satire.

Laughter is something that is never far removed in Greeley's fiction. In this book he even has Brendan and Kieran swap lawyer jokes. The novel itself is a comedy in that it does have a happy ending and like the classical comedies of antiquity, a romance with a marriage. After the death of Brien, tragic though it was, Kieran and Kathleen find the happiness together that they were deprived of by her family's manipulation of her life and Kieran's. In the words of Brendan: "Some loves by their durability over time and obstacles are very much like sacraments—metaphors, that is, for God's durable love for us" (339–340).

The archdiocese agrees to set up a lay review board for cases of sexual abuse by the clergy. Gerry Greene is removed from his parish. And James Leary, the vicar general, becomes a little more human. There is hope and renewal for the Church as long as there are priests like Brendan McNulty whose lives suggest a rumor of angels as do the lives of Kevin Brennan, Lawrence O'Toole, Jamie

Keenan, and John McGlynn.

In the four novels discussed in this chapter and in which these priests appear, Andrew Greeley, professor of social science at the University of Chicago, has written a social study of the Catholic Church since the Second Vatican Council. With incisive, comic, and dramatic satire, the purpose of which is always to correct evils, he has vigorously assailed the sins and weaknesses of the clergy. His characters are always well drawn and psychologically well motivated. With an economy of words and clarity of exposition he depicts the physiognomy, costume, ways of speaking, and gestures of each character so that even the minor characters, who often are types representative of certain kinds of people, seem to come alive. With great vivacity and wit, he delineates the human weakness of the hierarchy and their failings. His descriptions depict for the reader the cupidity, ambition, lust, and hunger for power of which people are capable when they rely on themselves instead of God's grace. An eminent moralist who never preaches but who rather illustrates the evils he attacks in the actions of his characters, Greeley permits the reader to draw the conclusion that while there is much wrong with members of the Church, there is hope for renewal. He strives always to reprove and correct those sectors of the Church that most need it and are most apt to avoid the challenge of change. Proof that he is successful in accomplishing his purposes is the commotion that has arisen in some quarters of the Church in response to his fiction by those who do not want their sin, weakness, inadequacy, ineptitude, and incompetence scrutinized and reproved.

Greeley's comedy reflects the manners, ideas, and conflicts in the postmodern Church. Based on Greeley's sociological expertise, the sociohistorical dimension of the comedy adds to the literary value of the work, which is a serious, but at the same time a comical study of the Catholic Church in the latter half of the twentieth century. In all four of the novels considered in this chapter, as in all Greeley's fiction, life is a mixture of comedy and tragedy. People die, sometimes violent deaths. Yet in what Greeley calls "the great cosmic joke" life always triumphs over death in a divine comedy which has a gloriously happy ending.

Greeley is a master of satire. He is not the first priest satirist to turn his literary talents on the evils of the clergy and other members of the Church. There are two others who come to mind. He has joined the company of Rabelais and Erasmus.

WORKS CITED

Greeley, Andrew M. *The Cardinal Sins.* New York: Warner, 1981.

———. *The Cardinal Virtues.* New York: Warner, 1990.

———. *The Catholic Myth; The Behavior and Beliefs of American Catholics.* New York: Scribners, 1990.

———. *Fall from Grace.* New York: Putnam, 1993.

———. *Making of the Popes 1978: The Politics of Intrigue in the Vatican.* Kansas City: Andrews and McMeel, 1978.

————. *An Occasion of Sin.* New York: Putnam, 1988.

————. *A Piece of My Mind . . . on Just about Everything.* Garden City: Doubleday, 1983.

Greeley, Andrew M., and Jacob Neusner. *The Bible and Us: A Priest and a Rabbi Read the Scripture Together.* New York: Warner, 1990.

4

The Passover Trilogy

In the early 1980s, Andrew Greeley represented the themes of the Easter Triduum, the Christian Passover, in a trilogy: *Thy Brother's Wife*, 1982; *Ascent into Hell*, 1983; and *Lord of the Dance*, 1984. The first book, *Thy Brother's Wife* echoes the Church's liturgy for Thursday of Holy Week. On this day, priests renew their commitment to the priesthood and the Church celebrates the commemoration of Christ's institution of the Eucharist, which provides the strength and sustenance necessary for keeping commitments. Similarly, this liturgy celebrates the commitment of Christ and his followers to each other. As one might surmise then, *Thy Brother's Wife* is the story of a priest and of the people who love him; the commitments they have made to God and to each other; and the Eucharist, which renews their commitments, and which are finally kept after some inconstancy. Wondering if he really has a vocation to be a priest, Sean Cronin considers abandoning the priesthood as he encounters the changes taking place in the Church after the Second Vatican Council, but after some inconstancy and a brief erotic interlude with his brother's wife, Nora, fervently resolves to remain faithful to the promises he has made. Similarly Nora Cronin, the wife of Sean's brother, remains faithful to the call of Christ in her life after she determines to keep her relationship with Sean free from erotic involvement.

Ascent into Hell is a Good Friday story echoing the liturgy of that day by portraying the crucifixion and spiritual death of a man who eventually rises from spiritual death to a new life in Christ. It is the story of Hugh Donlon, who probably never should have become a priest and who eventually leaves the priesthood, finding happiness with the woman he fell in love with before ordination. When the changes take place after the Second Vatican Council, Hugh loses faith in the institutional Church, and not having faith in God, he falls into the abysses of hell and even lower so that he has to climb up to make his ascent into hell on the way back to life and liberty. This novel celebrates the freedom that Christ won for his followers by his death on the cross.

The third work of the trilogy, *The Lord of the Dance*, is identified with the Holy Saturday Easter Vigil liturgy in which fire and water are conjoined, a symbol of the life-giving sexual union between a man and a woman. This is done in celebration of the new life that Christ won for his members by his resurrection and which is made available to them through the Church. In this story, Noele Marie Farrell, who is a correlative of the Church, being conceived at Easter and born at Christmas, brings new life to the members of her family who, because of their passions, are mired down in duplicity, deception, and death. She is a bossy and insistent teenager who will not relent until every member of her family is brought from the spiritual death in which they all languish, experience a resplendent resurrection, and find new lives.

Significantly, in all three of these highly satirical and humorous novels, which Greeley refers to as comedies of grace, grace is mediated by a woman who mirrors and reflects the feminine qualities in God's nature. It is one of Greeley's principal recurring themes that while God is neither male nor female he reflects both masculine and feminine qualities. In other words, God's love for us is both maternal and paternal with the maternal components of it being especially expressed in the Christmas story and through the Church—Holy Mother Church.

Illustrative of God's love and rich in satire, *Thy Brother's Wife* depicts what happens when an overly zealous and domineering person manipulates the lives of his family to fulfill his own ambitions without regard for anyone else. It is the story of Sean Cronin, whose father made the decision for him that he would become a priest, and of God's love which is mediated to him through Nora, his brother's wife.

In 1928 prior to the beginning of the novel, Michael Cronin married Mary Eileen Morrisey, whom her son Sean later describes as "a cloud of golden gentleness." Since Michael is a man who can be quite cruel and brutal and who regards women as possessions and instruments of pleasure, Mary Eileen turned for consolation to a sympathetic priest, who most probably sired her youngest son, Sean. Tortured by guilt and remorse, Mary Eileen suffered a nervous collapse, and tried to kill the infant. Proud man that he is, Michael, cannot tolerate having anyone know that his wife is mentally ill, or that he is not the father of her youngest son. For these reasons, he committed her to a private mental institution, faking a funeral when she wrecked her car. Only a few people know her true story, which is hidden even from her sons.

With Mary Eileen out of the way, Michael assumed total control of his sons' lives. When Sean was seven and Paul nine, Michael, without any reflection, decided that the older boy would become president of the United States and the younger a priest, "probably a cardinal." This was the genesis of Sean's commitment to the priesthood. Determined to buy careers for his sons in politics and religion, he planned their lives down to the smallest detail. When Paul was sixteen, Mike brought Nora, the orphaned daughter of an acquaintance, home to live with them, much to the resentment of Aunt Jane, Mike's alcoholic sister who took care of his sons. It was Mike's decision that Paul would marry Nora because according to Mike, Paul was to be the first Catholic president of the United States and Nora the First Lady "whether she wants to or not." (50).

At the beginning of the story in 1951, Sean is a seminarian and his brother Paul is missing in action in the Korean war. When it appears that Paul has been killed in Korea, Mike insists that Sean leave the seminary, where he is well on his way to ordination, and marry Nora. Before Paul is found alive, Sean makes the psychological shift needed to follow his father's desires and marry Nora to whom he was already attracted. When Paul returns home, the father's original plan is carried out with Paul becoming an attorney and marrying Nora.

Mike has such a powerful will and resolute determination that his sons and Nora always agree to his plans, even though they are not happy in doing so. Nora and Paul have an unhappy marriage, with Paul admitting that he is unable to love her as she should be loved and that she should have married someone like Sean.

Furthermore, Nora and Sean have a very strong mutual attraction, which they consummate during a two-week affair in Europe, while at the same time still intending to keep the commitments they have previously made—Sean's to the priesthood, Nora's to Paul. Although both Nora and Sean are stronger people as a result of their love for one another, they are guilt-ridden, until they finally accept God's loving forgiveness. Deciding to leave the priesthood and marry Nora, Sean refuses the office of archbishop of Chicago when the pope phones asking him to accept it. Nora, who is now free to marry since her husband's death, declines his marriage offer, insisting that he keep his commitment to the priesthood. Sean soon realizes that "having her, he would lose her. Not having her, he could love her forever" (348). Perceiving now that Nora is the "best sign of God's love" he will ever have, he agrees to becoming archbishop *because* of her love for him and his love for her (349). The lifelong doubts about his faith and his vocation now are gone. As the book ends, Sean enters the cathedral for Holy Thursday mass to renew his commitment to the priesthood. This briefly is the skillfully handled plot of the novel.

The characters of the book are well drawn. Patterning his behavior on that of his father, Paul resembles Michael Cronin not only physically but psychologically as well. Both are caught up in the sexual revolution of the 1960s and regard women as possessions and instruments of pleasure that they can use and dispose of when they are no longer appealing. Paul drives one woman, Maggie Shields, to suicide because he spurns her. Later her daughter, whom he beds down one night, dies in a hotel fire in a drug induced stupor, because he feels it would destroy his political career, if he carried the young woman's naked body out to safety. When he learns that the scandal surrounding the death of the young woman will become public, he takes his boat out in a storm on the lake and drowns.

From Michael, Paul learns that money can be used to buy friends, women, and political and social position. Since Paul is the son of a recently immigrated family that places more emphasis on material values than on spiritual ones, the novel is a satire on many of the immigrants who came to America. His cold, calculating callousness can be seen when he puts a contract out on a man who is blackmailing him for being a coward in Korea, deserting his command and afterward accepting a medal for bravery, which he did not deserve.

Paul's unprincipled behavior provides an opportunity for the novel to satirize the "functional justice" that occurs often nowadays in America. In an attempt to further his political career, Paul breaks into the office of a lobbyist to get information to incriminate some union officials that the government is trying to indict.

In the satiric treatment of a family facing suffering and destruction because of character failings, the novel resembles some of the great classic stories of Balzac. The fatal flaws in the personalities of the characters are like ticking time bombs waiting to explode. The thoughtful development of the characters is what makes the novel, for the plot is not complex. Sean, having been reared by Michael, also assumes some of his behavior. His attitude toward women is very poor, as one might expect from the son of a womanizer. He tends to be a bit of an antifeminist.

As the novel portrays the lives of the Cronins from all their various points of view, the reader is given a realistic picture of an Irish family which has risen far above its former immigrant status to a position of power and wealth. It is one of Greeley's favorite themes to depict how the descendants of the Irish immigrants to America have so quickly soared to success. In the case of the Cronins, money and the power it brings are very detrimental. Illustrating one of the worst ills that have plagued the Irish, Aunt Jane, Michael's sister and housekeeper, begins as a secret drinker and then is revealed openly as a drunk. Another Irish drunk portrayed is Senator Joseph R. McCarthy.

The main target of the author's satire in this novel is, as always, the Church. As the story delineates Sean's life in the seminary, parishes, and chancery office of the archdiocese of Chicago, the reader gets an insider's view of the Church as only an articulate and honest priest like Greeley can dare to depict. The reader must always bear in mind that the purpose of satire is to reprove and to correct. By holding up to derision the ridiculous things that happen in the Church, the author hopes to change the members of the Church for the better.

The seminary comes under attack in this novel as it has in previous ones. Because his family has great wealth, the seminary faculty is especially hard on Sean Cronin, making his life very unpleasant, in hopes that he will give up and leave. Despite his continual lack of faith in God and in his vocation, Sean perseveres in the seminary and is ordained a priest hoping somehow that things will get better.

When he leaves the seminary for his first curacy, his situation does not improve, but rather gets much worse. Simply because the old cardinal wants to prove that a rich man's son cannot last long in a poor black parish, Sean is sent to St. Jadwiga's, a filthy, run-down place with the yard of the rectory littered with trash, beer cans, and whiskey bottles. Nevertheless Sean makes a success of his stay there.

Eventually removing him from St. Jadwiga's, Cardinal Eamon McCarthy sends Sean to the Gregorian University in Rome to study the Church's history of marriage and sexuality. Becoming convinced that the Church must change, because it has "lost touch with the problems and needs of contemporary human beings" Sean, after a while in Rome, slowly begins to alter his views on many things (156). The satire builds as Sean observes the trickery and deceit that seem to be taken for granted in Rome where cardinals live in palaces.

When Sean confesses to a bored Roman priest that he has had sex with his brother's wife he receives only a light penance and a hasty, mechanical absolution. Later when he tells the Principessa Angelica Allesandrini, who had earlier tried to seduce him, about his affair with Nora, she replies that what he had done would not be sinful at all for an Italian priest.

Sean is transformed by his affair with Nora into a fearless man who is willing to face issues boldly. However he continues to lose faith because of his disillusionment with the stupidity and venality of the Church bureaucracy, and because of his flirtation with the Principessa, among other things. Consequently, he feels "the muddy waters of damnation swirl around him" (192).

Back in Chicago and serving as vice chancellor for the archdiocese, Sean finds that the American Church is falling apart. Defections from the priesthood especially stun him. Troubled by the chaos he sees in the Church, Sean begins to doubt God. He is especially distressed when the pope promulgates an encyclical against making any changes in the matter of artificial contraception.

One especially satirically humorous scene occurs when Sean, the new auxiliary bishop of Chicago, has dinner with three other bishops. In selecting a restaurant, Sean quips sarcastically that it would be a waste of money to go to any of the more expensive places because "the Episcopal palate . . . is almost as undeveloped as the Episcopal conscience" (234).

When the conversation turns to the birth control encyclical, it provokes one of Greeley's most scathing denunciations of the hierarchy. Sean says:

You can't be a good bishop unless you're an accomplished liar. We lie to Rome about how enthusiastically we receive their bullshit; we lie to the priests and the laity about how they should enforce such rulings; we lie to the press about what we really think. We even lie to ourselves, although we know that we won't be able to sleep at night because of what the goddamn encyclical is doing in our dioceses. Some of us are ready made psychopathic liars. The rest of us are the do-it-yourself variety. (235–236)

Now outspoken and fearless, Sean is ready to do battle with the ultra-conservative Soldiers of Christ, an international secret Catholic society of right-wing crazies who in their secret publications repudiate the Second Vatican Council. In a comic scene, he confronts their leader Father Camillo and forces him and his followers out of the Archdiocese. The reader gains some insight into the operations of some of the lunatic right fringe which are here satirized. Five husbands protest to Sean that their wives, members of this organization, will not sleep with them without permission of their spiritual guide, who is often Father Camillo himself.

Although Sean has become a very successful churchman, he still has no faith. Weary of "idiotic letters from Rome," he is ready to leave the priesthood, especially since he sees his fellow bishops as "dry, bloodless, unfeeling old men" (245–246, 312). Although bishops cannot get a dispensation from the priesthood, Sean decides to leave and marry Nora.

When the apostolic delegate announces that the pope commands Sean, in virtue of his vow of obedience, to become archbishop of Chicago, Sean snaps, "Tell the Holy Father to go to hell" (344). Since Nora, refusing to marry him, insists that he keep his commitment to the priesthood, he reconsiders his vocation. Astutely he comes to perceive that Nora is the sign of God in his life, that she represents the feminine qualities in God's nature, and is the mediatrix of God's grace for him. As the novel ends, the cathedral choir is singing "Ubi Caritas" as Sean prepares to renew his commitments to God and the priesthood.

Comic elements are frequent in the book. Although much of the humor is black humor, arising from the incongruous behavior of the churchmen satirized, Greeley's characteristic sense of good humor is found in the episodes in which Nora and Bobby Kennedy play practical jokes on each other, climaxing when Nora pushes the attorney general, fully clothed, into his Virginia swimming pool. There is also the usual joking and bantering about the Vatican bank.

In conclusion, *Thy Brother's Wife* is a satire depicting the reactions of the Cronins, a Chicago Irish family, to the acquisition of wealth and position, changing times, and a changing Church. Sean Cronin becomes a priest initially because of his father, but eventually he finds that he has a vocation and he perseveres in it. The satire becomes trenchant and even mordant as the Church is viewed through Sean's eyes as he advances from seminarian, to priest, bishop, archbishop and finally cardinal. The theme of woman as a mediatrix of God's grace is depicted in the love that Nora has for Sean. Humor is found throughout the story.

Ascent into Hell, the second volume of the trilogy, resembles *Thy Brother's Wife* because in both novels the parents manipulate the lives of their children and program a son for the priesthood. On the very day that Hugh Donlon is born, his father pledges that his son will be a priest in gratitude for his wife's surviving a difficult birth. Peg Donlon, Tom's wife, had already dedicated the child to God when she first felt him stir within her womb. Even so Tom doubts the wisdom of this dedication and wonders if Hugh might be better off with the young woman, Maria Manfredy, with whom he develops a relationship when in the seminary. Since the Donlons keep Hugh and Maria apart, eventually the girl marries someone else. The growing doubts about their son's vocation are finally justified when Hugh leaves the priesthood.

This novel excels in character study with the psychological development of all the major players being well motivated. As the story unfolds the characters are revealed to the reader as intricate multifaceted people who are very realistically portrayed. The central character, Hugh Donlon is a product of his environment, his parents, and his education. Because his parents instill in him the belief that things which are pleasurable and fun are sinful and that to please God one must do that which is most difficult, he decides to become a priest.

Because Tom and Peg Donlon pretend they are immune to passion and hide their real feelings behind a facade of piety and convention, they have no problem with the Church and are able to fool everyone except their three children. Hiding their passionate love for each other from everyone, Peg and Tom enjoy their sexual life together enormously. Because Peg feels that marital sex is sinful and she is ashamed of her "animality," she even wonders if God is punishing her when Hugh eventually leaves the priesthood.

Unable to hide their real natures as their parents do, the three Donlon children find it very difficult to fit into the Church. Because of Peg's somber view of God and Tom's strict principles, the lives of their three children are twisted and warped. Tim reacts at an early age to the repressed life of the family by stealing the chalice from his church sacristy and money from the parish carnival. Later, he is a constant source of worry for his parents because of his floundering marriage, his drinking, and his repeated difficulties with the Business Practices Committee at the Board of Trade. Eventually he loses nine million dollars and illegally uses customer's money to cover five million of it.

Marge Donlon, the sister of Hugh and Tim, is portrayed initially as a girl without morals. She leaves home and goes to San Francisco with an English dance director—her parents dislike the English— and then moves to Las Vegas where she works at a roulette table. Fortunately, Marge finds a life preserver in Lord Kerry, an Anglo-Irish peer, who appears one day at her roulette wheel, sweeps her off her feet, and marries her in the cathedral at Killarney two weeks after their engagement.

Hugh's reaction to his parents strictness and repression is just as dramatic. Never really happy in the priesthood, and still in love with Maria Manfredy, he has a sexual affair with a nun, which he resolves to break off. However, when she tells him she is pregnant, he insists he must marry her out of a sense of obligation and against everyone's advice. Acting in character, he must do that which is most difficult and which he really does not want to do. From the time he met Liz until her death, Hugh is dismally unhappy and seems to be sinking ever deeper into the abysses of hell. Eventually after the accidental death of his wife, Hugh is able to find his way back to life and happiness with Maria, the woman he loved before he became a priest. Before he does, however, he has much to suffer.

The continued changes in the Church and society erode Hugh's faith. Since he does not have a strong faith in God, when his faith in the priesthood falters, he is walking on perilous ground. Trying to live the celibate life in the midst of the sexual revolution of the 1960s and 1970s, Hugh is headed for disaster. His descent into hell begins with his frequent kissing with Helen Fowler, the wife of one of the parishioners; it escalates when Sister Elizabeth seduces him.

Interesting, comical, and at times hilariously funny descriptions of Liz and her liberal friends add to the satiric portrayal of the Church in the sixties and the seventies. Although Liz, a misguided liberated woman, is in graduate school, she is not devoting her energies to her academic program which she refers to as "Mickey Mouse stuff." Rather she is seeking "self-fulfillment." She is also intent upon straightening Hugh out, for she feels that he is old fashioned and she with her superior knowledge must teach him.

As Hugh becomes involved with Liz, he goes with her to Christ Commune, an assembly of misguided priests and nuns who are unfaithful to their commitment to chastity. Some of them are married, others living together, and some dating.

A high point in the comic satire is the Christmas Mass at Christ Commune with the lector wearing a Santa Claus costume and the music directress a south-seas sarong which does not become her figure. Brandied plum pudding and steaming wassail are the elements of the Eucharist, which are carried to the altar by priests bearing the messages "Joseph, killed by American bombs" and "Mary burned by American napalm" (152). At the offertory women in leotards do a modern dance with men in swim trunks. The scene is utterly ludicrous.

The zenith of the satire of the misguided liberal fringe of the 1960s and 1970s is the church wedding that Hugh and Liz finally have. After telling Hugh she wants to have a few guests, she invites her former religious congregation. The brief ceremony is performed with dignity and taste. However, as soon as Hugh and Liz turn from the altar, women, probably the nuns Liz invited, cheer like cheerleaders for a winning team. Liz, now three months pregnant, incongruously acts like a blushing bride. Her parents who consider the marriage sacrilegious are not there. Even Tim, Hugh's miscreant brother is embarrassed by the beaded and bearded crowd when he proposes a toast to the bride and groom wishing them a long and happy marriage. Before Hugh can reply to his brother's toast, one of the bearded members of the commune takes over with an anti-American diatribe, proposing the first toast to the victory of the Vietcong. The story becomes hilarious at this point for the members of the commune present shout "Ho, Ho, Ho Chi Minh" (207). Soon the orchestra arrives and begins to play as its first piece "We shall overcome." By now the reader is in stitches.

Greeley who is a master of such scenes has created in this one a real travesty, hilarious farce that illustrates how misguided people twisted Church reform in bizarre ways. The tone is one of mocking ridicule.

Because of Liz's discordant beliefs, frivolous crusades, and weird friends, Hugh's marriage to her becomes very unhappy. With Hugh replacing the religious congregation as the parent figure in her life, Liz blames him for everything that goes wrong in her life. Usually the differences between Hugh and Liz are insurmountable. Perhaps because their sex life is marred by memories of incest with her father, she resents the sexual demands that Hugh makes on her. What Greeley depicts in Liz is far more than just a caricature of a nun who jumps over the wall or of a liberated woman who regards all men as chauvinists. Her character is complex and very realistic in its development. Obviously confused, she has terrible pressures within pulling her in many different directions. Ironically, she thinks of Hugh as needing her help more than she needs his. To make matters worse, for some strange reason, she keeps Hugh away from his children so that they are strangers to him. She is an interesting psychological study, but definitely not a likable person. Tired of being what she refers to as "an unpaid day-care center" she hires a babysitter, joins a consciousness-raising group and begins to dress "like a double agent of the KGB" (248).

In addition to satirizing ex-nuns like Liz, the novel also takes a few shots at petty Third World tyrants and the American judicial system. By having Hugh serve as ambassador to the People's Republic of Upper River, Greeley is able to draw a caricature of Third World petty dictators and parody their barbaric activities, adding one more dimension to the satire of the novel.

Corruption in the American legal system is depicted satirically when Hugh is sent to prison for a crime he does not commit. Although he has fallen very low and done despicable things—made a god of money and power, taken revenge against people that had wronged him, taken drugs, had extramarital affairs that included sadomasochism and having sex with both a mother and her daughter, and many other evil deeds— he is made to pay not for them, but for Tim's illegal activities in the firm which take place when Hugh is out of the country serving the government in Upper River in Africa.

According to Hugh's lawyer, they will cut a deal whereby Hugh will pay a fine (he has already paid back the money Tim took from customers' accounts) and be put on probation. The judge agrees to the plea bargaining but has no intention of going through with it. After Hugh pleads nolo contendere, the judge, to settle an old feud with the Donlons, sentences him to eighteen months in prison.

The federal correctional institution where Hugh is sent is portrayed as a place that does not benefit the convicts who will never repeat their crimes, but costs the taxpayers dearly. It is a prison for those the government knows should not be incarcerated and where the penal techniques work because they are not needed. According to Hugh's new attorney Pete McQueen, putting a man in prison here signifies the victory of the prosecution attorneys over the defense attorneys and is "vengeance, pure and simple" (315).

Just as Hugh's undoing came through a woman, his salvation does also. Maria Manfredy is one of Greeley's most unforgettable characters representing one of the author's major literary themes that runs throughout his fiction—the feminine qualities of God's nature. Reflecting God's love Maria leads Hugh to accept the love, forgiveness, and freedom that God gives.

Maria, who refers to herself as "Sacred Love," brings light, warmth, joy, and humor to the novel as she turns simple things into revelations of God's love and grace. Her frequent jokes about her Italian background are quite comical, like the comment she made when the bishop in Ireland asked her what county she came from and she replied, "County Palermo." The jokes she tells about her Italian family are quite zany.

At the end of the book when Hugh has a religious experience, he discovers that God's loves him as Maria does but infinitely more and he is transformed. All his life he had been seeking God and now he had finally found Him with Maria and he will stay with her forever. Once again, God brings the surprise happy ending that every comedy must have.

Maria will appear in subsequent Greeley novels. In *Ascent into Hell,* Sean Cronin, from *Thy Brother's Wife,* appears as the very successful cardinal arch- bishop of Chicago who visits Hugh in prison and agrees that perhaps Maria *is* God's will for Hugh and perhaps he should not return to the active priesthood. Interestingly, Nora Cronin also from the author's previous novel, is mentioned in *Ascent into Hell.* The reader is delighted to learn that Nora is now married to Roy Hurley, a handsome sports announcer. This technique of bringing in characters from former novels gives the stories a depth of realism that would not otherwise be possible, since minor characters are therefore familiar and well-developed characters for the readers of the author's fiction.

In conclusion, *Ascent into Hell* is a comedy of grace in which Hugh Donlon breaks lose from the shackles of the legalistic mentality that bind him and rises to a new life of freedom in God's redeeming love as mediated by a woman, who represents the feminine qualities of God. The surprise and wonder of the happy ending, the frequent touches of good humor and the acrimonious satire with its black humor all combine to create a masterful literary work in which the character development is superbly delineated and the plot ultimately satisfying. As usual, the main character in the story is God, whose Loving Providence provides the happy ending.

Many of the elements found in *Ascent into Hell* are also in *Lord of the Dance,* the completing volume of the trilogy. This third novel corresponds to the celebration of the Feast of the Resurrection, specifically the Easter Vigil Liturgy, in which fire and water, symbols of the sexual union between a man and a woman, symbolize the new life of Jesus Christ generated by his resurrection and offered to all in his name through his Church.

Although there is a priest in the story, the protagonist is Noele Marie Brigid Farrell, a correlative of the Church having been conceived at Easter and born at Christmas, who leads all the members of her family to experience new life as they are resurrected from the anguish of spiritual death.

Noele is a breezy sixteen year old whose exuberance and joy lift her family from the tangled tissue of lies and despair into which they have fallen, since they immigrated from Ireland and have become successful in Chicago, with one son being a university professor and another a priest. The description of Noele is Greeley at his best:

She was a Celtic goddess of the nineteenth-century illustrations of Irish folklore books, strange, unreal, almost unearthly. Her long, bright red hair, contrasting sharply with her pale, buttermilk skin, swept across the room after her like moving fire. Her green eyes absorbed you as if you were a glass of iced tea on a hot summer evening; they were neither soft green nor cat green, but shamrock green, kelly green. She seemed a pre-Christian deity, a visitor from the many-colored lands of Irish antiquity. (9–10)

Noele's language adds a comic touch to the book with expressions like "yukheads," "geeks," and "bonged a load." When she asks God for a rose as a sign and a florist's truck drops a bunch of them on the hood of her car, she exclaims hotly, "Totally excessive . . . I asked for one, not a bouquet!" (162).

With a very strong tendency to be bumptious, Noele has no qualms about questioning the cardinal about his actions. When she leaves a room, she soars "like a comet blazing across the winter sky" (169). A "dazzling mixture of fragility and strength, of naïveté and wisdom," she wears lace underwear "the kind that Moms said prostitutes used to wear twenty-five years ago" (74, 517). Her uncle, Monsignor John Farrell says she thinks she runs the parish to which Father Ace McNamara, Captain Richard McNamara USN retired Ph.D., professor of clinical psychology at Loyola University, and weekend priest at St. Praxides, replies that maybe she is the Church, which, of course, is exactly what she symbolizes in the story.

When she is raped and sodomized by three men, Noele rebounds from the ordeal stronger than ever. She is described as "Violated and inviolable. Wounded and invulnerable. Battered and resilient, indestructible" (552). In short, she is the Church and all the demons from hell cannot prevail against her. "Noele knew the demons from hell could still touch her, perhaps even hurt her. But they would never prevail against her" (528).

Stronger than ever after her ordeal with the rapists, she commandeers her entire family, demanding that they all tell the truth and become freed from the morass of lies and sin into which they have fallen. Because of her insistence, they all are able to forget the past which has them entrapped and to begin new lives filled with hope for the future, as they celebrate the Easter liturgy together.

The novel has all the penetrating satire and comedy that one has come to expect of a Greeley story. Clerical culture, the media, the Mafia, CIA, and academia all share in the sting of the author's biting castigations and ridicule.

Monsignor John Farrell, now in his early forties, is at odds with clerical culture because he hosts a TV talk show on the local television station, making him the victim of clerical envy. When Monsignor Mortimer visits St. Praxides rectory, expressing the cardinal's animosity about John's having a program on secular television, the satire of the clergy begins. Jim Mortimer, distinguished only by his stupidity, and sounding and looking like a bull hippo, is in charge of the cardinal's own television channel. Because of his innate proclivity for being a sycophant and cultivating people with power, he was put in charge of the expensive and unproductive television station of the archdiocese of Chicago and commissioned as the cardinal's messenger boy. The message he delivers to John is that the cardinal is embarrassed by John's talk show in which he interviews all kinds of people that the Cardinal does not like. One such guest is Sister Celeste, a satire of the militant feminist nun, who has written a book called *Chauvinism and Peace* in which she makes peace seem like something malevolent, angry, and hateful.

When John reminds him that he also interviews people like Mother Teresa, Mortimer replies that the cardinal thinks Mother Teresa is a "faker" (21). The cardinal, in John's mind a psychopath, cannot tolerate it when anyone receives more publicity in the archdiocese than he.

Attack journalism, one of Greeley's favorite subjects for satire, is targeted for censure when Larry Rieves, the television columnist for the *Chicago Star Herald,* publishes a column for the newspaper giving John two thumbs down on his program in an attempt to ruin the program's ratings. When he even accuses John of neglecting his parish to work on his TV program, John realizes how damaging attack journalism can be and how little he can do to protect himself. The bitter sting of the columnist's venom hits home as many of John's fellow priests phone him to gloat over the article in the *Star Herald.* Regarded even by his brother Roger, a university professor, as "a clerical Phil Donahue," John hides his pain under the mask of clerical sophistication. Although John does an admirable job of defending himself, vicious remarks making fun of him appear in the newsletter of the Priests' Association. Yellow journalism is not just the prerogative of the professional media.

Troubled by the onslaughts, John turns for comfort to his sister-in-law, Irene Farrell, wife of his brother Roger. They come close to consummating their attraction for each other, when Irene, who admits she loves John, refuses to go through with it. Telling John that a priest is "someone who can love you without having to screw you," she declines his invitation to become sexually involved (308). Just the knowledge that she insists she really loves him, turns him into an aggressive personality.

With "a mixture of veiled self-righteousness and patronizing wit" clerical sanctions are applied to John when he attends a confirmation at Holy Savior Church in Greenwood Park, giving the author an opportunity to satirize the conduct of the clergy at these religious services (256). After a hearty dinner, the large number of clergy present for the occasion gather at the beginning of the ceremony for the formal procession into the church. They do not take seats, since they do not intend to stay during the liturgy. Instead they process until they are in the rectory for "more drinks and bridge or poker and a long night of loud and vulgar masculine conviviality" (257).

When John does not act as quickly as the cardinal thinks he should to stop the TV program, a phone message tells him that if does not cancel the show within twenty-four hours, they will appoint someone else as acting pastor of his parish. The scene is quintessential Greeley comedy. The reader cheers John on when he loses his temper, calling the chancellor a "crazy son of a bitch." Inquiring if the chancellor has any male hormones in his body, he tells him that there are canon lawyers in the archdiocese who can fight the case, until the psychopathic cardinal is gone. And as a final shot, John threatens to have a thousand angry teenagers picket the cardinal's mansion the next day. Slamming down the phone, John realizes that news of the conversation will spread and he will be "a pariah in the priesthood" for as long as he lives (441). Following the line of least resistance as he always does, the cardinal, who resembles "a dissolute Renaissance despot" capitulates (457).

Yellow journalism also plagues John's brother Roger Farrell, a university professor who is running for governor of the state of Illinois. Since Roger is a prominent political figure, Joe Kramer, who is writing an article for a college magazine, *The Republic,* interviews him. Given permission to see John's manuscripts of published books and articles, Kramer gets into his personal files and confidential papers and photocopies and removes them from Roger's office when the secretary gives him admittance in Roger's absence.

The president of the college where Kramer is a student seemingly supports the young man in his theft of Roger's papers for the school's magazine article. Because he did not remove the originals, merely the photocopies, and because it is perfectly legitimate to investigate Roger since he is well-known public figure, Kramer maintains that no theft occurred. Believing that he has an obligation to make the material public, Kramer is even convinced that it would violate his code of ethics if he, in fact, did not.

A short time later, Roger receives the photocopies of his material from the college president who assures him that no other copies of them are extant. When he has lunch at the Chicago Press Club with Bill Wells, the editor of the *Star Herald,* Roger soon learns otherwise. The lunch scene includes some of Greeley's most acrimonious satire of journalists with the description of the Chicago Press Club being outstanding:

The Chicago Press Club is shrouded in subterranean darkness. It is made to seem all the more mysterious because its walls are covered with mirrors. One can never really be sure whether one is seeing one's own likeness in the mirror or real people on the other side of the room. The effect created is one of a secret meeting place of a band of Renaissance plotters—poisoners, thieves, and murderers. In other words the membership of the Chicago Press Club. Here men decide the news before it happens, malign the reputations of public personages to curry favor with the arbiters of journalistic taste, assign book reviews to known enemies, cook up schemes of entrapment, abase themselves to visiting firemen from New York, plan sexual seductions of one kind or another, congratulate one another on their knowledge, sophistication, and cynicism, and drown their sorrows in expensive booze.

Anything to escape the cruel fate of going into the winter cold to cover a story. (268)

Eventually the photocopies fall into the hands of Rodney Weaver, the editor of the *Chicago Informer*, a small weekly publication. Indifferent to the threats the mob has made on the Farrell women if the story comes out, Weaver, fixed on the idea that the public has a right to know, plans to publish them, despite Roger's pleading with him not to. By now Roger is so desperate from what investigative reporting has done to him that he even considers suicide.

Another example of the effrontery of investigative reporters and yellow journalism occurs when Gery Jensen, the editor of *Fort Dearborn*, attacks Roger in a piece he published without interviewing him. His publication is cleverly described as "a slick magazine appealing to the limousine liberals of the lakefront Alps and the cocktail-party radicals of the suburbs, who sympathized with the poor and oppressed so long as they stayed within the city limits"(458). The magazine is ironically described as advertising "such left-wing products as fifteen-hundred-dollar stereo sets, twenty-five-thousand-dollar Mercedes automobiles, and half-million-dollar condominiums" (458). In the article, Jensen describes Roger as being superficial and without any future as a scholar. The satiric humor is delightful.

Also humorous and equally satiric are some of the episodes dealing with academic life. The inanities and foibles of academia are well delineated. Sex is a ubiquitous hidden agenda in the university with its academic slave market system, whereby it is customary for the senior male members of the faculty to prey on the junior female members and graduate students, who must satisfy their lecherous demands for sexual gratification or be expelled from the ivory tower and the ivy-covered halls. Roger's "slave" is Martha Clay, who is a mixture of feminine and feminist and who is willing to perform spread-eagled on his office desk, as he fantasizes various sexual games. There is much comedy surrounding Roger's sexual ventures with Martha Clay. The otherwise pompous professor, who analyzes everything in his life and who effects a   pose of intellectualism, fantasizes with Martha Clay that he is an extraterrestrial who kidnaps a housewife from a supermarket or a pagan ruler who seduces a missionary or something similar. Although Roger enjoys dallying with her, he regards her as shallow, but nonetheless tries to help her get tenure, even though he does not consider her a good candidate for a lifetime appointment. Here the book highlights the discrimination against women that routinely occurs in academe. The politics of promotions and tenure are scrutinized with satiric humor. When Martha finally achieves tenure, Roger reflects that it is almost as good as immortality.

Humorous exchanges take place when Roger talks to the provost who is characterized as a typical university administrator. In thirty years, he has only published one short book and two articles and never reads anything, not even the local newspaper. Contemptuously as he carefully muffles the phone, Roger calls him a "stupid cowardly bastard" (241).

Other administrators do not fare any better. The dean is described as "one of the great memo-initialing clerks of the century" (178). As usual with universities, the administration can find money for anything it wants to do despite continual pleas of poverty when the faculty makes a request for something.

Cops and robbers are also the butt of the novel's satire as they frequently are in Greeley's fiction. Rocco Marsallo, known as "the Marshal," is a "retired Mob crazy" whom Noele's father Danny Farrell and her boyfriend Jaimie Burns have to gun down, because the police are unable to protect the Farrell women. The portrayal of the police as ineffectual and unable to protect citizens from the terror of mobsters mirrors the society in which we live today when crime is rampant and criminals are leniently treated by the legal system.

The secret intrigues of federal government agencies such as the CIA also come under fire in the satire of the novel. Danny Farrell, who uses comedy to mask his anger, is employed by them and receives horrible treatment because of their secret machinations.

Some of the characters in the book deserve special mention for the humor they contribute. Brigid, Noele's lusty grandmother, is very colorful and at times quite funny. She and her husband the agnostic Burke—she had been his mistress for years during her marriage to Clancy, the grandfather of the family—keep the reader amused as they discuss their love life. She is always ready for what she calls "a good fuck." Considering herself to be beyond God's forgiveness, she believes and insists that she is damned and will for a certainty go to hell. Noele, however, insists that Jesus will be waiting for her when she dies and will invite her in. With the determined help of Noele, who symbolizes the Church, Brigid and all the other Farrells experience the surprise of Easter and the newness of life that Easter brings.

Much good humor is found throughout the novel. Little touches of it are everywhere in Greeley's language which is quite picturesque. For example, the first cold snap of December is " nasty snow-coated Canadian thug with a bitter snarl" (246). Noele's teenaged friends are "sweaty furniture in the house" (77), and the nun that teaches them is Sister Kung Fu. Roger's wife, Irene, with her "Bonwit eroticism" is "a Sears Tower kind of woman for a man who preferred the Prairie School." (65).

To conclude, the *Lord of the Dance* is an Easter story of resurrection. All the members of the Farrell family with the mediation of a young woman, Noele Farrell, a correlative of the Church, rise from the ruins they have made of their lives to new hope, new faith, and new love. The book satirizes many aspects of society—Church, government, the media, academia, feminism, and the Mafia among other things. The tone is one of comedy and ridicule as is appropriate to satire and is a fitting conclusion to the Passover Trilogy, three novels based on the final three days of Holy Week in which God's covenant of love is renewed. The themes of the three stories are similar: In all three people are searching for God who is searching even more assiduously for them until he finds them. The three novels can aptly be called "comedies of grace" in which God is the main character bringing a happy ending in each. All three are infused with irrepressible good humor and joy, even though at times the satire is black and caustic as the novels hold up to ridicule individual and societal failings. Very astutely Greeley draws on the great learning he has acquired through years of research as a social scientist and as a priest to depict society and individuals as they really are. He knows the human heart with all its vagaries, meanderings, deceitfulness, and capacity for evil, as well as its hunger and thirst for life and heroic virtue. Although the novels are excellent portraits of society and the men and women who compose it, as one would expect from an author who is acclaimed worldwide as an eminent and distinguished social scientist, Greeley the priest is always everywhere present in his stories. Only a priest who is skillful in the cure of souls could create such fiction in which the human psyche is so well analyzed and portrayed. The unique blending of social science and religion that Greeley is able to bring to his fiction, because of his background, makes his stories timeless and universal. Although most of them depict contemporary America, they speak to the hearts and minds of people universally.

WORKS CITED

Greeley, Andrew M. *Ascent into Hell*. New York: Warner, 1983.
———. *Thy Brother's Wife*. New York: Warner, 1982.
———. *Lord of the Dance*. Boston: G. K. Hall,1985.

5

Time between the Stars

Time between the Stars is the title of a series of novels that are set between the 1933 Chicago World's Fair, when a fourth star was added to the city's flag, and 1992, when the fair was supposed to be held again in Chicago with a fifth star to be added to the flag. Depicting the social and religious development of Irish Catholics in Chicago during this "time between the stars," Greeley has created a neighborhood of Irish American Chicago families—Ryans, Collinses, Caseys, Kanes, Murphys, and Keenans among others. Most of the families are closely related to the Ryans by birth, marriage, or friendship. The predominant member of the Ryan clan is Blackie Ryan, a.k.a. John Blackwood Ryan, Ph.D., Catholic priest and eventually a monsignor, bishop, and rector of Holy Name Cathedral; he is a central character, but not the protagonist, of the series. The stories of Time between the Stars in the order they considered are *Virgin and Martyr* (1985), *The Angels of September* (1986), *Rite of Spring* (1987), *The Patience of a Saint* (1987), *Love Song* (1989), *Saint Valentine's Night* (1989), *The Search for Maggie Ward* (1991), *Wages of Sin* (1992), and *Summer at the Lake* (1997).

Specifically wrestling with the collapse of women's religious congregations, *Virgin and Martyr,* surely one of Greeley's masterpieces, is an excellent depiction of the Church during the turbulent years following Vatican II. This novel gives birth to the zany Ryan clan which symbolizes the Church in the series. At the beginning of the book Backie Ryan, one of the major characters in Greeley's canon and who appears in many subsequent books, is teaching philosophy and Greek in a seminary; during the course of the book, he receives priestly ordination and, as he searches for Angela Carter, takes up sleuthing, for which he becomes later well known in a number of detective stories. Catherine Collins, the heroine of the story, is a correlative of the Church and Nicholas Curran, the man who loves her, is a correlative of Christ. We must, however, bear in mind that Greeley is not a consistent symbolist, for a story written with consistent symbolism would not be very interesting, but would merely resemble the medieval didactic plays. In reading Greeley, we cannot expect Nicholas or Cathy to be in every instance symbols of Christ and His Church, but the overarching symbolism is clear.

In telling the story of Cathy, Greeley satirizes women religious who let their enthusiasm push them into many excesses, including women's liberation and the so-called movement of liberation theology, which prompted many religious to go totally unprepared to the missions in Latin America and subsequently to suffer dire consequences. Led astray by priests who had also lost their orientation after Vatican II, and expecting their enthusiasm to make up for their deficiencies, they posed as revolutionaries who were trying to "liberate" a people who had not asked for liberation. To explain exactly what is involved by liberation theology, Greeley has this to say:

Liberation Theology—a bizarre idea that the Church, having utterly fouled up in Latin America by being on the side of right-wing extremists, can now redeem itself by going over to left-wing extremists just at a time when a younger generation of philosophers has begun to emerge in France who strongly question whether Marxism is all that radical. The Church in Latin America, with the unerring instinct to climb aboard a sinking ship, has opted for authoritarian Marxist societies under the guise of liberation. Some American Catholic thinkers, apparently constitutionally incapable of reflecting on the experience of their own people, have become enthusiastic supporters of liberation theology. Nowhere among the Latin American, the European, or the North American liberation theologians is their the slightest recognition of the fact that detailed political, social, economic analysis is required to understand social problems and begin to talk intelligently about their solutions. The problems of the poor countries, you see, have all been caused by the rich countries—particularly by the United States. Liberation insists essentially of blaming the United States and demanding that it expiate its sins. The only ones who are really liberated by liberation theology are the oppressive Third World governments who are liberated from taking responsibility for their own political and economic problems, since the gringo devil makes such a marvelous scapegoat. (*Everything* 55)

Liberation theology is one of the main targets for Greeley's ridicule, scorn, and anger in *Virgin and Martyr*. However, the legal profession, law enforcement, yellow journalism, and the educational system are also the butt of Greeley's raillery and ridicule in this novel as they usually are in his fiction generally.

Although he affirms in a note at the beginning of the novel that he has not written a sociological study, only an astute sociologist like Greeley who is also a priest could have written such a detailed portrait of the Catholic Church during this time of upheaval and change. In the future people will be able to read this chronicle and see just what was transpiring during this hectic time. Writing with the perspicacious mind of a social scientist, the penetrating soul of a priest, and the religious imagination of one steeped in Catholic tradition, his fiction is rich and resonates in the souls of those readers who have shared the same Catholic traditions as he.

The reader enters, not only into the religious imagination of Greeley but also into his sociological imagination, for according to the well-known sociologist

Kirby Wilcoxson, "Sociologists, especially those of Greeley's caliber, are necessarily possessed by a sociological imagination. . ." (112). To be precise, it was because of his sociological background that Greeley felt compelled to become a storyteller. Because of the depth and breadth of Greeley's sociological imagination, Ken Prewitt, also a social scientist, comments that he is not going to read any more of Greeley's nonfiction because "all the sociology is in the stories and far more palatable there" (*Confessions* 442). Since Greeley writes as a sociologist and as a priest, his fiction is woven from his knowledge of both sociology and theology as well as from his pastoral experience. This blend of sociology and religion makes for stories that are, as he describes them, "parables of grace." With his "freight train load of empirical data," as he refers to his knowledge, he writes stories that address the mind, heart, and soul of his reader.

After explaining to the reader in his prefatory note that *Virgin and Martyr* is not a sociological study per se, Greeley proceeds to inform the reader how he himself perceives the story. In his view, it is about "the temptation of confusing temporal and contingent political goals with the transcendent and the absolute in religious revelation." This is what, Greeley says, Paul Tillich called "idolatry" and Monsignor Ronald Knox referred to as "enthusiasm"—"the confusion of emotional fervor, however necessary with religious conviction." *Virgin and Martyr* illustrates this concept by showing how during the1960s and 1970s many in the Church became preoccupied with temporal and political concerns and lost sight of transcendent and religious goals.

Both the sociological and religious dimensions of the time period covered by *Virgin and Martyr* are well delineated. During the era in which the novel takes place, much confusion was triggered by liturgical changes, for it was during this time that the altar was turned to face the people and the mass began to be said in the vernacular. It was also the time of Vatican II, *Humanae Vitae*, and the great exodus of priests and religious from their vocations. In short, it was a time of tremendous chaotic turmoil and confusion. The book demonstrates that the momentum of change, once set loose, soon ran out of control as the Church slipped into what the novel refers to as a "black hole." Then, in the words of Blackie: "The densely compacted energies and forces that had been created in the black hole blew up. With the promulgation of the papal encyclical *Humanae Vitae*, American Catholicism became a supernova, an exploding fireball" (150).

Catherine Collins, the heroine of the story, typifies the nun of the 1960s and 1970s, who, by listening to the wrong advisers, becomes completely lost. At first, her story appears to be a tragedy, but it is actually a comedy with its happy ending, just as life is a comedy because love triumphs over death, since Christ is risen and promises resurrection and eternal life to all who believe in him. After floundering in a morass of misguided well-doing as a liberated nun and revolutionary, Cathy returns to her first love, Nick. This parable of grace demonstrates that although the Church sometimes wanders far from Christ with scandals of sex, money, and power, she always returns to her first love, Jesus Christ as Cathy returns to Nick. Like Christ, Nick is ever faithful and does not desert Cathy no matter how far she strays from him.

In this work, which is one of the best examples of Greeley's divine and human comedy, there are passages of biting satire and sparkling humor. As usual, Greeley, a master artist in creating characters that live in the reader's memory, draws the portraits of his characters with humor and satire. In fact, Greeley is at his best in creating caricatures which reveal the sins and failings of priests, nuns, lawyers, policemen, and journalists, among others. *Virgin and Martyr* is brilliant with such characterizations.

One of Greeley's very special characters is Blackie Ryan who appears for the first time in *Virgin and Martyr*. Much of what happens to Catherine and to the Church in these tempestuous times is recounted by Blackie who often serves as a persona for the author. Many people who read the novel see only the nuns and priests who dishonor religious life by breaking their vows and abandoning their vocations. They conclude that Greeley writes "steamy" stories of passion and sin. However, the attentive readers fix their gaze on John Blackwood Ryan, who in this novel and in the many subsequent ones in which he appears, is always an example of priestly celibacy and virtue, for he is ever steadfast as a rock and exceptionally faithful in keeping his commitments. The reason people overlook Blackie, is because he has a knack for keeping a low profile. Nick explains this at the beginning of the story when talking about their school days: "We didn't mind Blackie, who even then was a strange little kid, because after a few minutes he seemed to become quite invisible" (25). No doubt his ability to make himself unobtrusive contributes to his success as a detective later on, for his ability to become almost invisible is attributed to him in every subsequent novel in which he appears. As a detective he is reminiscent of Chesterton's Father Brown—short, pudgy, cherubic, with curly brown hair, apple cheeks and an expression of impenetrable composure. Despite his occasional ironic or cynical remarks, he is a lovable character. Some of his comments are quite humorous.

Speaking of the similarities between Blackie and himself, Greeley comments that although Blackie sometimes speaks for him, the character has an identity and integrity of his own. He is both younger than Greeley and has a different physical appearance and has a degree in philosophy instead of sociology. Blackie does have some of the characteristics of Chesterton's Father Brown which the Ryans claim he cultivates.

Although Blackie is quite disturbed by the misguided and destructive activity he observes taking place in the Church, he, nevertheless, remains unwavering in his dedication. After his cousin Catherine Collins enters the convent, he gives his views on things that are wrong in the congregations of religious women. In discussing the custom of referring to nuns as "brides of Christ," he remarks while humming "Veni Sponsa Christi," "It's a nice image . . . and it makes a nice Gregorian melody." "But it's only an image, and it's a terrible mistake to attempt to derive from it a complete theology and spirituality of the religious life" (143). And of course many nuns did exactly that. For example, Cathy wears Helen Ryan's bridal gown and elaborate lingerie when she comes into the chapel to become a bride of Christ. Blackie's sister Mary Kate Murphy even speculates as to whether Cathy writes a love letter to Jesus and tucks it in her brassiere, as many nuns have done in the past, when she goes forth in all her splendor to meet the Divine Spouse.

When the ceremony is over Blackie expresses his view that such ceremonies will continue only two or three years more, for he believes that women's religious orders are "finished" (146). On this occasion, Blackie is speaking as a persona for Greeley, who in the *Confessions of a Parish Priest* wrote that in this novel he "wrestles with the tragedy that traditional religious orders for women are finished" (94). Since every Christian is called to a "nuptial relationship" with God, Blackie disapproves of such ceremonies. In his words, "Intimacy with Christ is a possibility for all of us, and indeed a possibility that is at the core of the Christian life" (143–44). It is wrong for women religious to claim it as their's alone. He notes, however, that some communities have already pulled away from this kind of spirituality, because they realized that it might be offensive. In fact, the Murphys, Mary Kate and Joe, found the sermon that Father Ed Carny preached for Cathy's reception objectionable. This priest got so carried away by the symbolism of a nun being "a bride of Christ" that it caused Joe Murphy, Mary Kate's husband to comment "That may be the dirtiest sermon I've ever heard. I don't think they could put in it in the mails. It makes me horny for my woman" (144). Quickly agreeing Mary Kate replies,"Luxuriating on a wedding bed with Christ the bride-groom IS a little much" (144).

In the course of the novel, Blackie comments on many weaknesses of women's religious communities. Indicating a lack of respect for the privacy, dignity, and freedom of the individual, he observes that in the house where Cathy lives there are only two bathtubs and three showers for eighty-three people in a house that is poorly heated. Many of the customs of nuns are difficult to understand. Although they do not have enough good food to eat, the sisters are encouraged to fast excessively. Since cabbage, which is cheap, is their principal vegetable, the house always reeks of boiled cabbage.

For Lent Cathy keeps the medieval Black Fast—no meat, milk, eggs, or butter. Out of a strange sense of modesty, more properly named prudery, the nuns must put on their nightgowns before taking off their underwear. Cathy is reprimanded even for using tampons. In fact, conditions are so bad that many of the novices cry themselves to sleep at night. They are told their wills must be broken and that they are preparing for death.

Since Cathy does not like math, they inform her that she will become a math teacher. Because the congregation is determined to stamp out her abilities as an artist, Cathy's talent for painting is belittled and she is permitted to take only one art class in college. Someone reads her mail before she gets it and she has to smuggle out her letters to her cousin Blackie. Because of the severity of their life, increasing numbers of the novices drop out while others become ill. Most of the girls who remain even stop having menstrual periods. After Cathy has had no menstrual periods for nine months because of the rigors of this life, she finally collapses with an ulcer and malnutrition and is unable to keep solid foods down. At this point, when she is only one month away from completing her canonical year, her family is afraid she will drop out and have to repeat the entire year. Mary Kate Ryan Murphy, Blackie's sister and a Freudian psychologist, who provides a lot of humor to the novel comments, "Better to get the horse manure behind her once and for all" (166).

In discussing what is happening to Cathy with Nick Curran, who has loved her for many years and has hoped to marry her, Blackie laments that most of the priests and nuns, including Cathy, are not very well educated. Because most of those surrounding Cathy believed that to investigate and to think were an escape from responsibility, they did not provide her with an education or formation adequate for coping with a changing church. Although the religious orders were responsible for much of the poor education and formation of their members, Blackie also indicts the colleges, one of the favorite targets of Greeley's ridicule. As a case in point, the theological school where Cathy is working on a doctorate, wanting to be on the cutting edge, evenly divides its professorial chairs among blacks, women, people from the Third World, and gays and lesbians.

Greeley also lampoons parish life by showing the worst of it in Careyville, where Cathy is assigned to teach seventh grade as her first teaching position. Here we have a good example of the black humor that Greeley often employs. According to Blackie, this parish is "just over the border into the nineteenth century" (195). In the vibrant language the reader has come to expect from Greeley and Blackie, Cathy went there "with all the innocence of a first communicant embarking on a one-person exploration of the Gobi Desert when Genghis Khan and his horde were on the rampage" (197). It was her idea to teach " the salvation history theme" and "Gabriel Moran's theory of extracting values from the young people themselves" (196). All of which, in Blackie's opinion, was "gibberish."

The Careyville assignment was a total disaster. Frightened by the bald obese giant of a pastor who was "a kind of red-faced Humpty Dumpty," Cathy felt compelled to laugh at his crude stories. Firmly convinced that the reigning pope will call a new council to reverse the decision of Vatican II, he limits Cathy to teaching only what is in the 1885 catechism. The nun in charge of the school in Careyville, Sister Martina, a caricature of a religious sister, is a small, skinny, ugly woman who wears elaborate and expensive underwear and sleeps in a custom-made bed, and "looks like a teenager playing the Wicked Witch of the West in a spur of the moment Halloween sketch" (202).

The curate, Father Tierney, a caricature of priests who have trouble with Punch and Judy, leers at Cathy, speaks in a whine, always needs a shave, and drinks to excess. One night when he is drunk, he tries to rape her as he says some dirty words and squeezes her breast. A jab of her knee into his groin makes him writhe on the floor, screaming in pain, as Cathy indignantly tells him that it he ever tries it again she will cut his balls off. The scene is amusing to the reader but tragic for Cathy who now becomes a very angry woman.

Summer institutes are also satirized by Blackie. Hoping to get a handle on "the black hole" that had been created, the most confused of the priests and nuns attend the institutes. Blackie, Greeley's persona, notes that most of the religious orders did not know how a professional should be trained. Mistakenly they believed that a couple summers spent in an institute studying a course or two would give their people the advanced training they needed. When Cathy is sent by her superior to attend courses at a summer institute in Chicago, Blackie seizes this opportunity to vent his opinion of institutes. His denunciations could not be more vitriolic. Nuns at the institutes act like adolescents, which, according to Blackie, is a punishment the church earned for keeping these women "emotional adolescents" (244). Conversation revolves around who has obtained a dispensation, who is engaged, and who has married. Although Blackie has not yet been ordained he is distressed over the violations of lifelong commitments made by these religious.

When distinguished Catholic speakers are brought to the institute, the questions the participants put to them are inane and enough to disgust any scholar. They ask things like "Is there anything left to believe in?" or "Why can't I fuck?" (186). Critical thinking runs shallow as they quickly accept a hodgepodge of ideas without reflection. Quick answers and simple theories are the order of the day.

To Blackie, many people were hurt because of the summer institutes, especially Cathy, because of those who "would destroy beauty and excellence" (185, 187). Quickly Cathy picks up the jargon of the institute—"maturity, relevance, honesty, openness, trust, freedom, truth, multinationals, imperialism, greed, peace, justice." "The ideas were rushing around in her head like ice cream in a milk shake machine—and they had about as much constancy and substance" (194). She is victimized by her relationship with Roy Touhy, whose inflammatory rhetoric of "militancy" and "identifying with the poor" becomes the focus of the institute crowd. Unfortunately, Cathy chooses him to guide her doctoral dissertation at the theological school where he has a chair in religious studies. He teaches her that the resurrection of Christ is irrelevant to liberation theology. As Cathy explains, "It is death that matters. For a death in the name of the cause of human liberation is a resurrection in itself. If we wish to follow Jesus—and I always have and still do—we must be prepared to die in the ranks of the revolutionary vanguard" (264).

To Blackie, Touhy is one of the "pure frauds." (185). Greeley's portrait of him shows how a priest can go wrong and then destroy the lives of others. He lectures on the evils of America and quotes Chairman Mao that "morality like political power, grows out of the barrel of a gun!" (238).

Encountering Touhy when he escorts Cathy to the institute to protect her from predators, Blackie observes him to be a mean, despicable fraud. In response to Touhy's calls for revolution, Blackie ironically comments, "There's room in the tradition for his theme. The last time the church embraced it was when it proclaimed the Crusades. Kill a Moslem for Jesus" (238).

With the biting and caustic satire that characteristically flows from Greeley's pen when he is attacking evil, Blackie's description of Touhy is trenchant and humorous.

I imagined Roy as an Irish Dracula, lean, sallow, bloodlessly handsome, with a high forehead and slightly receding hairline, which seemed to give him small horns on the top of his head. He wore a tailor-made black suit and dark tie and lacked only the cape and the fangs to give Bela Lugosi a run for his money. Moreover, his voice was a nasal whine, the sort one would expect in a creature returned from the grave. And he treated students like his life depended on sucking their blood and draining away their vitality. (188)

Touhy's character can best be observed in the wedding he arranges with Cathy. The wedding scene is one of the most humorous and satirical episodes in the novel. Since Blackie, faithful priest that he is, tells Cathy that he will not attend her wedding to Touhy, because he cannot take part in anything that shows contempt for the Church, the wedding is described as seen through the eyes of Blackie's sister, Mary Kate Murphy, and her husband. According to Joe the wedding is "like a visit to an institution for delusional schizophrenics" (282). It is a "horror show enacted in Central Park under a hot sun and a hazy blue sky, with balloons, banners and dancing boys in leotards (no dancing girls, please note), a bearded, long-haired celebrant [Touhy] dressed in gold watered silk, readings from Mao, Marcuse, Norman O. Brown and, of course, Roy Touhy" (282). There is no mention of God in the ceremony. While police watch from a distance the wedding party sings revolutionary songs.

Wearing cardinal red monastic robes tied with a gold cord, Touhy preaches a homily lasting a full forty-five minutes in which he frequently quotes himself. Afterward while the wedding party drinks cheap wine and nibbles on stale cheese, Roy Touhy delivers a second address in which he talked about Cuba, the Vatican, Vietnam, freedom, and maturity with absolutely no mention of his bride, who is wearing a simple brown homespun dress and a long veil that conceal her beauty. Throughout the entire proceedings, Touhy is the center of attention instead of the bride. He is a risible and ludicrous character and the reader laughs him to scorn.

Mary Kate, the psychiatrist, quipped that any wedding ceremony that needs to hide the bride's lovely figure is "sufficiently sick to call for the immediate institutionalization of all involved." Continuing with her typical humor she concludes: "The climax, you should excuse the expression, came when Cathy proposed a toast to her new husband in a timid and anxious voice" (284). To Mary Kate, Cathy is suffering from "middle-twenties penis hunger"and Touhy is a classic autoerotic who married himself in the strange ceremony.

In a delineation that is vintage Greeley, Cathy is also described humorously with an economy of words, as Blackie gives his opinion of her: "Typically direct and to the point, Cathy was as flaky as a bowl of breakfast food, kinky as a telephone cord, and indecisive as an archbishop. But once she had made up her mind to do something, she acted with the brisk vigor of a 747 touching down" (14).

When she was believed dead and reported to be a virgin and martyr of the Church, Blackie quips ironically and humorously, "St. Catherine of Chicago, virgin and martyr—my cousin Cathy . . . A virgin? Well practically a virgin, a couple of orgasms in this day and age could hardly be held against you" (3). In the words of his sister Mary Kate, Blackie "perceives that her life was a half-intoxicated drive down a mountain road, on the one side of which was comedy and the other side commitment. He understands that at one edge of the road there was superficiality and at the other zealotry, and that Cousin Cathy spent a hell of a lot of time on the edges" (44).

Suspecting that Cathy's marriage to Touhy is a sham and that the couple has no sex life together, Blackie sends Mary Kate to visit Cathy. In a very funny scene Cathy's marriage to Touhy ends as Mary Kate visits the couple and shows Touhy up for the scoundrel he really is. Cathy is now "fat, slovenly, no make up on her unhappy face, her hair ratty and unwashed, her cheap house dress wrinkled and unattractive" (291). Mary Kate discovers that Roy married Cathy so she could be his housekeeper, provide him with money, and to write his books for him. Convinced that Roy's book (in fact, really hers) will be as significant as Augustine's *City of God* or Aquinas*'s Summa,* Cathy has become the slave of a man who hates women and is constantly degrading them. She is in Mary Kate's terms, an extension of Roy's "auto-erotic ego" (293). As Mary Kate had surmised at the time of the wedding, Roy is a homosexual and has a male lover at school, a young black assistant professor.

The scene that follows is hilarious and typical of the comedy the reader has come to expect of Greeley. Laying a trap for Touhy, Mary Kate predicts that when he comes home he will be vicious and cruel to her. Cathy disagrees. But when Touhy arrives on the scene, he immediately begins to denigrate and degrade Mary Kate, who puts on an act of being a weak and vulnerable woman. As he accuses her, the psychiatrist, of being a parasite on society, she plays along with him pretending to be defenseless in the face of his brutal attacks. Her account of the affair tells another story: "I had hit it rich. The more vulnerable a beautiful woman, the more uncontrollable Roy's rage against her. His mother must have been a real ball-buster" (294). The reader is amused when Cathy becomes angry at Touhy's abuse, especially when he accuses Mary Kate of "complete moral and intellectual bankruptcy" (294). The scene become riotous as Cathy jumps on Roy and blackens his eye before Mary Kate pulls her off and he can escape out the door with both women yelling at him.

In time, bitterness and anger lead Cathy to radical feminism and a rejection of a male priesthood. She comes to the point when she quits going to mass and attends "a eucharistic banquet" conducted only by women (267). Feeling oppressed by the clergy, she now believes that "our only valid prayers, are the prayers of our life in revolutionary meetings and on the streets" (266–267).

As soon as she is free of Touhy, Cathy falls victim to another unforgettable and despicable character—Father Ed Carney. Having gained Cathy's trust when he was principal of her high school, he had pushed her into entering the convent even though she was in love with Nick Curran. Victim as well as victimizer, after sixteen years in the priesthood, Carney's religious congregation took away his parish because he had participated in the civil rights demonstration at Selma and attracted national attention. He was sent to a black parish. Under his guidance and while participating in peace marches and demonstrations against the Vietnam war and racism, Cathy adopts liberation theology. It is Carney who, desiring a martyr for his cause, later sells her to the insidious and ghoulish Felipe Gould to be raped and murdered.

With his typical skill of drawing incisive thumbnail sketches, Greeley describes Ed Carney as a "Hans Kung with muscles, a Ted Hesburg who did not change sides after every presidential election" (5). As head of the Movement for a Just World and as a missionary in Latin America he smuggles currency for the Mafia. Carney persuades Cathy to join him and his revolutionary group in Central America. She goes with nothing to offer but enthusiasm.

Religious enthusiasm ran in Cathy's family. Greeley's description of Erin Collins is humorous but at the same time tragic; because of her fanaticism she failed completely at being Cathy's mother. "Mrs. Collins was in her early fifties then, a slender woman with pale skin, a thin face and long white hair, clad always in black and looking like a poster for a Lady MacBeth—or maybe one of the witches. Her eyes were permanently wide in the kind of expression of awe you would expect from someone who had just seen a vision of the Sacred Heart, and her voice was soft and breathless, as though she expected the cardinal to walk in any minute" (31).

Following Erin's example of dedicated enthusiasm, Cathy, while she is still a nun wearing a veil, gets politically involved and tangles with the police and the media. Once again Greeley satirizes both the police and the media. As Cathy and Father Ed and others are holding a prayer vigil for peace on New Year's day in front of Holy Name Cathedral, a policeman accosts Cathy calling her a "fucking bitch" and rips off her veil, while telling her to leave. Immobilizing her with a blow of his club to the stomach that caused her to collapse on the sidewalk, he proceeds to arrest her for not leaving. She is thrown in jail with prostitutes and drunks. When this brutal episode is shown on the evening TV news, the Ryans, who symbolize the Church, rush to her aid. The newspapers recount the story of Cathy the "hippie nun," who was a passive resister because she was unable to get up from kneeling in prayer quickly enough.

Cathy was savaged a second time. When she was working in Senator McCarthy's headquarters the police rush in and beat her up, accusing her of dropping human waste out the windows of the hotel. When Nick finds her beaten and broken and tries to help her, in her misguided state she calls him a "fucking pig" and spits in his face. (252). In this satire of the media, it is pointed out that TV crews fake scenes of police brutality for the evening news because their assignment is to get such coverage. In Nick's words, "If there isn't any news, then you create it" (250).

In a scene that takes place in the law offices of Minor, Grey and Blatt the legal system is satirized. Joe McNally, the Mafia attorney who represents Carney, uses his influence with the mob to try to force Nick to settle Cathy's estate, before the seven-year period allowed by the state of Illinois is up. Thinking that they will squash young trial lawyer Nick like a bug, they hope to wrestle from him Cathy's fortune for Ed Carney and the Movement for a Just World since she is presumed to be dead (5).

When about two years after Cathy's supposed martyrdom, Counselor McNally argues before a woman judge for the declaration of the death of Catherine Collins, the corruption of the legal system is held up for ridicule. The Mafia had influenced the judge probably by promising her a seat on the federal bench if she would rule in favor of McNally. As the proceedings unfold, Father Ed Carny is smiling in anticipation of the money that will come to him, when suddenly Cathy appears, goes to the judge's bench and offers her help. "And who are you, young woman?" The reader gives a hearty chuckle when Cathy replies in that tone of the pious novice at which she was so practiced, "The decedent, your honor" (436).

When Blackie and Nick go to the mother house of Cathy's religious congregation for a ceremony in honor of the presumed dead virgin and martyr, a great deal of comedy occurs. The invitation to the event is to Blackie "about as appealing as an invitation to a ball in Seville while the black death was raging in the city" (13). After describing the chapel at our Lady of the Hill as "hemorrhoidal Gothic" (65), he observes, "This whole scene must be preserved in some Disney World of the twenty-first century . . . as evidence of just how far we've sunk from Chartres" (66). The former novitiate building is now a home for aged nuns where, ironically, many of the nuns will die in the same building where they began their religious training. They had not had a postulant in the past three years; there were sixty five in Cathy's class of postulants.

Doctor Benetta, the president of the college, a civil engineer who was unable to get tenure at a state institution, looks like "an up-and-coming hit man." He begins the ceremony with "ten unmemorable remarks about sanctity from an engineer's point of view" (67). Bishop Cafferty, "a thin, short Telly Savalas, whose wild eyes suggested an escapee from a halfway house for the harmlessly insane," gives a rambling speech on Pius XII, John XXIII, and Paul VI (66). After the unveiling of the statue of Cathy, made by her friend Rosie O'Gorman O'Malley, Bishop Cafferty offers a prayer and then begins to "warble" "like a drunken canary" as the charismatics present join in. Annoyed by the entire proceedings, Blackie remarks to Nick that Cathy would have laughed if she had seen the ceremony.

At lunch in the refectory a priest wearing a poncho, long hair, and a beard makes a speech that they should "vote a motion of censure against those legal lackeys who were responsible for keeping Cathy's money out of the hands of the poor to whom it belonged "as a matter of justice" (70). Upon Father Ed's suggestion, Nick tries to speak to the group, but he is silenced by hissing.

After viewing an exhibition of Catherine's paintings, "which were so bad as to deserve to be buried in the ground and indeed without any of the rites of Christian burial," a girl in the crowd is miraculously healed. An adolescent in a wheelchair begins to cry "as though she were having a charismatic seizure" (71). This is met by rising hysteria when the girl gets up and walks. In this scene Greeley shows his dislike for the charismatic renewal as he does in other stories.

Another major change takes place in the Church during the period of time covered by the book—the change in the sexual mores of the Catholic people. In reading about the sexual practices of the characters in Greeley's fiction, one must always remember that Greeley is writing as a sociologist and not as a moral theologian. The moral theologian tries to show what is good in life; the sociologist tries to depict life as it is being lived. In other words moral theology is prescriptive and sociology is descriptive. When Greeley relates that Mary Kate and Joe Murphy have decided that in spite of the papal encyclical *Humanae Vitae* they are going to practice birth control, Greeley is merely reporting the decision that many Catholics made at that time. It does not show that he supports this position; rather, it simply describes what he as a sociologist observed took place after the encyclical was promulgated. Blackie describes what happened throughout the Church as a result of the encyclical as follows: "And a few months after Robert Kennedy was buried in 1968, our gloriously reigning supreme pontiff brought the era of papal-led reform to an end with his encyclical on birth control. Changes continued, of course, but now it was out of control. The densely compacted energies and forces that had been created in the black hole blew up. American Catholicism became a supernova, an exploding fireball" (150). And again: " The birth control encyclical caused the black hole to explode, priests and nuns were running for secure cover, some in marriage, some in the pursuit of the annual ideological fads, some in drugs" (285).

The novel also depicts the change in attitude of many Catholics toward pre-marital sex. The female character Monica is "an old-fashioned Catholic" but she thinks having sex with a friend is at most a venial sin that does not keep her from receiving communion.

Cathy Collins undergoes many changes. She gives up her messiah complex of wanting to liberate Latin Americans and finds her true identity as she comes to the realization that she cannot identify with the poor unless she first identifies with herself. Cathy does in fact learn to identify with herself. After she is tortured and raped in the mythical country of Costaguana and barely escapes with her life, she is able to neutralize the horrors she experienced and begin life again. She is a resurrection person who with the grace of God finds happiness. This divine comedy ends with the marriage of Cathy and Nick. She will reappear in subsequent novels in Time between the Stars as a happy wife and mother. *Virgin and Martyr* makes the point that we can all be resurrection people and put the past behind us, no matter how bad it was, and begin life anew.

In conclusion, presenting as it does an accurate and in depth account of the Church in the years following Vatican II, this novel will be read long after some of Greeley's nonfiction works are forgotten. The characters of the book are well drawn and believable and the events of their lives quite plausible. With the use of satire, ridicule, and humor, Greeley gives vent to his anger, his fury at what inept and insensitive priests have done to the Catholic laity, many of whom have suffered as Cathy did, perhaps not in the same ways, but with the same pain. *Virgin and Martyr* is one of Greeley's masterpieces.[1]

In the second novel of Time between the Stars, Greeley again depicts a woman who has suffered greatly because of the treatment she has received from the Church. *Angels of September* is the story of Anne Marie O'Brien Reilly, a woman in her early fifties who receives savage treatment from the Church throughout most of her life but through grace—the unmerited favor of God—finally puts the past behind her and becomes a resurrection person. Women find this novel especially compelling, for, unfortunately, many of them relate closely to Anne Reilly, having experienced similar treatment themselves. The story, in Andrew Greeley's own words "is about guilt so powerful it finally seems to objectify and personify and obsess a woman and her art gallery" (*Confessions* 456). It is also a parable of grace about the justice and mercy of God.

With great skill, Greeley interweaves the various events in Anne's life. Rather than beginning *ab ova* with Anne's childhood, the author starts *in medias res* with the middle-aged Anne suffering from the trauma of long-experienced guilt. Little by little the author reveals her past and the causes of her guilt as Anne tells her story to her Freudian analyst Mary Kate Ryan Murphy.

In Anne's art gallery, Father Desmond Kenney's painting Divine Justice, depicting the fires of hell and the suffering of the damned, is on display, triggering strange phenomena and deeply troubling Anne. One of those suffering in the picture actually looks like Anne—not surprising since we later learn Kenney had her pose for his paintings. When strange things begin happening in the gallery, Anne wonders if Kenney is haunting her from beyond the grave. He had been the parish priest at Mother of Mercy Church in 1935 when a fire destroyed the parochial school killing many children, including Anne's two sisters, Connie and Kathleen.

After the fire, Kenney taught in the seminary for a while and later went to live at Cardinal Mundelein's residence and was probably there the night the cardinal died mysteriously, some say killed by his homosexual lover. Shortly thereafter Kenney went insane, gave his artwork to the archdiocese in 1949, and entered an asylum where he died thirty-three years later. With consummate humor Blackie comments on Kenney as he throws a satiric punch at liturgists: "Instead of putting him in an asylum, today we'd make him a consultant to our Liturgical Art Commission" (6). According to Blackie, Kenney never should have been ordained in the first place. As Blackie explains, "His career is still cited in the archdiocese as evidence that you cannot be an artist and be sane" (7).

The fire, which took place when Anne was a child of about seven, the reader learns, was the catalyst of Anne's abiding, tormenting guilt. Mistakenly she "remembers" starting the fire by setting some newspapers ablaze. However, she and the reader discover that she was not in school the day of the fire, but was at home with an illness.

Father Desmond G. Kenney, referred to by the press as the "Hero of the Mercy Fire," testified on the witness stand that the fire was God's punishment: "God's divine Justice punished us for our sins of the flesh" (185). Perhaps, as he said this, he recalled how, as early as the summer of 1942, he began to torment Anne Reilly about the fire, when he was staying in her aunt's guest house. Previously she had confessed to him in the Sacrament of Penance that she had started the fire. Violating the seal of the confessional, he uses this mistaken information to force Anne, a fourteen-year-old pubescent girl, to take off all her clothing and pose for him. Threatening to tell the police about her starting the fire, he screams at her calling her "an evil whore," accusing her of killing all the innocent children in the fire, while insisting that she will suffer eternally in hell. This loathsome priest tells Anne that her body is "a stinking swamp of evil, a vile trap for men, like every other woman's body, all shiny and beautiful on the outside and filled with corruption and the stench of dead men's flesh inside" (347). Day after day he forces her to pose nude for his paintings of women suffering in hell. All the while he keeps repeating that a woman's body is "a vile stinking swamp, a cesspool of filth and corruption and death" (347). "All the bodies of women should be locked up in convents forever!" (347).

As soon as she had undressed one particular day, he kissed her and caressed her while shouting that she was a demon from hell. Slapping her to the floor, he yells, "You'll have a miserable and unhappy life, you'll die a terrible death and suffer in hell for all eternity. You're no longer human; you have no rights as a person. Anything I do to you is part of God's punishment" (348). When he then broke down and sobbed, Anne comforted him. Although she never posed for him again, the pain he had inflicted would not go away.

Anne's first marriage is to Jim Reilly, a high school athlete who reached his peak his senior year. His mother promised to give him fifty thousand dollars the day he married Anne, since she thought Anne would be able to change him. He is a mean-spirited person who is determined always to get even for anything that he considers as an offense to him. For fifteen years Anne tolerates his meanness, his excessive drinking and physical abuse. Their sex life is very unsatisfactory, but when Anne gives him a marriage manual to read he declines, saying that they have no need of it.

Because her husband is using birth control, Anne's soul is troubled when she attends a parish mission at her church. Here begins Greeley's satire of the inept missions that have deeply injured many people who have attended them in the parishes. Husbands and wives do not attend the mission together; rather women attend the mission the first week and then the men go the following week. Two priests, who are not good preachers, give the mission. Poor preaching in the Church is one of Greeley's pet peeves and rightly so, for his surveys show that the laity are dissatisfied with the poor quality of the Sunday homilies. The mission priests give a series of sermons on banal topics, such as Communism, bad confessions, damnation, birth control, God's justice, and Fatima, which could have been presented to the least-educated parish, even though everyone in Anne's parish had gone to college. Although her pastor had told her that she was not sinning when her husband used contraceptives, she begins to feel a lot of guilt at the mission, especially about not having had enough remorse at previous confessions. These feelings of guilt lead Anne to confession to one of the mission priests, ironically called Father Placid, to whom she does not mention Jim's use of birth control. When the priest demands to know the ages of her children and learns that the youngest is one and a half, he rudely and blatantly asks why she is not pregnant. When he learns that Jim is using "unnatural practices," Father Placid tells her that God would be "perfectly justified" in sending her to hell or "in taking her two children away" from her. Completely distraught she promises to stop having sex with her husband when he uses unnatural means to prevent conception.

Opposing her husband for the first time, Anne refuses to have sexual relations with him, explaining what the priest had said. Jim gets mean, calls her a "frigid bitch," and slaps her around. In six weeks' time she is pregnant with Davie and her marriage is falling all apart. Ironically, Father Placid later married the nun who was superior of his parish school.

When Anne tells priests in confession that her husband beats her, they respond by saying that she probably deserves it and advise her to pray for her husband and try to be a better wife. One priest even tells her that when a man beats his wife, nine times out of ten, she deserves it. The beatings become more frequent and more savage and accompanied by verbal abuse. When Anne learns that her husband is visiting brothels, she mentions it to a confessor who insists that it is probably her own fault.

Although Jim dominates her completely, even insisting that she vote for his favorite political candidates, he grudgingly gives his permission for her to return to graduate school. Since she attends the University of Chicago, her mother-in-law wants to know if she has become a Communist. With a touch of ironic humor Anne replies, "Like Milton Friedman and George Stigler" (228). Of course, neither Jim nor his mother knew either of the men, so the irony is wasted on them.

When Anne receives her master's degree in March 1965, Jim refuses to attend the graduation or let their children attend. When she returns home after the ceremony , she finds that their son David is unconscious with a broken nose; Mark has one arm broken and Jim is still beating him with a strap. Their daughter Beth is locked in her room crying. Jimmy has disappeared. Since Jim had previously groped Beth when he was drunk, Anne fears incest.

When Anne appears on the scene, Jim turns on her violently shouting, "How many of those Communists did you fuck today, you fucking cunt?" (228). Their son Jimmy saves her from further abuse and possibly death by returning with the police.

After the horrible violence against herself and the children on graduation day, Anne, now thirty years old, walks out on Jim and goes to stay with her Aunt Aggie. As a devout, old-fashioned Catholic, Anne has always believed that God wanted her to stay with Jim. No doubt Jim is aware of this belief and it probably provoked him to mistreat her, knowing that she would not leave him because of a beating. With her life and the lives of her children in danger, Anne has no choice but to leave.

This satire on the Church's attitude toward battered wives continues when her mother-in-law's priest, Monsignor Crowley, asks Anne to forgive Jim. This she will do, but only if Jim gets into an alcoholic treatment program and takes psychiatric counseling for a year. Anne starts proceedings for a separation.

As part of the separation process both Anne and Jim have to seek counseling with their own parish priest who inquires if Anne plans to marry again, advising her that there is no chance of an annulment under the present legislation in the Church. Believing that she would always be married to Jim, she has no intention of finding another husband.

The story takes an ironic twist when Jim charges her for desertion and adultery and demands legal custody of their children. Before the Church gives them permission to separate, Jim sues for divorce. It is at this point in her life that the Ryan clan comes to her aid with attorney Ned Ryan who represents her in the divorce proceedings. The Ryans, as mentioned previously, represent the Church in these novels.

Anne moves to Washington to attend graduate school and eventually earns a Ph.D. and a job teaching at American University. At this time, Senator John Duncan enters her life by driving her home from a meeting one night. His wife of thirty years is in a mental institution where he visits her every weekend, blaming himself for his political life which he believes might have destroyed her mind. When John Duncan later calls Anne and invites her out, she agrees to see him. Looking back on this period of her life at a later time, Anne comments, "I was a virtuous Catholic woman for whom the idea of adulterous sex was unthinkable. I did not yet know myself well enough to realize that the hormones and the emotions pay little attention to what is thinkable and what is unthinkable" (279).

Anne's love affair with John Duncan causes her much guilt, making her to assume she will go to hell if she dies suddenly, especially since she feels rejected by God already for previous sins. Although Anne feels that she is defying God, who, as she sees it, rejects her, she keeps saying her morning and night prayers, even when in bed with John Duncan, a devout Protestant who wants to pray with her. Because she does not want to increase the number of her mortal sins, she never quits going to Sunday mass, but she determines she will enjoy the time she has left before the demons come to claim her.

When John's wife dies, he asks her to marry him. Sadly she explains to John, whom she has grown to love very much, that she cannot marry him because in the eyes of the Church she will always be married to Jim Reilly. She explains that she would be excommunicated if she married him. Because many changes have taken place in the Church since the Second Vatican Council, he asks her if it is not possible that the rules will change. Her answer: "Even God couldn't dissolve my marriage to Jim Reilly" (307). As usual, Greeley, to borrow one of his expressions, has a lot of ironies in the fire.

Nevertheless, Anne goes to the chancery of the archdiocese of Washington to inquire about the possibility of getting an annulment. The priest there asked her a "litany of inquiries," which had nothing to do with the ordinary life of ordinary human beings. They had been put together in a dusty and arid old room in the

Vatican by men who had been taken away from their families as small boys and who had never known the sting of desire or the joy of love (309).

Under the present legislation, the priest informs her, there is not much chance of her getting an annulment. When she replies that there is not much compassion in the rules, he replies superciliously, "The Church is not interested in compassion, Mrs. Reilly. Our presumption is in favor of the sacramental bond. We must protect the sanctity of the bond, even if the cost is human suffering. People are not important, sacraments are" (307). He emphasizes that if she remarries she will cut herself off from God's love for the rest of her excommunicated life.

After breaking with John Duncan, who subsequently marries someone else, Anne returns to Chicago and a teaching job at St. Columbanus, a Catholic College. When three years later Anne receives a document from the Matrimonial Tribune of the archdiocese of Chicago, asking her six pages of questions relating to the annulment of her marriage to Jim Reilly, she sees a young priest to inquire what was happening. He explains to her that Jim Reilly is seeking an annulment of their marriage. Because Anne, such a short time before, had renounced John Duncan because of the Church's marriage laws, she is furious. "What kind of sick games are you playing with human lives?" she inquires (358). "The Catholic Church has an incredible facility for doing offensive things, especially to those who love it," (357) he replies, emphasizing one the themes that runs throughout Greeley's fiction.

Explaining the Church's new attitude toward marriage, the priest comments, "Marriage is a sacrament because the permanence of the union between a man and a woman reveals the permanence of God's commitment to us" (359). When the union is not permanent it is not a sacramental marriage, because one of the partners was incapable of establishing a permanent union. When she inquires if she had married John Duncan could she now be getting an annulment, he answers in the affirmative saying that if she had applied three years previously in Chicago, instead of Washington, she would have obtained it then. He concludes, "Because you were a good Catholic laywoman and did what the Church told you to do, you've been abused, cheated, treated unjustly, unfairly. I wouldn't blame you if you walked out of this office and out of the Catholic Church and never had anything to do with us again" (360).

Storming out of the rectory, Anne informs him that she will do just that. However, a week later she returns, with the completed questionnaire he had given her and apologizes, saying, "It may not be much of a Church, Father, and I'm furious at what it's done to me, but it's still the only Church I have" (361). It is at this time she learns that the priest is Blackie Ryan.

More pain is in store for Anne at the hands of the Church. The President of St. Columbanus, Father Matthew Sweeney, begins taking Anne out. Since the evening is always concluded by a handshake or a peck on the cheek, Anne is quite surprised when he asks her to marry him, explaining that he has applied to Rome for a dispensation, is resigning as president of the university, and is leaving the priesthood the following week. He will continue on as a tenured member of the faculty of St. Columbanus. He is convinced that for his personal growth he must marry. When she considers the matter and turns him down he cries until she says yes. When he told her that he was free to marry, they had a private ceremony in the university chapel. As a result of the marriage, she lost her teaching position at St. Columbanus, because, she is told, the parents and students would be scandalized if she continued teaching there because she has married a priest.

Matt Sweeney, who is permitted to continue teaching at St. Columbanus in spite of the marriage, begins attending meetings of the Catholic Charismatic Renewal. After two and a half years of marriage, he attends a weeklong charismatic retreat, during which time Anne concludes that she must love him, since she misses him during his absence. When he returns from the retreat, he hits her with a thunderbolt. Since the pope denied his application for a dispensation, they are not validly married and he is determined to return to the priesthood. He had lied to her, when he assured her that he was free to marry.

Anne's two marriages are declared null and void by the Church. The first one because the Church decided she and Jim were not emotionally or psychologically capable of contracting a sacramental marriage; the second because the Church had never given consent for Matt to marry. Moreover, she missed out on marriage with John Duncan because she was following the rules of the Church, which would have granted her an annulment in Chicago, when she was denied one in Washington, if she had only known about it.

Devastated but not defeated, Anne manages to buy an art gallery with the help of her son and is there when the story opens. Strange and fantastic things begin to happen when she displays the artwork of Father Desmond Kenney at the request of the archdiocese to whom he had left it. Smoke, soot, explosions, chilling cold winds, unusual weather events, doors suddenly locking shut, figures in paintings seeming to change, objects mysteriously moving from one place to another—these are some of the phenomena that occur. Anne and the reader must hesitate between a rational and a supernatural explanation for the cause for these events, as one does in fantastic fiction.

As Blackie tries to find a solution to the mysterious occurrences at the art gallery, the author develops this character. In contrast to Father Kenney and the other priests that do great damage to Anne, Blackie is a good priest who comes to her aid. Many readers regrettably fail to see Blackie's many good qualities, because he has a tendency to make himself almost invisible. The reader should know that Blackie is Greeley's idea of what the ideal priest should be—faithful, obedient to his bishop, embracing celibacy, filled with compassion, eager to serve the people of God, and very self-effacing. However, Blackie does have human weakness like the rest of us: he loves chocolate, raspberries, cookies and has a big appetite, especially at breakfast. Unlike most of us, however, he finds his refreshment in reading patrology—the Fathers of the Church.

With a great deal of exciting adventure, Blackie and Mike Casey the Cop, imitating his namesake St. Michael the Archangel, rescue Anne from the demons that pursue her, with the help of the other September angels—Mary Kate and

Deirdre. These four angels—priest, lover, psychiatrist, and patrol officer—represent the Church at its best as they deliver Anne from the devastating forces that overwhelm her. With their help, Anne becomes a resurrection person. With Mike she finds the fulfillment she has always needed and desired. This couple, together, with the rest of the Ryans (Mike's mother was a Ryan) continue to appear in the subsequent novels in the series Time between the Stars, fostering the illusion that they are real people. Interestingly, Maria and Hugh Donlon from *Ascent into Hell*, reappear in *Angels of September*. The reader is pleased to learn that they now have a child, Mary Margaret, and that Maria is now a bank president. Cathy Collins, the heroine of *Virgin and Martyr,* the reader learns, has two children by Nick Curran, her husband—Nicole and Jack. Greeley has the remarkable ability of keeping track of his characters and what becomes of them once their story is told. They are never forgotten and can appear suddenly in a story, when they are least expected.

Greeley's typical satire and satiric humor contribute much to *Angels of September.* Probably few women have been caused as much pain and suffering by the churchmen as Anne; possibly all women have suffered some of the things she experienced. However, this novel demonstrates that the Church and its attitude toward divine justice and the mercy of God have really changed since Vatican II. Gone are the days when nuns warn students the last day of classes in June that they will go to hell if they miss mass one Sunday during the summer vacation and then meet up with a fatal mishap. According to Blackie, the Church in those days was less confident of God's love. As he says, "We merchandised a lot of guilt in those days." And as for going to hell? How does Blackie define hell? "Hell is not responding to God's love. . . " (73).

Speaking of the savage treatment Anne Reilly received, her psychiatrist Mary Kate Ryan Murphy makes a very astute observation: "Her monumental guilt attaches itself to the actual or imagined violation of various and sundry Church regulations, laws, norms, canons, and other obligations—past and present. And heaven knows the Church has gone out of its way to screw her as well as screw her up" (106–107).

Greeley does not limit his satire to Catholics. Another of the favorite targets of Greeley's humorous and often pungent satire is the police. However, Greeley is not opposed to all cops, just bad ones. Mike Casey, who appears in quite a few novels, is an example of what a good police officer should be, and in *Angels of September* he is one of the four angels who come to Anne's rescue. Contrasted with him is the bad cop, Police Captain Jeremiah Mullens, described as "kinky" and whose only adjective is "fucking." In talking about Anne and her marriage to ex-priest Matt Sweeney, he says in all seriousness, "She's been married twice, you know. Once to a fucking priest" (87). The play on words here is typical of Greeley who likes to jolt his readers with his language to shock them into taking a different perspective on events. As he says, "Scatological and obscene words . . . however inappropriate they may be in certain contexts and however much they may be a matter of taste and no taste, are not sins at all" (*When Life Hurts* 79).

Another bad cop is depicted in a comic incident when Mike and Deirdre Lopez, his colleague and a patrol officer, while in an unmarked police car, spot a policeman harassing a confused black motorist from out of state. Traffic is backed up for half a mile when Mike yells, "You stupid idiot," and tells the officer to get the car off the street. Not knowing who Mike is, the cop counters by calling him "fuckhead." When Mike drives on, the infuriated and indignant cop follows them, stops them, gets out of his car with a drawn gun and waddles "arrogantly toward them, as though he were imitating a sheriff in some inane vintage southern movie." When the cop announces that he is going to frisk them both, but thinks it would be fun frisking the girl first, Mike tells him to put his gun away. Snarling the cop replies, "Don't give me orders, fuckhead. Who the hell do you think you are?" "Deputy Superintendent Michael Patrick Vincent Casey is my name, and your name, copper, is mud. M-U-D, mud" (412).

There is a lot of such humor in the book. Once when Anne hears footsteps in the gallery and suspects some paranormal happening, she throws open the door and shouts, "What do you want, you miserable son of a bitch?" Mike Casey is standing there with a malted milk. On another occasion Blackie comments that all the females on the force are in love with Mike. "The female police dogs aren't" was Mike's quick response (414).

Many kinds of comedy appear in the book, but the overarching comedy is the comedy of life, the divine comedy—or what Greeley refers to as the "great cosmic joke in which life successfully puts down death" (*Love and Play* 336). Anne's sufferings are great and mostly caused by the Church, but it is also the Church that comes to her rescue in the persons of the "angels of September"— Mike Casey the Cop; Blackie Ryan of Holy Name Cathedral; Blackie's sister Mary Kate and her husband, Joe Murphy, psychiatrists; and Deirdre, a patrol officer. With their help Anne is able to neutralize the horrors of her life and emerge a triumphant resurrection person. Life triumphs over death; comedy over tragedy. In Greeley's own words, "Catholicism is a Comic Religion (and not in the sense that many of our leaders are unintentional comedians). It believes in hope. It believes that life is stronger than death, love stronger than hatred, good stronger than evil. The Catholic religious sensibility—if not always formal Catholic theology—has always known that the storyteller/God is a Comedian" (*God in Popular Culture* 113).

The comedy continues in *Rite of Spring* (1987), a retelling of the quest for the Holy Grail, which is the theme of Greeley's first trilogy which comprises *The Magic Cup*, *Death in April*, and *The Final Planet*. In the ancient Celtic legend and in Greeley's versions of the legend, the hero searches for a cup and a woman, which are identified with one another and which represent God. The hero soon learns that his princess is also seeking him.

Brendan Ryan, the forty-two-year-old protagonist of the romance and cousin of Blackie Ryan, recounts how the beginning of his "fall from grace" occurred when he first saw Ciara Kelly. After twenty years of marriage, his wife Madonna had obtained what Brendan refers to humorously as "a lunch counter annulment," leaving him free for a second chance at romance and love. Once he is free, he wastes no time in pursuing a new life.

Interestingly, Brendan is part of the law firm of Minor Gray and Blatt where both Eileen Kane and Nick Curran practice law. The reader is delighted to learn that Nick Curran and his wife, Cathy, are expecting a baby, as are Eileen Kane and her husband, Red. They were late pregnancies for both women. When Brendan observes the pregnant Eileen and Cathy, he wishes ardently for a wife to impregnate. Sex and pregnancy had been rare events in his life with Madonna, his former wife, who did not care for either one.

In presenting Madonna and her family, Greeley portrays the quest for respectability that has characterized many Irish families in America. The portrait he presents shows the zany and absurd lengths to which some Irish will go to impress others. The wedding of Madonna and Brendan is a classic comical Greeley scenario. Lourdes Clifford, Madonna's mother, assumes that the couple will marry and begins discussing wedding plans with Brendan, before he even proposes. Then Brendan and his parents are pushed aside as Lourdes and Madonna design the production, which includes twenty-six members in the wedding party, seventeen priests in the sanctuary—many of which are "decrepit lap dog clergy,"(83) trumpets and violins, a papal blessing, a large bouquet of roses at the end of each pew, and over one thousand guests at the reception that follows. It is as if they are trying to impress all of Chicago as the Cliffords are determined to prove that the Irish have become respectable, but as the author comments, "It took another generation to realize that respectability wasn't worth the candle" (80).

The Shannon Rovers' Irish Warpipes band escorts Brendan and Madonna into the church. Everything shouts nouveau riche from the green, white, and orange ice cream—the colors of the Irish flag—to the Notre Dame motif in the decorations. Adding to the absurdity of the scene, the Notre Dame victory march is played as the couple takes their place at the head table at the reception. Of course, the Cliffords had spread the word ahead of time that the wedding was costing them twenty thousand dollars. Lourdes's insistence on having everything completely "respectable" drove Madonna to daily attacks of nausea and chain smoking.

Referring to the wedding as "the day of our monstrosity," Brendan recalls how little help they got from the Church. The pre-Cana conference was a pretty dismal affair—a priest gave them abstract theology; a doctor offered technical sex instruction; and a married couple assured them with "cloying sweetness" that it is fun to have children. The priest who fills out the ecclesiastical forms the night before the ceremony is "barely civil." By this time Madonna is not speaking to Brendan.

Because his military guard of honor did not clash their swords at the right time, Lourdes will not speak to Brendan at the reception. As for Dr. Clifford, he took great pleasure in having the dance music interrupted ever so often by the Notre Dame victory march.

Since they were not at all prepared for sex or the conflicts of married life, "the wedding night was a disaster" (84). With extreme prudery, Madonna merely tolerates sex as an obligation that has to be fulfilled. Her sentiments: "Come on, don't play around with me; get it over with" (85).

Closely allied to Irish respectability and the lack thereof is the Irish proclivity for drinking too much alcohol. In *Rite of Spring,* Greeley deals with the topic of excessive drinking. King Sullivan, Brendan's childhood friend, is destroyed by alcoholism.

As is usually the case in Greeley's fiction, the police are satirized in *Rite of Spring.* The cops who investigate the murders on Brendan's boat assume that Brendan has been murdered without checking dental records or the height of the victim. As usual, the police use obscene language to try to establish their masculinity and authority. The following incident is typical of Greeley's humor. On one occasion, Eileen addressed a man called Art Savage in this way: "Sit down, Savage" (183). This remark caused a dumb cop to lash out with the following: "What's the matter with you, man? . . . "I'm not black, but I wouldn't let that white bitch call me a savage" (217).

Again the cops are inept when they find that Brendan is alive after the explosion on his boat. They falsely accuse him of the murders that took place on board his boat and harass him. When the story moves to Ireland, the reader learns that the Irish Garda also has its share of stupid inept cops. They also have cops whose language parallels that of their American counterparts; the Irish versions of the four-letter words contribute to the comedy of the book.

A caricature of a German Jewish psychiatrist, Dr. Otto Freihaut, "a Black Forest elf," gives another comic touch to the story (227). Convinced that psychic phenomena do not exist and that Brendan has imagined Ciara Kelly and the ghost of his wife Madonna which appeared to him, he diagnoses Brendan as suffering from mental illness. In commenting on this psychiatrist and his false diagnosis of Brendan, Blackie says with much humor: "Patently, *Herr Doktor* has considerable anal retentive rigidities. . . . Not that I know what that means, but I'm always impressed when my sister, the good Mary Kate, speaks that phrase trippingly on the tongue" (233).

Another comic character is Cindasoo, who speaks Appalachian English and is in the "Yewnited States Coast Guard" (246). Introduced in this book, she appears in subsequent fiction by the author. She saves the day when she puts a bullet right between the eyes of Crazy Mal Malocha of the Mafia, who tries to kill Brendan

The Murphys, the Caseys, the Kanes, Blackie, and the rest of the Ryans are part of the growing neighborhood that Greeley is creating to symbolize the Church in *Rite of Spring* and in subsequent stories in the series Time between the Stars. As Brendan struggles to possess his grail, these characters come to his aid. Since an earlier chapter is devoted to Greeley's version of the grail quester legend, it suffices to make only a few comments about the grail quest in *Rite of Spring.* Brendan states his belief that Ciara Kelly is his life and his destiny. As fertility was a very important part of the ancient Celtic grail legend, Brendan constantly pictures Ciara as pregnant with his child.

Searching for his grail, Brendan enters into the old mythic world of the west of Ireland with its great heroes. As he battles Irish terrorists for his woman, Brendan sees himself as a modern Finn MacCool. Like the heroes of Greeley's grail trilogy, he is transformed from a conservative person into an Irish beserker. Other parallels are found between this and Greeley's earlier grail romances. For example, Ciara saves Brendan's life as earlier Greeley heroines saved the lives of their heroes. Furthermore, it is not a coincidence that the final scenes of *Rite of Spring* are set on the Strand at Inch, but parallel those of earlier stories.

When he finally gets his grail, Brendan will wed Ciara—the proper ending for a comedy. After Blackie has provided the sacraments of the Church, the couple will settle down in a house at Grand Beach not far from the Kanes, Caseys, Murphys, and other Ryans. Brendan's intentions toward Ciara remain what they have been from the first moment he saw he; he wants her for his wife and the mother of his children. In finding Ciara his first love, Brendan finds God and God's will for his life. Transformed by the second chance that God has given him, he is a resurrection person. He is no longer the "dried-up old bastard" that his daughter Jean called him at the beginning of the story, but rather he is filled with tenderness and transforming love. The reader expects that in future he will join the rest of the Ryan clan who are correlatives of the Church, as they demonstrate their caring love for people in need.

Patience of a Saint brings us to the very core of Andrew Greeley's thought as a sociologist and as a priest. Although Andrew Greeley would be the first to tell you that he is not at all inclined to be a mystic, in this novel the main character is one. Furthermore, although Andrew Greeley is a celibate, in *Patience of a Saint* he has written the intimate story of the marriage of Red Kane and his wife, Eileen. The question why naturally arises. The answer is that the novel is a parable—a story illustrating a religious lesson. *Patience of a Saint* is also the vehicle for sociologist Andrew Greeley's ideas on human sexuality and marriage, since these topics are a very essential part of sociology. The course on marriage and the family is one of the most popular Sociology courses in the university curriculum. We must also keep in mind that Greeley is not writing or illustrating a theology of the mystical life.

The book begins with a description of Red Kane's religious experience. The incident is typical of Greeley's fiction, a humorous one.

Wacker Drive is not exactly the Road to Damascus. Nonetheless, it was on Wacker Drive that the Lord God hit Red Kane over the head with a cosmic baseball bat.
. . .
Moreover, the Lord God used the same one-two punch which he had done in Saint Paul. The latter worthy was knocked from his horse perhaps by a lightning bolt. Red Kane, not having a horse was bowled over by a large Cadillac limousine that narrowly missed him as it made a rapid right turn against a red light and sped away at high speed.

"Eileen!" Red cried as he jumped out of the path of the car, lost his balance, and fell with considerable lack of dignity on his rear end. (3)

For the sake of the lesson to be learned from the parable, Greeley emphasizes

God's immanence, but does not depict his transcendence. To Greeley, life is a comedy and God is a comedian. Love triumphs over everything negative in what he calls the "great cosmic joke" (*Love and Play* 336). Love and life conquer hatred and death. This is very important to keep in mind, for if one does not understand Greeley's point of view in this regard, one might be inclined to feel it is impiously irreverent to mix the comic with God.

At the time of this experience, Red Kane, fifty years old and hiding behind "a mask of cynicism" with all his dreams turned to ashes, thinks of himself as "the last of the Irish journalist drunks in Chicago"(24). A fallen away Catholic, he is an agnostic. His marriage is in dismal shape. Only very rarely does he make love with his wife, having had about ten mistresses in the past thirty years and currently has a mistress, Melissa Spencer, whom he does not love. Abysmally poor are his relationships with his children.

So what is Greeley trying to prove with this story? The answer is very clear. That human passion is a metaphor for God's love for us and that God loves each one of us like a man loves his wife, but with far greater depth and intensity. However, this is not a new idea, but it is one that has been largely disregarded. The analogy that God loves us in this way is one that is actually scripturally based, having been expounded by St. Paul in Ephesians 5:21–33. Moreover, the concept that Israel is the spouse of God is one that runs throughout the Old Testament. As Greeley says, "That human passion is a sacrament and an instrument of divine passion is a notion as old as Yahwehism" (*Confessions,* 443). In the Song of Songs the analogy between human and divine love is clearly indicated and writers such as St. John of the Cross, one of the Doctors of the Church, recognized this and continued to express the same theme in, for example, works like *The Spiritual Canticle.* However, the Church has not enthusiastically embraced this concept, to say the least, because of its views on sex and marriage.

As for the Church's attitudes toward human sexuality, Greeley comments, "I suspect Catholic historians of the future will describe the Church's obsession with sex and particularly with an attempt to deny the pleasures of sex to married men and women as a chapter in our history compared to the Inquisition and the Crusades" (*Confessions* 340).

Actually, the winds of change are already slowly beginning to blow through the Church. Pope John Paul II, at least since the time he was assigned as a priest to the university parish of St. Florian, has worked to help young people find happiness in marriage. While at St. Florian's, he was in the habit of taking groups of university students, comprising both men and women, on all-day hikes and outings to the mountains or lakes. According to Bernstein and Politi in their biography *His Holiness: John Paul II and the Hidden History of Our Time*, Wojtyla, dressed casually in a polo shirt and shorts (to keep him from being identified as a priest since priests were not allowed by the government to lead groups of young people outside the church), discussed intimate details of love and marriage with the students.

According to Bernstein and Politi, the reflections and conversations from these outings led to the publication of *Love and Responsibility* in 1960, by which time Wojtyla was already a bishop. This book caused quite a stir in the Church "because no one had ever heard of a bishop dealing in print with subjects like sexual excitement, unsatisfied wives who faked orgasms, or the fundamental importance of a man's making sure that his mate climaxed" (82). Although he got most of his information from the confessional and his reading, some of his students wondered if perhaps he had been previously married.

Commenting on *Love and Responsibility*, Bernstein and Politi find Wojtyla audacious in that he, as a priest and a celibate, could speak so freely on sexual intimacy. They observe that Wojtyla had done much research on human sexuality.

Although his footnotes in *Love and Responsibility* cite few sources other than his own philosophical writings, it is apparent from the text that Wojtyla had done his research on human sexuality, especially on matters of anatomy and physiology. The views of "sexologists" are frequently mentioned, as are the "teachings of sexology." As for his audacity in creating a theory of sexual relations without any direct experience, his whole life had been stirred by questions about love, of which sex is so much a part: the miracle of love between man and woman, love of one's fellow human beings or of the parent for a child, love as the basis of societal values; love as Christ's dowry to his disciples. His audacity—a trait he had in abundance in any case—lay foremost in his willingness to speak bluntly and with feeling about what occupied his mind in a time when such language was considered daring in a priest. (*His Holiness* 82)

Those who think it incongruous for Greeley to write so plainly about sexuality should perhaps consider what has just been cited from Bernstein and Politi about John Paul II.

Greeley's views on sex and marriage are clearly formulated and expressed in his writings which include two non-fiction books—*Sexual Intimacy* (1973) and *Love and Play* (1975), reprinted in one volume, *Sexual Intimacy: Love and Play* (1988),—and in his novels which illustrate his ideas. To Greeley "sex is edifying and religious and important" (*Confessions* 443). In his book *A Church to Come Home To*, written in conjunction with the theologian Mary G. Durkin, his sister, he laments that the Church is making little effort to develop and articulate a positive vision of marital intimacy. In his view, the quest for marital intimacy is a religious quest. "It is a quest for God and needs God's continual presence if it is to be successful" (108). The way a man and a woman experience marital intimacy brings God into the world.

The image of two in one flesh and of a man and woman cleaving to each other as the way in which God intended that holiness should enter the world reminds us that the Yahwist author of the Genesis story undoubtedly was familiar with a marital relationship which at some time or the other caused him to realize that a perfect relationship between a man and a woman would reflect God. For, as the later Genesis I author puts it more theologically, "two in one flesh" allowed Adam and Eve to be in the image of God. (107)

In his sociological study *Sexual Intimacy*, Greeley makes a point that the real sexual revolution of our time is "the very modern and very recent idea that marriage, friendship, and the principal of genital satisfaction could all exist in the same relationship" (59). As a result, the spouse becomes a "playmate" (59). This change in the marital relationship, Greeley observes, causes people to expect more of marriage than in former times, as for example in nineteenth-century France, where a man had a wife to give him children, a friend, usually male, to provide him with interesting conversation, and a mistress to satisfy his sexual desires. This is exactly the situation in which Red Kane finds himself at the beginning of *Patience of a Saint*. However, his life changes dramatically after his mystical encounter, because the tremendous inflowing of love that he experiences motivates him to love his wife, his children, and everyone else. He wants to love as he has been loved in his mystic moment. Before examining *Patience of a Saint*, it is a good idea to clarify some of Greeley's ideas on human sexuality and marriage so that when he illustrates them in the novel, it will be easier understand what he is doing.

One point Greeley makes about marriage is that sex is the bond that holds the couple together. This should be obvious to anyone who is married, but it needs to be emphasized in a Church, which has a celibate hierarchy. The bonding that comes from sexual union makes it possible for a couple to stay together and rear the children they have conceived. Moreover the happiness a couple derives from their physical union compensates, in great measure, for the troubles of daily life. According to Greeley, and most married people would agree, "The most delightful lovemaking among married couples is precisely that which is explicitly designed to alleviate loneliness, discouragement, and weariness. It is then that love most effectively communicates to the other that he is worth something, that he is desired, admired, and loved" (*Sexual Intimacy* 157).

The benefits of the marriage relationship extend beyond the couple themselves, for as Greeley sees it, the quality of a married couple's love is "the most effective way they have of revealing God's love to the rest of the world" (*Sexual Intimacy* 180–181). This is because the greater the pleasure that they give each other, not just in bed, but in all the facets of their marriage, the more God is present with them (*Sexual Intimacy* 191).

One of Greeley's principal views on marriage is that for a marriage to be successful it must be playful. Sex itself must be playful and an "exercise of relaxed, confident, creative, spontaneous mutual fantasy and celebration" (212). In his book *Love and Play*, he emphasizes the necessity for play in marriage and insists that playfulness can only occur in a sexual relationship in an atmosphere of permanent commitment. Furthermore, in Greeley's opinion "Christian lovers dance and play together because they believe that life, for all its tragedy, is still ultimately, a comedy, indeed, a comic, playful dance with the passionately loving God" (214).

The game of sex celebrates the victory of life over death. It is because it is celebratory that it becomes playful. Without a celebratory aspect, Greeley maintains, sex will become "grim, somber, and deadly serious." What do we really celebrate? Greeley answers, "Sex, then, is a celebration of both its own over-whelming pleasure and power and all the other good things that the powers of light and life have made available to us" (307). But sex is more than celebration; it is also communion and thanksgiving. Or as St. Paul says, sexual union is a great sacrament, a great *mysterion* that reveals the intimacy of God's union with his creatures. We may be content to write off our sex life as a prosaic, pedestrian biological function. When we do that we miss something the great mystics and the great lovers, the great poets and the great visionaries down through the ages have perceived. When a man and woman are locked in an embrace they come for a few brief seconds close to the core of the greatest mystery of them all (*Love and Play* 260).

Despite all its mystery and wonder, Greeley maintains, sex is also funny. To be specific: "Sex is a game, all right, and an uproariously funny one at that. . ." (206). What is so funny about sex? "To begin with," Greeley responds, "the naked human body is funny. It may be radiantly beautiful, but is also slightly ridiculous" (323). As he explains, stripped of clothing, people are stripped of pretenses. Sexual arousal is even funnier than nakedness (325). Furthermore, people lose their dignity in sexual encounters. There is, according to Greeley, no dignified way to have sex.

When a man and woman make love to one another they also temporarily make fools out of themselves. They may suppress this fact and pretend what they are doing is serious, sober and dreadfully important. When this pretense is maintained in the face of almost over-whelming evidence to the contrary, the relationship between the man and woman offers the raw material for much of the high comedy the human race has produced. The intercourse interlude within such a relationship is responsible for almost all of our low comedy. Funny things happen when a man and woman make love to one another. They can pretend that it's not hilarious and thus protect their fragile egos, but such a pretense misses much of what goes on in the situation and absolutely precludes the possibility of sex's being playful. (328–329)

When people feel secure with one another they are able to laugh at the incon-gruities of sex and find healing in laughter. Laughter dispels fear and sex is "scary business" because, as Greeley says, "In sex we put ourselves on the line both phys-ically and psychologically in a way we do in practically no other kind of activity" (332). In fact, the fear of sexuality may be linked to our basic fear of death. We respond to our fears with laughter. "We laugh at death and we laugh at sex because if we don't laugh at them they may well overwhelm us" (333–34).

In sum, Greeley's view of human sexuality is very positive and inspiring. He further believes that religion must provide meaning for human sexuality. In *Patience of a Saint* Greeley concentrates on giving sexuality religious meaning by showing how Red Kane grows in holiness as his love for his wife increases. Red experiences the love of God and immediately changes his life by giving up smoking, drinking, and his mistress. Most significantly, however, he falls in love again with Eileen, his wife. As he courts her with much humor and laughter, their sexual life becomes playful and celebratory. Red works hard at establishing a good relationship again with his children. On his job as an investigative reporter for the *Herald-Gazette,* he becomes a crusader for justice. In short, he is striving for sanctity, although he would probably be the last to admit it.

The story of Red's love affair with his wife Eileen is interwoven, as Greeley's readers have come to expect, with a fascinating and tense adventure story filled with mystery and suspense. The usual elements of comedy are present throughout the book—comedy of situation, expression, characterization, and satire. The main targets for his caustic humor and derision are the media, inept clergy, the legal system, including law enforcement personnel.

The *Patience of a Saint* is the story of second chances in which Red Kane is a resurrection person like the other protagonists we have already observed in Time between the Stars. Reaching out to help Red, the Ryans represent the Church through the ministrations of Mary Kate Ryan, the psychiatrist, and the priest Blackie Ryan, her brother. Because of the caring of all those who surround him, Red is able grow and overcome his weaknesses and the things that separate him from God and his family.

When Red falls in love with Eileen again and starts to pursue her amorously, Eileen suspects that there must be something wrong with him, since they have not made love in months. The tremendous love Red feels for Eileen is "a healing grace" (82). Realizing that God loves him the way he loves Eileen turns their sex life into fun and games as they act out their fantasies in the bedroom. When he makes love to her in "comic pseudo French," she giggles with delight (80–81). He comes to realize that God is in some way linked to Eileen. "Eileen was like God and not like God; God was like Eileen and not like Eileen" (83). According to Eileen, Red treats her like she is someone sacred. To Red his wife is "a particularly compliant and luminous lover—like a sanctuary lamp in a darkened church" (292). She whispers to him, "You treat me like you are a priest touching a sacred vessel" (164). As time goes by, Red comes to identify Eileen more and more with God until the two become linked and confused in his mind.

Frequently after they make love, Red can hear Eileen weeping in the night. She confides that she blames herself because he committed so many adulteries during the years of their marriage. When she confesses that she is still afraid of losing him, he wonders if perhaps God feels the same about him and is afraid of losing him too. Because of his earthshaking religious experience, he is able to tell her what God is like: "God is a tender, passionate lover like me at my very rare best" (313). When Eileen notices how very patient Red has become with their children, she calls him St. Redmund of Lincoln Park.

Confused by his mystical experiences, Red visits a priest, Larry Moran, to get some advice. When he explains to the priest what has happened to him, the priest replies that mystics—including St. Teresa of Avila and St. John of the Cross, both Doctors of the Church—are schizophrenic. Here Greeley is satirizing the liberal radical priests who think that religion is only serving the poor. Moran insists, "Ours is a religion of service to the poor and not mystical experience. . ." (296).

When Red says that he thought the Christian ideal, according to St. Thomas, was supposed to be a blend of contemplation and action, the priest only shows contempt for Aquinas, saying "Fuck Saint Thomas" (296). Moran is also, Red learns, opposed to the charismatic movement because he believes most of them spend their time in contemplating their own spiritual navels.

Later, on another occasion when Red talks with Larry Moran, who refers to himself as a psychologist, the priest advises Red that he and Eileen should forget about their relationship and get involved with the poor.

You and Eileen should find something useful, something relevant—God, Red, those are the wrong words—something socially challenging to do. Open a soup kitchen somewhere, if nothing else. Take the first steps in your own life toward committing yourself to the building up of a just society. . . . The careers at which you are both so good are, after all, worthless; they don't really help anybody." He rose from the desk, as a sign of dismissal. (321)

The reader laughs Larry Moran to scorn, especially for his failure to realize the potential journalists and attorneys have for making a tremendous impact on society for change. Sadly Red comments about the Church, *"Now that I may need it more than I ever have in my life, the best I can find is a priest-psychologist turned alienated radical"* (303). Wondering why priests say "fuck" as much as cops do, Red disconsolately goes away from his interviews with Larry Moran.

Other facets of the Church are satirized by Red Kane in the column he writes for the newspaper. Obviously the reader assumes that Red is speaking here as a persona for the author. Observing that the "scruffy" Vatican bureaucrats in the streets of Rome are never seen smiling, Kane goes on to suggest that perhaps the reason the leaders in the Church are "so vehemently obsessed with sex" is because they are not having any fun and they want to be certain that married people don't have any either.

According to Red Kane, the Vatican bureaucrats are "so hung up on sex" that they do not preach the good news of Christ. He concludes that "the Roman Church goes into a paroxysm of grief every time a man and woman have a pleasant night together" (300). "Their mission in life, and their vocation, is to drive joy out of world" (301). Expressing his ambivalent feelings toward the Church, Red notes that it was never there when he needed it, and when he didn't want it, it was all over him "harassing, threatening, warning, disturbing" (303).

In this novel, as usual, Greeley satirizes the media, the legal system, and the police, among others, such as the Irish who drink too much. Since Red is a journalist and knows the media thoroughly, he is able to lampoon it very effectively. Of course Greeley is also, among many other things, a journalist, having written newspaper columns for over thirty years. Having started out with great dreams of being a crusader, Red saw his dreams die between the time Kennedy was assassinated and Nixon was elected as president. With bitterness he describes his profession: "We know that all reporters are whores or they wouldn't be in the business. That's not so bad. Any good journalist knows it in his heart.

We also see that the pimps for whom we work no longer know how to run a good whorehouse. And that's enough to drive a man to drink (94)

Perhaps the reason Red has been drinking so heavily is because of the corruption in his profession. In time he learns that even his mentor Paul O'Meara sold out to the despicable Harvard Gunther, keeping quiet about the incriminating things he knew about the man, rather than printing them and bringing him to justice. In Kane's view, a reporter should tell the truth, but others in the business remind him that they are in the news business not the truth business. Showing the evils of advocacy journalism in which reporters put a spin on the news to depict events, not as they are, but as the reporter wishes them to be, presents a well-founded satirical picture of the media. Reporters like Paul O'Meara take money from criminals for the news they report and for that which they suppress.

Roscoe Bane, whom we have encountered in an earlier novel, appears again in *Patience of a Saint*. The story shows how prosecutors can indict almost anyone they wish and haul them before grand jury in order to aggrandize themselves and even earn a ticket to a term in the governor's mansion. The wealthy and celebrities are especially good targets for such indictments because of the free publicity their indictments bring to the prosecutors.

In this story, a black athlete, Hurricane Housten, is indicted and is defended successfully by Eileen. When he is acquitted, Housten, in a humorous scene, does a dance in front of the jury bench like a football player after catching a touchdown pass, kisses Eileen, and even swats her rear.

The ineptitude of the police is also well depicted. When she is pregnant Eileen is caught in the street riots and becomes the victim of tear gas. When Nick Curran goes to her rescue, the police remove their badges so they cannot be identified. Another victim of police violence is Red Kane's father who was shot by a police officer in the back of the head and killed as he marched in a Memorial Day parade. An especially humorous scene transpires when Red's daughter and her boyfriend are arrested and incarcerated for stealing Red's car.

Comedy permeates the entire story of *Patience of a Saint* with humorous characters, situations, and remarks. In this book, as in all of Greeley's fictional universe, God is the quintessential comedian and life the ultimate comedy.

Love Song is a classic romantic comedy with a happy ending, resulting in the union of two lovers who overcome tremendous obstacles and find happiness in marriage. The book takes its inspiration from the biblical Song of Songs, also known as the Canticle of Canticles or the Song of Solomon, although there is no certainty that Solomon composed it. The male lover of Greeley's book, Conor Clement Clarke, a venture capitalist and sometime poet, has composed a paraphrase of the biblical song, strophes of which interlace the text of the romance. Just as the biblical Song of Songs has traditionally been interpreted in two ways, so must Greeley's story be understood on two levels. The first level of meaning is the literal interpretation of the words of the song as they pertain to the erotic love of a man and a woman. The second level is the allegorical one in which, as in the biblical Song of Songs, one must see the love of Christ for the soul, and the soul's longing to unite with him. Therefore Conor Clarke is a Christ figure in the story as he pursues Diana Marie Lyons, who is not really very lovable. Refusing to consider her failings as impediments to their love, Conor pursues her with an unconditional love which, in turn, becomes her salvation. From a truly human perspective one would probably consider Diana to be hopeless, but Conor's love—Christ's love—redeems, transfigures, and transforms her into a beautiful bride.

An additional dimension to this romance is that it illustrates Andrew Greeley's ideas on sexual intimacy which are expressed in his nonfictional works such as *Sexual Intimacy* (1973) and *Love and Play* (1975), reprinted in single volume as *Sexual Intimacy: Love and Play* (1988). Following Greeley's prescription for happiness in love, Conor is playful with Diana. On one occasion, imagining that they are in the Vienna woods, he pretends he is an archduke and she an exotic spy on a secret assignation. As tries to lure her into his secret harem, she feigns an attempt to obtain a copy of a secret naval treaty. To complete the scenario, their waiter, they decide, is Sherlock Holmes in disguise with a German accent. Although they are very playful, Conor is quite serious in his search for a wife who will give him children and share his entire life with him. He believes that he has found her in Diana Lyons.

The conversations of the lovers are studded with lighthearted often comic banter and are reinforced with a great deal of sexual tension, suggestive remarks, and erotic innuendoes. The tension and humor are also found in Conor's paraphrase of the Song of Solomon. For example, when he consults Father Roland Murphy about his paraphrase of the Bible, the priest tells him he cannot render the words of the Shulamite "Nigra sum, sed formosa" as "I'm black and I'm really built" (27).

Since she and the Grecian goddess are both rather cold, haughty, and chaste, Diana is well named. Deciding that she does not need sex and marriage, she decides to remain single and to adopt a Cambodian refugee at a later date when she is ready to have a child. A five-foot, nine-inch-tall beauty, Diana is a lawyer to please her father, on whom she has a fixation, and who is an embittered old man because of his adverse dealings with Conor Clarke's father. With her Spartan no-nonsense approach to life, Diana lives to please her father, who will not even tolerate a television in the home she shares with her parents, until she, as the assistant U. S. attorney for the Northern District of Illinois, has found enough evidence to indict Conor Clarke. She must wreak revenge on him for the injury his father inflicted on hers.

Fortunately Diana's mother is a Sicilian woman, a war bride, a warm and earthy person, who is typical of the Italian women in Greeley's stories who are much more natural, relaxed, and generous in love than his Irish heroines. Because of her mother, who reveals her Sicilian temperament and zest for life when Diana's father is not around, the reader is given a ray of hope for Diana and her love for Conor.

Temperamentally Conor is very different from Diana. Warm-hearted and generous, even lavish and extravagant, he is a poet, a romantic. With a great zest for life on a grand scale, Conor is a flamboyant and energetic person overflowing with joie de vivre. Just the opposite, Diana, who is not a sympathetic character, is suspicious and narrow with a tendency to be adversarial and judgmental. A perfectionist, considering herself to be a "dull, respectably lower-middle-class professional," she plans to live a celibate life as an employee of the government in public service (100). On the purely natural level, the prospect of a happy marriage between these two is very poor, but Greeley does not work on the natural level. Since his stories are parables of grace, there is always hope in them. In the end, grace will transform Diana into a beautiful bride.

As is often the case in Greeley's fiction, this novel satirizes the legal system and "functional justice." It demonstrates that the legal system is often corrupted by the use of immunized witnesses and plea bargaining for light sentences. Diana is told by her boss that she must forget her ethics classes in law school and "learn to play hardball" (134).

Diana is sure that Conor is a rich criminal and has to be "dragged down and destroyed" (190). Since the media are just looking "for professional women they can portray as castrating whores," her boss warns her that if the case explodes in her face she will have her "ass in a sling" and lose her job (194). This barb is typical of those thrown at the media in this book, since it is a favorite target of Greeley's satire.

Especially satirized is the way in which the legal system and the press go after celebrities, considering them to be fair game for indictment because they are successful. The legal system leaks information to the press so that the person in question is convicted in the media before he ever goes to trial. The book shows how the press has the power to destroy people with the lies and innuendos they print. This is a theme that Greeley returns to in book after book.

Two of Conor's confidantes are Naomi Rachel Stern Silverman, a psychiatrist, and her husband, the Rabbi Ezekiel Silverman. In plotting, Greeley likes to include a Jewish character in his stories; in this book he has given the reader two. The wise rabbi and his wife are able to shed many insights into his relationship with Diana.

Finally, in spite of Diana's uncertain feelings toward Conor, the couple finally mates in the swimming pool in the two-million-dollar home that Conor has bought, without her knowledge, as a future home for them. Announcing that the raft is their marriage bed, he declares this is their unofficial wedding day which they will soon make official. The playful love seen illustrates sociologist Greeley's theories about intimacy and play which one finds in his nonfiction. Learning that sex is a game Diana assures Conor, "I can be as good at this game as I am at golf. That's what it is: a wonderful game" (282).

As she grows in love for Conor, Diana's love for God deepens. Because of Conor's love for her, Diana tells God that she now understands how he loves her. Here Diana elucidates one of the most important themes in Greeley's fiction and one which is found in almost all his stories: God made us for love and he loves like we do only more so.

Consulting Monsignor Blackie Ryan about the difficulties he is still experiencing with Diana, Conor learns from the priest that Diana has a problem with
envy. Knowing this, Conor still wants to marry her at Easter. In his conversations
with Blackie, he confides in the priest that he had sex with Diana but does not feel
guilty about it, since he plans to marry her. Although Blackie informs Conor that
he does not approve of premarital sex, he does not think that they committed a
serious sin because they were both "drenched with reproductive hormones"and for
this reason they probably did not have sufficient freedom to commit a serious sin
(291). Encouraging them to marry soon because of their family problems, Blackie,
who is a persona for the author, also makes a statement that is one of the major
themes of Greeley's fiction: "Madonna love animates the universe" (292). It is
a theme that is illustrated continually in Greeley's novels.

In a scene that touches on the very heart of the story, Blackie meets with
Conor's friends, the rabbi and his wife, and they discuss the plight of Diana and
Conor. Even though it is now publicly known that Diana has been trying to get
information from Conor to use against him to indict him of a crime, the three of
them believe that Conor still loves her. She has done something despicable and the
rabbi believes that her redemption and salvation will be achieved only through
Conor. This is the main thrust of the book. Naomi, the psychiatrist and wife of the
rabbi, trying to effect Diana's redemption and salvation, informs Conor that Diana
is now in a serious and self-destructive condition.

Agreeing with the rabbi and his wife, Blackie, assuring Conor that Diana is
possibly the "best sacrament of God's love" in his life, urges him to forgive and
pursue her. Following this advice, Conor plans to propose to her, requesting that
the marriage take place the second Saturday after Easter. However, when he
phones, she refuses to talk to him, because she feels totally worthless and does not
want to be forgiven since she is not sorry for what she has done to him.

Symbolizing the Church, the members of the Ryan clan—O'Connor the Cat,
Eileen Kane, and the rest—minister to her showing love, concern, and a willingness to overlook the bad publicity she has received from the media. Observing
the caring people that surround her, Diana finally begins to wonder if perhaps the
"hound of heaven" might be pursuing her. The reference to the hound of heaven
comes from Thompson's poem about how Christ, the Hound of Heaven, pursues
the soul until he catches it. Earlier in the book Conor confessed to her that he will
always be pursuing her like a hound. When she inquires, "Hound of Heaven?" he
replies, "Something like that" (204). Here we have a definite statement indicating
that Conor is in fact a Christ figure for Diana. Additionally there are many other
indications of this relationship in various subtle ways.

Finally, coming to the full realization that it is God who is pursuing her with
his grace, she acquiesces and surrenders, praying, "Dear God, you are trying to
overwhelm me with grace, carry me off in it, drown me in it" (416). Diana knows
in her heart that "God would stop at nothing" (416). With a touch of humor
Cindasoo, O'Connor the Cat's Irish Protestant friend, with her strange mountain

accent, sizes up the situation and remarks, "We'ns have a saying: the first hound dog up in the morning get the possum" (416). In the end of the book, the Hound of Heaven does get his possum and Conor gets his bride—all the elements of a classic comedy.

Conor is a Christ figure throughout the story and Diana is the bride who betrays him. References in the text are made to the kiss of Judas and the thirty pieces of silver he got for the betrayal. Like Judas, Diana despairs and considers suicide. Conor's love saves and redeems her; Christ's love saves and redeems his Church.

The story of Conor and Diana is a parable of grace, and like the Song of Songs in the Bible it is the story of Christ and the soul. St. John of the Cross in his *Spiritual Canticle* explores the same theme. Only when the soul comes into the agonizing dark night and loses everything, does the Beloved unite himself to her. His love is, as the Scripture says, "strong as death" (Song of Songs 8:6). He loves her even when she is unlovable. The union of Conor and Diana symbolizes the union of God with the soul. Sex is sacramental, a fact Greeley never tires of telling his readers. In conclusion, *Love Song* is one of Greeley's finest parables and an inspiring comedy with a happy ending. One final note, Greeley tells us in chapter 18 of *Happy Are the Merciful*, a subsequent detective story, that Diana Clarke is now a "top flight lawyer." It is one of the delightful touches of the author's fiction that his characters are not forgotten but have a way of popping up later in the most unexpected places and the reader finds out what has become of them.

Perhaps the first thing readers notice about *St. Valentine's Night*, the next book in the Time between the Stars series, is the map of Beverly Hills, a magical neighborhood in Greeley's Chicago, placed as it is in the very front of the book. Because the map is given such prominence, St. Praxides in Beverly, which the reader first encountered in *Lord of the Dance*, may be said to be the main character in *St. Valentine's Night*. In most of Greeley's novels, a neighborhood is important to the development of the story, for example St. Ursula's in *Ascent into Hell* and *The Cardinal Sins*. In *St. Valentine's Night*, the neighborhood dominates the story—even the bad guys are from the neighborhood as well as those who offer love and healing.

Just what is a neighborhood? Greeley says it is "a place where you come home to to be renewed. It's a place where you matter. It's a place where you are important because people know you and they know your family. It is a place where you're loved" (*Conversations* 65). Only in the United States and perhaps a few counties in the west of Ireland does the Catholic parish, known as the neighborhood, taken on such significance. According to Greeley, "The neighborhood parish is one of the most striking manifestations of community that exists anywhere in the world" (*A Church to Come Home To* 74). The parish is "a place of our own, a place where we belong and hence, most certainly, a place to come home to" (75). It is a religious, social, cultural, recreational, and political center. St. Praxides in *St. Valentine's Night* is all of these things and represents Chicago's

Christ the King parish where Greeley had his first assignment after his ordination to the priesthood. Writing about this place, he says, "I will never get over Christ the King. It is still my parish, still my neighborhood, and always will be" (*Confessions* 155). Just exactly what do St. Praxides and Beverly exemplify? Greeley explains how he felt about Beverly looking back on his experience there.

Beverly . . . was the upper crust of the Irish middle class. It represented one of the three or four places In the city where the Irish had made it big not merely as individuals but as a group. In Beverly we were no longer the poor immigrant or the honest "cap and sweater crowd" (as one priest said proudly of his parish), or the hardworking laborers or the responsible clerks, salespeople and high school teachers. Here were the professionals, the managers, the successful small businessmen, the stockbrokers, the lawyers, the judges, the union leaders. Here it was not only possible for all the young to go to college, it was unthinkable that they should not. Here the Americanization of the Catholic immigrant group was entering its final phase. The Irish had arrived. (*Confessions* 155–156)

Best of all, speaking of this "magic parish," Greeley writes, "I can always go back in the world of fiction if not in the world of fact" (*Confessions* 165). "I can go home again. . . . And bring millions of people with me" (166). And this is exactly what Greeley does in *St. Valentine's Night*.

Neal Connor, "a washed-up and burned-out TV journalist" (*St. Valentine's Night* 23) and a borderline agnostic, on a trip to Chicago for the funeral of Mayor Washington, encounters at O'Hare Lisa Malone, the protagonist in the Blackie Ryan detective story *Happy Are the Clean of Heart*. She invites him to come back to St. Praxides for the celebration of the thirtieth anniversary of their 1958 class graduation from grammar school. When he agreed to come, he expected to find the neighborhood "deteriorating into a resegregated slum, a fate he told himself that it richly deserved, just as a hated woman deserved to grow old and ugly" (5). He personally had not really liked the neighborhood. When he was in high school and a young priest referred to it as a "magic neighborhood," Neal had sneered and replied, "A spoiled rich neighborhood" (5). Because his father was only a cop, he had felt inferior to others in the parish, when he was an altar boy serving with Blackie Ryan. Consequently, he moved away to Arizona as soon as he was able.

Arriving at St. Praxides for the anniversary mass celebrated by Blackie Ryan, Neal immediately encounters the neighborhood in the familiar faces of his old classmates. Meeting Megan O'Keefe Lane has a special emotional impact on him. Having carried her out of her burning family home to safety when they were children, he had saved her life. Although a bond developed between them at that time and eventually ripened into love, her family insisted that she marry Al Lane, whom, they thought, had much more to offer. Because Megan's father was a lawyer for the mob, they were especially driven by the Irish push for respectability and did not want her to marry a cop's son. A few days before she was to marry Al Lane, Neal almost persuaded her to elope with him.

The neighborhood that Neal encounters is a well-developed one. Almost all the characters that appear in the previous stories of Time between the Stars are there—Cathy and Nick Curran; Mike and Anne Casey; Red Kane and his wife, Eileen, who is now Judge Kane; Blackie Ryan; Joe and Mary Kate Murphy; Ned Ryan and his dying wife, Kate, and his new wife Helen; Lisa Malone, and the growing brood of children of these people. Father Ace who was assigned to St. Praxides in *Lord of the Dance* in the 1970s is back again in the parish, now as pastor. Donald Bane Roscoe, attorney for the Northern District of Illinois, whom we encountered in *Love Song,* continues his legal maneuvering in *St. Valentine's Night*. One character who is merely mentioned in this book and who will appear in subsequent stories of the series is Dr. Maggie Ward Keen, whose sixtieth birthday is being celebrated.

After his arrival in the neighborhood, Neal discovers that Megan Lane is now a widow who is having financial difficulties. He immediately feels that the neighborhood is trying to match him up with her, and although he feels physically attracted to her, he also feels like he is being trapped. Since Neal was not married in the Church and his wife left him twelve years before, everyone in the neighborhood thinks it would be just perfect if he and Megan were to renew their relationship and marry as they had not been able to do in the past. Even Blackie Ryan, Neal believes, is trying to be a matchmaker. Although Neal feels a powerful attraction to Megan, especially at the midnight mass at Christmas, he is very much undecided about pursuing a relationship with her. His ambivalent feelings continue until the end of the book when they are finally resolved with the happy ending that comedy desires and Greeley's readers have come to expect.

As he draws closer to Megan, Neal also grows closer to God. Having not received communion in twenty years until the anniversary mass for the class, he even doubts the existence of God as he sips from the chalice.

When Neal discusses his attraction to Megan with Blackie, his childhood friend, Blackie says the whole neighborhood is watching Neal and Megan waiting to "cheer or weep," depending on the outcome of their relationship (172). The romance intensifies with Megan seducing Neal. Feeling trapped and suspecting that the whole neighborhood is aware they are lovers, Neal ponders the situation: "Megan is the field which is the neighborhood. Like the ancient kings of Ireland, I have plowed the field and it has absorbed me. I have fucked a whole neighborhood" (282).

Puzzled by his ambivalent feelings toward Megan, Neal again discusses the relationship with Blackie Ryan. Specifically he asks the priest if it is a sin for him to have sex with Megan. When Blackie tries to get Neal to draw his own conclusions to formulate an answer to his question, Neal asks Blackie what he would tell him if he were his confessor. Blackie responds that he should either marry her or remove her from his life.

In this story as in previous ones, we see a woman who is loved becoming identified with God, so that in finding Megan and eventually taking her as his wife, Neal will regain his faith, but not before much exciting adventure transpires and the mystery of the story is solved. Almost all Greeley's stories contain a mystery that must be unraveled and exhilarating exploits brimming with abundant good humor and penetrating satire—elements that Greeley's readers have come to expect in his fiction. The bad guys of *St. Valentine's Night*—the Outfit (a.k.a. the Mafia) and the Latin American drug dealers—provide a lot of comedy with characters like Cos the Card and Tommy the Clown. Although their families have moved on to greener fields, the Outfit, which has a presence in almost all Greeley's novels, still maintains a foothold in the neighborhood. Nowadays many of them have college degrees, since they also have climbed the American ladder of success. Humorously they fake Italian accents which can be quickly dropped. The scenes with Luis Garcia, the Latin American bad guy, and his family resemble a story from the old TV series *Miami Vice*. There is a bit of black humor thrown in when Maria Annunciata, Luis Garcia's girl friend, announces that there will no more killings until after Christmas.

An amusing bit of situation comedy takes place when Megan's children visit Neal and invite him to move in with them. When he does move in for Christmas, he experiences what it would be like to have Megan and her children as a ready made family. Christmas is usually a happy time in Greeley's fiction for it radiates the Madonna love that suffuses Greeley's universe with its essence being that God loves us like a mother. In *St. Valentine's Night*, Christmas happiness is threatened by a harrowing misunderstanding between Megan and Neal. But not to worry. Greeley's reader knows that love and life will triumph at the end of the story.

The humor continues throughout the book. The story contains many funny things, almost like jokes. For example, when Neal is speaking to Megan about being a TV correspondent he makes the following ironic comments about the media:

"The secret of our game is not to be relaxed but to give the illusion of being relaxed."

"I guess I am pretty good at that, she admitted with a touch of bitterness. "Poor Megan, isn't she just wonderful and with so much on her mind.'"

"Sincerity is what counts," he continued. "Once you learn to fake that, everything else is easy." (87)

Politics usually comes into focus in Greeley's fiction, and this story is no exception. In *St. Valentine's Night*, Donald Bane Roscoe, U. S. attorney for Northern Illinois, who always hopes to further his career of possibly becoming governor of the state of Illinois, is up to his customary stunts of trying to get publicity by indicting anyone he can. In this satire of the legal system, Roscoe even uses a certain man's attorney to get information against him. However, his attacks on Megan are unsuccessful, even though the FBI gets in the act harassing Megan and her children, because Roscoe wants to indict her and force her to face a grand jury. Much to the amusement of the reader, Judge Eileen Kane uncovers Roscoe's corrupt legal practices and censures him. Coming to Megan's defense, Neal also has a away of dealing with him; he makes a television series about him which will damage his career.

With its satire of the legal system, *St. Valentine's Night* resembles many of

Greeley's other stories. It also resembles them in that it is the story of a second chance, of lovers in the prime of life who find happiness with each other, when that happiness eluded them in the past. As in other stories of Time between the Stars, the Ryans are a metaphor for the Church. The neighborhood is a source of grace for Neal and Megan as God's love surrounds them and draws them closer to each other and to himself. Another similarity between this story and others is that Megan saves Neal's life by pulling him out of his car in which he is trapped as it sinks into the lake. Greeley has a predilection for a heroine who saves the life of the man she loves; it happens in quite a few of his stories. Perhaps the final word about *St. Valentine's Night* should be this comment made by Blackie Ryan: "No one is born . . . and no one dies without the embrace of God's love" (338). This is certainly true in all Greeley's fiction.

Significant in that it introduces a new family into Time between the Stars, the Keenans, who serve the same function of being correlatives of the Church that the Ryans do, *The Search for Maggie Ward* (1991) is a fascinating tale of adventure and romance with elements of the fantastic and the paranormal. The protagonist of the story is Jerry Keenan, the grandson of Jeremiah and Maggie Keenan and the son of Mary Anne and Tom Keenan, an attorney who is a good friend and an associate of Ned Ryan in the legal profession. The Keenans first appeared in *The Cardinal Virtues* (1990), which was discussed in an earlier chapter.

In response to his publisher's request that he create a new priest in his fiction, Greeley created two of them—Packy Keenan, Jerry's brother, and Jamie Keenan, Jerry's son. Although Jerry is already a priest in *The Search for Maggie Ward* when Jerry is writing a book about Maggie, he does not figure in this story of times gone by, except for Jerry's quoting some of his opinions about the Church. As the story unfolds Jamie has not yet been born and Packy, who also appears in *The Cardinal Virtues*, is a seminarian. Since the Keenans have an apartment in Holy Name Cathedral parish of which Blackie is rector, they know him quite well. In fact Jerry made paper airplanes for Blackie when he was only two years old.

The Search for Maggie Ward is also significant in that Greeley employs it in many of the techniques and conventions of fantastic fiction. The fantastic, defined as something which is rationally inexplicable, occurs frequently in this story and is presented in such a way that it becomes obvious to the literary critic that Greeley has studied the masters of fantastic fiction and learned from them how to create a fantastic story. Two of the techniques he employs are the use of ambiguity and the grotesque. The story is often ambiguous as to whether or not something super-natural is occurring. The text suggests both a natural and a supernatural explan-ation and lets the reader opt for one or the other or to continue to hesitate between the two. The use of grotesque and supernatural imagery contributes to the creation of the fantastic as we shall see when we examine the story in greater detail

In the restaurant at the Tucson train station on July 22, 1946, forty years in the past, Jerry meets Andrea King, a waif of a girl who is both hungry and short of money. Taking her to a hotel dining room for breakfast, Jerry notices almost immediately that fantastic things, things that cannot be explained rationally, seem to be happening.

When Andrea says that she wishes she did not believe in God, for then she would not be forced to live suspended between earth and hell, Jerry begins to wonder about her because she is uncanny and does not seem to belong to this world. Since Phoenix is on his way as he drives home to Chicago, he offers to take her there where she says she has a job. En route, they visit a church where she falls on her knees and prays fervently "like someone pursued by demons" (42). When Jerry tries to photograph her, she jumps out of the picture. The few times he managed to catch her in a photograph, he is surprised to see that she is missing from the pictures when he gets them developed.

Although he begins to think of her as a "ghost girl" (88), she seems very real when she eats heartily. To his amazement, she has an unnatural and incredible ability to know things about him that Jerry does not tell her. The hesitation as to whether she is a real girl or a supernatural entity continues throughout a large part of the book. Even Andrea herself wonders if she is not invisible at times. She even ponders whether she exists or is only a dream. To add to the fantastic atmosphere, Jerry sings an uncanny song as the two of them travel to Superstition Mountains and the Lost Dutchman mine. To the bewilderment of both the reader and Jerry, Andrea keeps saying that she is a lost soul.

After they arrive in the Superstition Mountains, the fantastic elements augment. Stories of mysterious deaths associated with the legend of the Dutchman's treasure contribute to creating an atmosphere and a tone of the supernatural. Strange things also begin to happen to Jerry and Andrea. As a sinister storm is brewing, Andrea mysteriously comments, "It's coming for us" (185). What follows is a sequence of fantastic and grotesque horror worthy and reminiscent of E. T. A. Hoffmann, the German nineteenth-century fantasist who is credited with being the founder of the modern fantastic genre.

As lightening snaps and cracks all around them like "thunder gods," Andrea and Jerry are hurled from the car which now refuses to start. She is torn from his arms as they are both thrown into the main building of the ghost town of Clinton where all hell breaks loose. Drawing on a wide panoply of literary techniques, the author paints a picture of incredible horror and the ghastly grotesque. He suggests both a natural and a supernatural explanation for the rationally inexplicable events that occur but does not decide in favor of either one, leaving it open for the reader to decide whether something supernatural really occurs or not.

While Jerry watches, Andrea's clothing is ripped away as she screams in terror. Strangely and suddenly the men Jerry had lost under his command in the war come back as ghosts to accuse him and blame him for their deaths. As he protests his innocence, one of his men, Rusty, turns into a baby who is drowning. Such transformations are common in fantastic fiction. Another one of his men, Tony, is transformed into a sailor whose skull has been crushed. Then Jerry's clothing is ripped off and steel-tipped whips tear off his flesh; the wall at his back is "hot like a frying pan" (188). Suddenly these phantoms are gone, replaced by ghosts from the local area's past. Then ghosts of his grandparents Jeremiah and

Maggie Keenan appear. Finally, Jacob Waltz, the famous old Dutchman himself appears—together with the people he murdered and the victims of an Apache massacre, accusing Jerry of being responsible for their deaths. In trying to understand what is taking place, he speculates that perhaps it was happening on "a different plane of reality" (189). Pinned to the wall, Jerry watches as gold coins begin piling up around him burying him in gold; he listens as the Dutchman tells him where the mine is. Suddenly the Dutchman vanishes and Jerry's military buddies, the drowning baby, and the sailor with the smashed head return to haunt him and condemn him to hell because he is charged with "violating the sanctity of these sacred mountains by fucking a cunt who had already been damned to hell" (190). The judge is Andrea's husband, the prosecutor, her child, and the war dead are the jury. Grandmother Keenan, who is drunk, is his defense attorney. Horrified Jerry watches. "Andreas body flayed but still breathing, a twisted, squirming mass of agony and disease was staked out on the floor in front of him" (190). Her child speaks to Jerry, " 'Fuck my mommy now,' the baby screamed. 'Is she a good lay when she's rotting flesh?' "(90). According to the baby's father, Keenan is condemned to "screw a skinless corpse for all eternity. This scene reminds one of some of Clive Barker's scenes in *Hellraiser.* It is truly an exemplary passage of modern fantastic horror, one worthy of the masters of the genre.

With screams that Jerry is guilty, the specters participate in a *danse macabre* in which they force him to dance with Andrea. When he looks at her, she has no eyes, only empty sockets like the phantom in E. T. A. Hoffmann's *Die Elixiere des Teufels.* As the dance progresses, he is passed from "one set of obscene hands to another" (191). While they are dancing with Andrea's flayed body, a magic sword arises from the depths of his being. Fighting desperately for Andrea's soul and his own, Jerry tells them that he is not going to hell, but might perhaps go to purgatory.

This is a key chapter in this book, which had a prepublication title of "War in Heaven." Suddenly Michael the Archangel appears urging Jerry to fight to save Andrea. When he refuses to let the demons have her, they insist that she is already damned. Stronger still, Jerry insists that the judgment has been reversed. Fighting all night long, he becomes weary. When he can hold out no longer and is just at the point of giving her up, the angel appears again now as a "blond-winged giant in navy dress whites and the five stars of a fleet admiral." This time Michael wields a Browning automatic rifle, which Jerry hears shooting as everything goes dark.

When Jerry revives, Andrea is gone. Since it would have been almost impossible for her to walk down the mountain road carrying her suitcase and he cannot find her anywhere, her disappearance is fantastic, causing him to wonder if she had been carried off to hell with her few belongings.

The fantastic elements continue throughout most of the book. The hotel where she said she had a job never heard of her. Unanswered questions suggest supernatural answers. Had she succumbed to the evil forces of the ghost town? Was she indeed dead and on her way to hell? Was she being punished perhaps for murdering her husband and child and doomed to wander the earth like the Flying Dutchman? Jerry wonders if he imagined the entire episode. Was it a nightmare? Since there are no marks on his body, in spite of what he endured from the whips, he wonders if he is having a nervous collapse? Is he crazy? Is Andrea real? All the questions are posed, but no answers are given. The reader and Jerry must hesitate between natural and supernatural explanations. Very successfully Greeley has mastered the techniques of fantastic fiction.

Continuing his search, Jerry can find no sign of the mineshaft into which he had thought he had fallen. In the main hall where the *danse macabre* took place, there is no dust on the floor and he wonders if he had imagined earlier that dust was there. Perhaps the dance removed the dust. Finally he finds a piece of cloth in a corner that might be a piece of Andrea's blouse. Finding this item, which establishes her presence, is a literary device of fantastic writers made famous by Théophile Gautier in "Le Pied de Momie" in which a telltale mummy's foot is found bearing witness that a fantastic event actually took place.

Now begins Jerry's great search, his quest to find his lost grail and to find answers for the perplexing events that have occurred. Greeley does use the grail imagery again in this book, but there is also a bit of Don Quixote in Jerry who calls his woman "Dulci" for Dulcinea and his car Roxinante after the woman and the horse in *Don Quixote* by Miguel de Cervantes. The love affair of Jerry, the grail quester, and his beloved is the essence of the story. Their encounter and union is what Greeley refers to as a "limit experience," a term borrowed from Father David Tracy. What does Greeley mean by this expression? A limit experience is a religious experience that discloses reality to us and stirs up wonder in us about divine grace. It is essentially an experience in which all one's perceptions have been shattered and new ones are being structured. Limit experiences, or horizon experiences, as Greeley sometimes calls them, can be triggered by sexual differentiation when it is sacramental and "for most people sexual love is likely to be the most intense if not the only limit-experience in their lives" (*Mary Myth* 537).

So what does this have to do with *The Search for Maggie Ward*? Although a limit experience occurs to most of Greeley's protagonists, it is especially apparent in this story of Jerry's love affair with Andrea a.k.a. Maggie Ward. They are both completely transformed by their sexual and sacramental union.

Jerry is the supposed author of the story about Maggie Ward. The fact that he is now an author, as well as an attorney as his family had wished, is one of the results of his limit experience. As he writes the story of Andrea/Maggie he discusses the writing of the book with his wife who refers to Andrea as "that dreadful girl." Interestingly his wife promises him the best orgy he ever had when he finishes the manuscript. It is not until the end of the book that the reader knows that Andrea a.k.a. Maggie is his wife and the mother of his children, one of whom is the very special and ideal Priest Jamie Keenan, whom we encountered in *The Cardinal Virtues*. They also have daughter who is a physician and a granddaughter who is eighteen, the age that Maggie was when they first met and fell in love. The technique of speaking about the writing of a book in the book itself is one that is used frequently in fantastic fiction.

When Jerry, aged twenty-four, meets the young Andrea/Maggie, he is an agnostic having completely lost his faith in God. She is like a lost soul or a phantom spirit returned from the dead. In addition to the religious tension, a good deal of sexual tension exists between Jerry and Andrea/Maggie from the inception of their relationship. When they meet, Jerry is still a virgin and Andrea has had very little sexual experience. Not even knowing how babies originate, she was seduced by a contemptible man, who consequently felt compelled to marry her and subsequently mistreated her. Both her husband and her child are now dead.

Although Andrea/Maggie is convinced that she is damned to hell for all eternity, she still believes in God and tries to convince Jerry of his existence by pointing to all the good things of life. After they have been together but a short time, Jerry demonstrates the rebirth of a small amount of faith by expressing his view that God had sent him to protect Andrea. At this time, he is still having nightmares about the men he had killed in the war. With the blossoming of their love, he confides in her that he had once wanted to be a priest, but that his parents had insisted he become an attorney in the family law firm. His brother Packy is studying for the priesthood.

As they arrive at the Picketpost House in Superior, Arizona, Jerry begins thinking of building a future with the strange girl. Registering as Mr. and Mrs. Keenan at the hotel, he rents the honeymoon suite. As the couple has dinner, we observe that they are beginning to have a limit experience when Maggie asks him, "Do you feel sometimes that these last two days have all been a dream—that the dreamworld and the other world. . . ." He picks up her thought saying, "That maybe the boundaries have slipped somewhere?" (107).

Thinking how happy he would be to spend eternity with her, he concludes that a God who created such love between a man and a woman might be able to wipe away all tears. Andrea/Maggie also falling deeply in love remarks that it is "like the whole sky is on fire with love" (110).

Sometime after she drifts off to sleep in the master bedroom of the suite, Jerry, who is asleep in the adjoining room, hears her scream in terror and completely naked rushes to comfort her. She too has nightmares because, as she explains, the demons who are waiting for her in hell are pursuing her relentlessly. Jerry's comforting Andrea/Maggie turns to gentle lovemaking, which is beautifully recounted. Reflecting on his sexual union with Andrea/Maggie, Jerry comments that his religion teachers in high school and college would have said that had they died then, they would have gone to hell for all eternity. He knows that the priest who is pastor at the time he is writing the story of his love believes that to be true also, as do the documents coming from the Vatican. Although he had halfway believed such ideas before he went to war, he had not refrained from having sex with a woman out of fear, but because his father had taught him to respect women. Pondering the matter, Jerry proceeds to imagine what judgment the various members of his family would make in the present time over his sexual encounter with Andrea/Maggie. His brother Packy, now a priest, would say that since their passion was so great, he could not imagine that serious sin could be involved. His daughter the clinician would say that such hastily consummated unions could lead to dysfunction at a later date. His son Jamie, the priest, would say it is between the couple and God.

Not surprisingly, the convent educated Andrea/Maggie decides that what they have done is sinful and they will not do it again, for since she is already damned, more sin will put her deeper into hell. When Jerry tells her that he doesn't think it is sinful, she counters by saying that God considers it sinful—to which he replies somewhat humorously that he is an atheist. At the end of the day, Jerry writes an entry in his diary that the experience was "grace not sin" (155).When he awakens in the night, Andrea/Maggie is softly sobbing. To comfort her, he promises to take care of her always.

Jerry's faith begins to grow stronger as he begins to tell Andrea how much God loves her. He says: "What's God like? He's like me, you gorgeous little nit-wit—loving inept and dumb. Run from that if you want, but don't make up an imaginary hanging judge who won't give you a second chance." This is basically what Red Kane told Eileen. As Jerry continues to reflect, he comments, "Loving, inept, and dumb—that was the God into a belief in whose existence I had talked myself" (163). Forty years later as Jerry reads through his diary he sees a note that Andrea/Maggie had penned there when they were first lovers. "I hate you Jerry Keenan. I had given up all hope and you've driven me to hope for hope. I had believed that love was impossible and you've made me want to love again" (165).

After Andrea's/Maggie's disappearance, Jerry hunts for her using all the clues he picked up from her conversations. Realizing that she is his grail, he must find her. When Jerry's search leads him to a grave that was supposedly Maggie's in a city cemetery, because the Church refused to bury her believing that she had killed herself, Jerry wonders if she had been sent to him to recall him to the faith. He also wonders if part of her purgatory was the fear that she was already in hell. Deciding that he will return to the faith, he stands at her grave and says "All right, Maggie, . . . you win. I believe again. I don't promise that I'll bounce back into mass next Sunday, but I'll make my peace with God because you said I should" (287).

Jerry is changed; he will never be the same again. Loving her opens his soul to the world and to emotions that he had never known before. As he prepares to study law with the Jesuits, he realizes that he has come to know God. Convinced now that God loves him the way he loves Maggie, he consults with Father Donninger, one of the Jesuit priests at the law school. From this priest, who confirms Jerry's belief that Andrea was a grace for him, Jerry learns that God readily waives punishment on sins of the flesh because of human weakness. Shortly after this conversation and about seven months after Andrea's supposed death, Jerry goes to mass and communion for the first time in two years.

When Jerry finally finds Maggie, it is Christmas Eve. Frequently wonderful things happen in Greeley's fiction at Christmas, for according to him the entire universe is filled with Madonna love. When he finds Maggie, she is living in a very simply furnished and chilly cold-water flat and has a miniature Christmas tree with a single string of lights and a small crib set. On the wall a print of Raphael's *Madonna* brightens the room. The presence of the symbols of the Mother of Jesus are there to remind us that God is passionately in love with his people, loving them like a mother loves her very special child.

Almost at once, Maggie inquires if Jerry has returned to the Church and if he is writing. Then she tells him "God keeps giving us second chances as long as we live. . . . A young man taught me that in Arizona" (360). When the two lovers are finally united again, the sacramental nature of their love is very obvious.

> She threw back the blanket and knelt above me. Like a new postulant sacristan holding a chalice, she took possession of my most tender parts.
> "Maggie," I groaned in protest.
> "You're so beautiful," she began to kiss her chalice, slowly, sweetly, reverently.
> . . .
>
> " So you lie there," she said, suddenly very angry at me, "thinking you've found your Holy Grail who's going to keep adventure and romance in your life till you're eighty at least. And you're wrong. I found my Holy Grail, right here in my hands, my sweet, good passionate —she drew a deep breath—"terrible, beautiful man." (433)

A true comedy in the classical sense, the story of Jerry and Maggie Keenan is a beautiful love story, which is still continuing forty years later as the two lovers reminisce about their happiness and the fruitfulness of their marriage as it is reflected in the lives of their children, especially in the life of that very special priest son Jamie Keenan.

The comedy is rich in good humor. Greeley is naturally humorous and it shows in everything he writes. Sometimes the comedy is the result of the funny things the characters do and say. For example, when Jerry and Packy still think that Andrea/Maggie might be a ghost after she mysteriously returns a small bit of money to Jerry. Packy, who plays Sancho Panza to Jerry's Don Quixote, says:

> "Think of how many houses she had to haunt to make that money."
> "She's probably a waitress somewhere."
> "A haunted restaurant? I can see the ads: 'Ghoulish Goulash, served by the prettiest ghost girls this side of Transylvania. Bring your own garlic." (338)

Sometimes the comedy results from comic characters like Dr. Feurst, Maggie's psychiatrist who is a prize example of Greeley's ability to create a humorous character with just one sentence. He is "a Jewish elf from the Schwarzwald, a bald, vest-pocket Santa Claus with a propensity to massacre English syntax as his laughter indeed shook his belly like a bowlful of jelly" (398). Punctuating his English frequently with the expression "vatdahell," he even puts his finger next to his nose when he talks, just like Santa. Later Maggie contributes to the comedy of the book by imitating the accent of Dr. Feurst in her conversation with Jerry.

At other times situation comedy blended with comedy of manners causes the reader to chuckle like, for example, when Jerry begins attending Loyola University law school and encounters the rules the Jesuits have set up for the students. He describes the retreat that all the students are required to attend. A conference Friday evening, three conferences on Saturday, mass on Sunday and two more conferences, and the papal blessing, which is supposed to prepare them for instant heaven if they should die that day, comprise the retreat, which was devoted largely to sins of the flesh. No one had informed Father Donninger, an "odd duck" who "looked like an aging and withered Gary Cooper," that two-fifths of the students were married (323–324). The conferences warned them about the dangers of necking and petting.

The humor becomes more scathing when Greeley begins to satirize the failings of the clergy and religious. A highly humorous and derisive scene occurs when Jerry visits an area priest in Arizona right after Andrea disappears. A drunken Irishman who is more interested in knowing if Jerry had sex with the girl than helping to find her, the priest tells him he is condemned to hell and sprinkles him with "a tidal wave of holy water " and waits to see what happens, thinking perhaps that he is a demon (202). Solemnly in all seriousness, the priest informs Jerry that the woman was a succubus from hell sent to take his immortal soul. Unless Jerry spends the rest of his life in a monastery doing penance, the priest insists he will be damned forever, because otherwise the succubus will fight with God for his soul and will win. When the priest starts to weep, Jerry decides the man is in bad need of a drink. As a parting shot, Jerry tells him that Michael, the Archangel, dressed like a fleet admiral carrying an automatic weapon, had helped him battle for Andrea's soul and his own.

More religious satire is found when Jerry visits St. Dominic's school hoping to learn something about Andrea's background. Sister Regina viewed him "with the same fastidious dismay with which she would consider a fly in the convent butter supply" (219). Jerry surmises that she treats everyone this way except a superior in her order. Instead of helping him, she dismisses him. Jerry comments, "I went silently into that good night, you say? Not for want of appropriate curses for the old bitch" (220).

When he returns to St. Dominic's to try once more to get information, the cabby who takes him there tells him that St. Dominic's has the reputation of being a "hell hole" and that the nuns there "enjoy being mean" (223). Since Sister Regina, the Superior, is not there this time, he talks with the principal, Sister Marie, who is described as having "that hair-shirt-wearing fanatics glow" in her eyes (224). The nun identifies Andrea King as Margaret Mary Ward, whom she says had "bad blood," and refers him to Sister Patrice, the librarian for further information..

When Jerry inquires about Margaret Ward, the old nun replies that Maggie's family was frequently named in the newspaper and that her mother was a great beauty. As for Maggie she read too much.

"Read 'most every book I had. Got herself educated despite them. Course they held that against her too. A child that reads too much may get undocile thoughts, eh, young man?" She cackled again. "Become provocative. Even think for herself. Ask questions we aren't able to answer. Can't have that, can we young man, eh?"

The satire continues as Sister Patrice explains about Margaret Ward:

"Why, even though she had the prettiest voice in the school, they wouldn't let her sing in the choir or even try out for a part in the play. Fired her from the debate team because she won all the time. . . . Ever try to argue with her, young fella? . . . Someday the order is going to have to pay for such cruelty."
Her merry eyes snapped with delight at the prospect of the order being punished. I too hoped that I would be around for the assignment to appropriate regions of hell of sister Mary Regina and her stooges. (228–229)

Obviously Sister Regina and her associates in this novel are sociopaths who take a perverted pleasure from being unkind. Since such types have been all too prevalent in the Church, Greeley continually targets them and their behavior with damning and cutting commentary. As we have already seen in many other of his novels, he makes the sociopaths in the Church the target of some of his most caustic humor and satire.

These are but examples of the comedy in *The Search for Maggie Ward*, one of the most beautiful love stories that Greeley has written and a valuable contribution to his divine and human comedy. It illustrates especially well Greeley's theory of sexual differentiation as evoking limit experiences. A memorable character is Maggie, and the reader should turn to *The Cardinal Virtues* to see the delightful and humorous woman she becomes when she is mature. There one can also see the extraordinary and impressive priest Jamie Keenan, Maggie's gift to God and his Church and know that God indeed writes straight with crooked lines. We will encounter Maggie again in *Summer at the Lake* together with the other Keenans.

One of the darkest and most dismal families in all Greeley's fiction is the Flynn family in *Wages of Sin* (1992). From the title, the reader surmises that sin has a lot to do with their lives. The Scripture says, "The wages of sin is death." And we find death and destruction in this novel. But there is a corollary to this verse which says "the gift of God is eternal life." The hope of eternal life is extended to the blackest sinners of the family before the novel ends, so that the reader feels that if they can make it to heaven, anyone can, which is exactly what Greeley wishes to communicate to his readers.

The plot is driven by the eighty-year-old father of the family Patrick Lorcan, a despicable codger whose legs are paralyzed from a stroke, but whose tongue is extremely active is the scathing, hateful, and vulgar judgments he makes about the members of his family and their friends. He is especially nasty in his crude and debasing remarks about women, in particular in denigrating Maura Meehan

Halinan, the woman his son Lorcan Flynn, the protagonist of the story, loves. Old Patrick Lorcan is like a character from the fiction of Franz Kafka. Indeed, he reminds one very much of the unnamed father of George Bendemann in Kafka's story "The Judgment." Both old men are destructive in dealing with their sons; they are nasty in their remarks about women and they flirt with the woman their son loves as if in competition with him for her favors. However, since Pat Flynn is a character in a novel instead of a piece of short fiction like Bendemann, Greeley has more opportunity to show the different facets of his personality and for this reason has created a character who, although he resembles Kafka's character, is far worse. If Kafka had written a novel about George Bendemann instead of a short story, George's father would probably have been even more like Lorcan Flynn's. Both characters are remarkable for the utter darkness that saturates their souls.

The story begins in 1989 with Lorcan Flynn—his marriage of thirty years has been recently annulled—telling the psychiatrist Mary Kate Ryan Murphy about the problems he has had with his father and of his recurring dream of Maura Meehan. In the dream he is lying on beach towels with Maura when his father appears, laughing hysterically, and the girl goes away with him. The rest of the book is spent unraveling the mystery of Maura.

As the story unfolds, the author depicts the upscale Irish who have arrived in Chicago society. Lorcan's son, Patrick Michael Flynn II is a physician and a psychoanalyst-in-training at the Chicago Institute of Psychoanalysis. In an earlier age he would have been perhaps, a police detective, a criminal lawyer, or a canon lawyer at the chancery. Still earlier he would have been a bartender or an undertaker or even a precinct captain. Greeley portrays the rise of the immigrant families in society.

The reason Lorcan cannot remember what happened between him and Maura is that he became seriously ill and almost died. During his illness, an explosion rocked the home of the family that reared Maura, killing them all except her. Since Maura was not at home, her life was spared, but she moved away before Lorcan recovered his health. As the story open, he has not spoken to her since the episode on the beach towels.

Since Lorcan's daughter Marie marries the son of the widowed Maura/Moire, Lorcan again encounters the love of his youth. When he asks her what happened that night so long ago on the beach towels, she explains that his parents found them kissing on the beach towels and screamed at her calling her crude names. His father struck her twice on the face before she ran off. Moire thinks that his mother was drunk at the time.

While Moire is staying at Lorcan's house shortly before the wedding of his daughter and her son, Lorcan and Moire consummate their love. At the wedding of their children, Blackie preaches a beautiful homily about the love of God, the crux of which is "God loves Rob and Marie even more intensely than they love one another, and all the rest of us too. . ." (286). The night after the wedding, Lorcan and Moire, hoping to marry, spend the entire night together.

The next morning, Lorcan's father phones him and the old man greets him by saying, "Did you screw the trash real good last night?" His father then adds that Lorcan must have been too sick to remember what he had told him that night he caught them on the beach towels. As Lorcan suddenly begins to recall, his father says, "That tart is your sister. I screwed her mother and got her preggers. So you fucked you own sister" (292). As a result of this conversation, Lorcan withdraws from Moire without explanation.

Dinny Rooney, whom Lorcan had hired as an investigator, brings him many of the facts of the case. In the end, it turns out that Lorcan's father who was a bit of a playboy had an affair with Betty Allen, who is now a wealthy socialite. She was already pregnant when she made love to Pat Flynn, and Maura is not his child. She had told him he was the father of her child since the real father was too poor to help her. Consequently, Pat Flynn's father paid her off. The mystery of the explosion that killed the Meehans, who reared Moire, is finally solved. Lorcan's mother who was emotionally unstable because of her husband's adulteries and from fear of losing Lorcan, set the house on fire, desperately wanting to kill Maura/Moire. The family had not obtained psychiatric help for her, because, in their opinion, nothing was wrong with her.

The plot is quite complicated because the IRA, the Mob, the FBI and Donny Roscoe all get involved in it. The rest of Lorcan's family resemble old Patrick Lorcan and his wife, with the exception of Lorcan's children, who turn out to be very good people, and his sister, Eileen, who moved to Seattle to get away from their father. To get some idea of how contemptible they were, just consider that one of Lorcan's brothers even tries to incriminate Lorcan in the explosion of the Meehan house to save his own neck in some financial dealings.

Donny Roscoe is up to his usual tricks trying to indict whomever he can for the publicity of it. In this book he is after Betty Allen and her husband, one of the biggest financial names in Chicago, and tries to force Lorcan to testify against them, which he refuses to do. Much pressure is put on him and his family to get him to testify. The FBI arrests Lorcan's sister-in-law for perjury because when they come to her home, she tells them that her husband is not at home, when he, in fact, was.

The satire of the FBI agents who burst in to Lorcan's office is genuine situation comedy. Since Lorcan is aware that they try to engage people in friendly conversation until they can catch them in a lie, and then charge them with perjury, he orders them out of his office or he will have them arrested for trespassing. Since they do not leave, Lorcan calls the police. In an hilarious scene the cops come and read the FBI agents their rights. When the FBI agents resist arrest, they scuffle with the police even damaging property in Lorcan's office. As the black cop struggles to put handcuffs on Special Agent Foster, she screams at him, "Let go of me, you fucking pig!" (95). Then McGrath calls him a "fucking nigger bastard. "Special Agent McGrath," Lorcan intoned, "you just ended your career as a G-man." (95) This is typical of the humor and satire that Greeley includes in his fiction and that is quite pronounced in *Wages of Sin*.

Lorcan's daughter-in-law Maeve Anne O'Leary Flynn also provides a comic touch to the story with her fake Irish brogue and quaint manners. She and Lorcan engage is some very farcical banter. On one occasion he replies to her, "Ah, woman, would you stop blathering like a cow with loose bowels and in the name of all the holy saints above tell me what the point is!" (179). Expressions like "dragonfly shite" make Maeve's conversation quite amusing. (241). Some of the other characters also come up with comical expressions like Lorcan's father when he denigrates his son: "You are not old enough to know shit from Shinola" (107). Or again when Lorcan's attorney Larry Whelan tells Lorcan that he knows some people who "wont be particularly eager to play horsey for Donny Roscoe's Lady Godiva" (174). Greeley is always good at the well-turned humorous phrase and this story is sprinkled with them as is the rest of his fiction.

In Greeley's comedy life always triumphs over death. This theme is expressed at the funereal for Pat Flynn, Lorcan's father. Blackie Ryan presides over the wake with Cardinal Cronin in attendance. At the final services for Pat Flynn, held in the chapel of Queen of Heaven Cemetery, Blackie continues along the same lines as he had at the wake, making allusion to Patrick's having been a airplane pilot. " 'It is inappropriate,' the little priest said, his purple stole hanging lopsided from one shoulder, 'to sing "Off we go, into the wild blue yonder," in this chapel. Nonetheless, we can hum it in our minds as we bid this temporary farewell to our friend Patrick' " (310).

We will be young again. We will laugh again. Once again, in this story, Blackie, Mary Kate Ryan Murphy, and even Mike Casey, the cop, as correlatives of the Church, minister to Lorcan and his family. When all is said and done and Lorcan knows that he is free to marry Moire and she is not his sister, he pursues her, even though she has turned him down. As the book ends he is on his way to her home. Greeley's reader, knowing that God always gives second chances, expects that he will capture his grail and make her his wife. Life will triumph over death, love over hatred.

A second chance is also given to Leo Kelly and Jane Devlin Clare in *Summer at the Lake*, in which, during a wonderful Catholic summer of love, happiness, and passion, they are able to renew their love affair that was quashed thirty years earlier by the machinations of her family in its quest for Irish respectability. Other players in this story of love and mystery are Monsignor Patrick James Keenan, who is considering leaving the priesthood to marry Jane, psychologist Dr. Maggie Keenan Ph.D. and her husband of thirty years Judge Jerry Keenan, now in their seventies, and their children and grandchildren, numerous members of Jane's family, and various neighbors and friends. Since Jerry is an academic, a professor of political science and Packy is a priest, the satire in this story centers around academia and the Church. The police and the legal system are also targeted. In this story, the Keenans play the same function as do the Ryans in earlier works in *Time between the Stars*—they are correlatives of the church. The story goes from one character's point of view to another's and weaves back and forth from the present to thirty years in the past as the details in the lives of Leo and Jane and their friends emerge. Greeley is especially skilled in unraveling a plot like pealing off the layers of an onion.

The keynote of the story is sounded at the beginning by Jane who muses:

> Maggie Ward Keenan, who thinks she knows everything, says that Leo and I should have a Catholic summer, one in which we allow the summer heat to rekindle the warmth of the love that once existed between us. She quotes a liturgy from some place about the bride being buxom and bonny in bed. Well I suppose I'm buxom enough but not very bonny in bed. Not much practice in a long time. (13)
>
> Maybe she is right about being Catholic. We do know in our hearts that our lover is kind of like God to us. I wish I could really believe that. I certainly was not God to my husband nor he to me. If I invite Leo back to our empty house, would he come? Should I try? Would You want me to? (14)

Jane had married Phil Clare, a sociopath, after he raped her and got her pregnant. Not appreciating her, he spent his time chasing other women and neglecting her. Her family, who thought Leo was not good enough for her, contrived secretly to get his military orders changed so that he was sent to the war in Asia, hoping that he would be killed. When he was reported dead, Jane married Phil, who after many years of marriage deserts her for another woman, leaving her free to marry again.

Leo is also free, because his wife whom he did not marry in the Church, has left him. Having returned to Chicago to take up the position of provost at the university, he spends the Memorial Day weekend with his old friends Maggie and Jerry Keenan. This is the beginning of a glorious summer for Leo and Jane.

In an earlier summer, 1946, to be exact, Leo and Jane had a "limit experience" together when they went skinny dipping one night, before they were separated by the terrible forces that her family unleashed to keep them apart. It is an experience in which they sense the Reality that lies just beyond and within creation and which transforms them.

Much sexual tension and banter pass between Jane and Leo, who keeps telling her that he will have her before the summer is over. For her part, she is afraid she will be a disappointment to him sexually, since her husband was not satisfied with her. She realizes that Leo is a grace for her, but she is a bit afraid of that grace. Leo, also afraid of grace and a typical Greeley male protagonist, is afraid of women being "both attracted by the mysterious cave they offer (metaphorically as well as literally) and also frightened of it" (71).

Their love affair climaxes when Leo breaks into the home of a very distraught Jane to prevent her from taking her own life. After he removes the pills from her hands, he comforts her while she sobs in his arms. Then hungrily and demandingly he embraces her. "Super solemn high fuck for the fifty-year-old woman." (344)

Their lovemaking is joyful and playful. When morning comes they swim naked and then make love in the first rays of sunlight. When they climbed out of the pool "giggling and holding hands like children," Leo muses, "Maggie would have compared us to the newly baptized on Easter morning" (350). Another limit experience for Leo and Jane. Leo realizes that he has risen from the dead and Maggie is a resurrection person too. Their love, God's love, has transformed them.

Summer at the Lake takes a very positive perspective on love and human sexuality. This is reflected by Maggie Ward Keenan in statements like "Catholicism . . . believes in love and the goodness of the human body" (65). "And if passion leads people too far, it was always understood down in the villages and the parishes that the passion itself is not wrong. Rather it hints at how God feels" (65).

Patrick, the priest, expresses his thoughts and Greeley's on sexuality in one of his homilies for Assumption.

To say that Mary's body is in heaven, my friends, is nothing more than to say that the human body is destined for glory. Our bodies with all their weaknesses and frailties, their propensity to weariness and sickness and eventual deterioration are nonetheless sacred. There is nothing in the human body that is not sacred, neither birth, nor growth, nor love, nor aging, nor death. In Jesus all creation is saved, in Mary that salvation is celebrated. Moreover she represents for us God's life-giving, life-nourishing love, the blessing of the flock and the field, of the womb and the breast, the flourishing of life and love in all creation. Mary tells us about God: "whose glory bare would blind / or less would win man's mind / through her see him / made sweeter, not made dim / and her hand leads his light / sifted to our sigh." (357)

It is especially fitting that Patrick, the priest, expresses and expounds one of the major themes that runs throughout the canon of Greeley's fiction—there is nothing in the human body that is not sacred. Patrick is also a resurrection person; as the story ends his total rededication and commitment to the priesthood is expressed in his comment, "It takes awhile to realize that you are possessed by the priesthood" (406). He is not the only one of Jane and Leo's friends and family to be resurrected. All the Devlins are given a second chance at happiness and an opportunity to rise above the darkness in which their mother enveloped them and from which they are set free. The summer at the lake—a numinous summer—was a time of reconciliation and new beginnings.

Patrick, committed to renewing the Church, will, in future, continue to protest against the things that he finds wrong with it. The satire of churchmen, as detailed by Patrick, is often acrimonious and irascible, as Greeley's readers have come to expect. Thinking of leaving the priesthood at the beginning of the novel, Patrick cites as his reason "the insane Church and its stupid cowardly leaders" (11). Weary and worn out, he has come to hate his work "and hate the assholes who are running the Church especially the little old self-pitying Pope who messed up the impact of the Vatican Council with his damned birth control encyclical ten years ago and the paranoid soiciopath who has pretty well destroyed the Archdiocese" (67). Although he had hated the seminary, he endured it, because he wanted very much to be a priest. Now he is especially infuriated with "the nut case Cardinal" (88).

Packy is distraught over the birth control issue. According to him, young people have to decide between large families or no sex or no sacraments. In his view, it is not natural for a man and his wife to sleep in separate bedrooms. "If marriage is a sacrament, husbands and wives should make love often so as to reflect the constant passionate love of God for his people" (89).

With the promulgation of the encyclical *Humanae Vitae*, Packy discharges his anger on those who had "sold out the leading Cardinals of the Council who had been on the Birth Control Commission" (257). He feels that the pope has double-crossed them, because the Italian curialists wanted revenge for the restriction of their power by the Council. In his rage, Packy continues: "Our own gloriously reigning psychopath [archbishop of Chicago] had someone write him an innocuous statement and then went off to Alaska the day the encyclical was issued" (258). As Packy sees it, the encyclical is not about sex, but about power, the power of Rome over the sex lives of the people. "The Holy See, trapped in its Aristotelian view of the nature of human nature and indifference to what scientists since Aristotle had discovered about human nature, had dug a trap for itself" (258).

What Packy desires is for is an entirely new structure for the Church "so it is not run by men who will sell their soul . . . for a place in the Papal power elite" (329).

Perhaps not as abrasive as Packy's commentary on the Church are Leo's derisive remarks on academia which contribute much to the comedy and satire of the book. Speaking of the slave market of graduate school women of academe, Leo comments ironically that although he had never used them for sexual purposes, he knows "all the magic words that make such seductions seem to both the victim and the exploiter not only politically acceptable, but indeed acts of high revolutionary virtue" (54). Fights over hiring, tenure, and promotion, three major concerns of the university, are also dramatized from the point of view of Leo as provost. He makes the following tongue-in-cheek conclusion: "Sometimes I think it would be a tremendous improvement in the life of a university if the faculty had to work for a living" (145) This is a reflection of Leo's view that "a provost is committed ex officio to the doctrine that all academics earn too much money and meet too few students" (56).

Since universities are always facing financial crises, Leo insists that if a person gives enough money to them, they are always willing to certify the donor as respectable regardless of how the money was acquired. (98) When Richard Devlin, Jane's brother, appears in his office wanting to donate a million dollars to set up a chair in honor of his drunken brother Herbie, Leo thinks to himself, "We had named chairs after far worse bandits" (140). "Was this thug, former thug, what-ever, actually going to write me a check for a million dollars?" (140) He did and he got his chair.

In a more amusing vein, once when Jane introduces Leo, she says, "This is Doctor Leo Kelly." "A professor doctor, not a *real* doctor (161). A real put down for academe and its degrees. In passing we note that Leo, who has a tendency to poke fun at academics, drives a black Volvo, which he describes as a "provost's kind of car" (60). He also say tongue in cheek that he is reading Iris Murdoch's *The Sea, the Sea*, because he, as an academic, has "a certain obligation to read 'intelligent' novels by other academics" (355).

When Leo interviews a candidate, an intellectual snob and egotist, for a position in the Biology Department the reader is in for some good satiric humor. Although he plans to recommend him, Leo raises certain questions which he knows will keep the man from being hired. The candidate stupidly raises the question as to whether Leo, "as a devout Irish Catholic," is qualified to pass judgment on him, revealing the anti-Catholic bias that many in the academy have. After sparring with words and insults, the biologist insists that Leo cannot approve of his work on evolution. Leo is amusing as he retorts,

"Your ignorance of Catholicism astonishes me. We are not biblical fundamentalists. As long ago as St. Augustine, which was a millennium and a half ago, we were already open to the possibility of evolution. We weren't the ones who are responsible for the monkey trial"
I had never read that passage in St. Augustine, but that was beside the point. (227)

After some political maneuvering with the Dean, Leo decides to let the Biology Department make the decision on the man's hiring, but points out to the Dean, that ten years ago academics like the biology candidate were proclaiming that they were a new breed and were going to reform the academy and the entire country. "Now all they care about is their own careers—and they are as self-righteous as ever" (245).

The justice system and the police also are subjects of satire. Since the police hate the urban rich who summer at the lake, they arrest Leo and accuse him of driving the car that killed two of Leo's friends. Refusing to believe that Leo is an officers candidate in the Marine Corps they refer pejoratively to him as a "kid who sucks ass around Tom Keenan's," because of his friendship with the Keenan family (28). It is a constant theme in Greeley's fiction that those who are poor have a great dislike for those who are more affluent. Brutally putting handcuffs on Leo's burned wrists, the police arrest him for homicide as they laugh at his screams of pain.

Federal agents, trying to get Jane to testify before a grand jury against her erstwhile husband, are up to their usual capers and are compared to the gestapo. Because Lucy tells them that her mother, Jane, is not at home when they push their way into the family home, they arrest the girl for perjury.

The Irish fondness for alcoholic beverages is the cause of the deaths of four out of six who die in the story. "What a curse it is. Yet we continue to drink" (149). Both Jane's mother-in-law, Iris Clare, and her own mother, Ita Devlin, "a fearsome alcoholic bird of prey," die of alcoholism. No wonder these women's sons were also drunks. Leo's description of Jane's family is one of the author's classic one-line descriptions that gives colorful but very accurate characterization. "The Devlins treated life like it was a barroom in which a brawl was about to erupt" (96). Elsewhere they are described as "an unacceptable family, crude, uncultivated 'Shanty' Irish" (38).

All the elements Greeley's readers have come to expect in his stories are present in *Summer at the Lake*. As the book ends with a strong expression of hope, the surviving members of the families experience a resurrection as the mystery surrounding the deaths of Jim and Eileen Murray and the fatal car crash in which they died is resolved and the truth frees them all. The story line in *Summer at the Lake* follows a pattern that is a favorite of Greeley's. A person in middle life, most often a male, usually disillusioned, often agnostic having lost faith, returns to the neighborhood that was home many years in the past. In returning, the character encounters many problems and usually a mystery that must be solved before happiness can be found. And happiness is found as the character succeeds in finding the "Holy Grail," which is another way of saying the character finds a mate and God, the two being inseparably bound together. With this union the comedy is complete. The Church helps to smooth out the difficulties the lovers experience in the persons of people who are correlatives for the Church. In *Summer at the Lake*, that the Keenans symbolize the Church is explicit. Leo says, "The Keenan house was my parish, you see. In it I could be myself the way I never could at home" (127). Maggie Ward Keenan also expresses this idea: "And the Keenan family is the Church that rallies around us waifs and protects us and gives us life—complete," she jerked her finger at Packy, "with its own built-in cleric" (351).

Life triumphs over death, love over hatred. In all nine stories of Time between the Stars, lovers are united in marriage resulting in the happy ending of comedy. God is the comedian who writes straight with crooked lines and whose "cosmic joke" causes life to triumph over death, and love to prevail over hatred. Since this series presents a very complete depiction of the life of the Chicago Irish and the Catholic Church in the twentieth century, anyone in the next millennium, who wants to get a good picture of what that life was like during this time, can find it in Time between the Stars. Greeley's knowledge of popular culture is extensive and he displays it in every story from describing the fashions in women's clothing including the trends in underwear, to depicting the operations of the Chicago stock market, to exhibiting the political corruption of the city and the federal government, to uncovering the bungling of inept and incompetent churchmen. Inspired by a love for truth, he never fails to depict life as it really is with all the sins and failings of the secular society and the Church, letting the chips fall where they may, in hopes of sparking a reform and changing them for the better.

NOTE

1. For further commentary on *Virgin and Martyr* see Allienne R. Becker, "*Virgin and Martyr:* A Story of God?" in *Andrew Greeley's World: An Anthology of Critical Essays*

1986–1988. Ed. Ingrid Shafer. (New York: Warner, 1989).

WORKS CITED

Bernstein, Carl, and Marco Politi. *His Holiness: John Paul II and the Hidden History of Our Time.* New York: Doubleday, 1996.

Greeley, Andrew M. *An Andrew Greeley Reader.* Ed. John Sprague. Chicago: Thomas More Press, 1987. Vol. 1.

———. *The Angels of September* 1986.

———. *Confessions of a Parish Priest.* New York: Simon and Schuster, 1986.

———. *Death and Beyond.* Chicago: Thomas More, 1976.

———. *Everything You Wanted to Know about the Catholic Church but Were Too Pious to Ask.* Chicago: Thomas   More, 1978.

———. *God in Popular Culture.* Chicago: Thomas More, 1988.

———. *Love Song.* New York: Warner, 1989.

———. *The Myths of Religion.* New York: Warner, 1989.

———. *The Patience of a Saint.* New York: Warner, 1987.

———. *Rite of Spring.* New York: Warner, 1987.

———. *Saint Valentine's Night.* New York: Warner, 1989.

———. *The Search for Maggie Ward.* New York: Warner, 1991.

———. *Sexual Intimacy: Love and Play.* Chicago: Thomas More, 1973. 1975. New York: Warner, 1988.

———. *Summer at the Lake.* New York: Forge, 1997.

———. *Virgin and Martyr.* New York: Warner, 1985.

———. *Wages of Sin.* New York: Putnam, 1992.

———. *When Life Hurts.* New York: Doubleday, 1989.

Greeley, Andrew M. and Mary G. Durkin. *A Church to Come Home To.* Chicago: Thomas More, 1982.

Pasquariello, Ronald D. ed. *Conversations with Andrew Greeley.* Boston: Quinlan, 1988.

Sprague, John, ed. *An Andrew Greeley Reader.* Vol. 1. Chicago: Thomas More, 1987.

Wilcoxson, Kirby. "The Sociologist as Storyteller: Science and Fiction in the Novels of Andrew Greeley." *Andrew Greeley's World: An Anthology of Critical Essays 1986–1988.* Ed. Ingrid Shafer. New York: Warner, 1989. 111–118.

6

God Game and the Angel Trilogy

Frequently Andrew Greeley's novels contain elements of the fantastic—the rationally inexplicable—as evidenced by the mysterious events in *Angels of September* and *The Search for Maggie Ward*, for example. This chapter considers four highly fantastic stories: *God Game* (1986), *Angel Fire* (1988), *Angel Light* (1995), and *Contract with an Angel* (1998).

Scintillating and effervescent with its sparkling wit and debonair good humor, *God Game* (1986) is a tour de force spotlighting Andrew Greeley's virtuosity as a fiction writer and a novelist. This story of alternate realities was not written for a wide audience but rather for the elite circle of readers who can appreciate the subtleties of an intellectual writing for other intellectuals, of an academician writing for others of his breed.

The most outstanding characteristic of *God Game* is the constant Romantic irony with which the story is created. What is Romantic irony? It is one of the techniques that may be used to create fantastic fiction, as shall be explained. Since it is not often employed by authors who write in the English language, the masterful use of Romantic irony, as in this story, reveals Greeley to be a writer well-skilled in his craft and one whose knowledge extends to foreign literary artistry and craftsmanship.

Since this chapter deals with Greeley's fantastic fiction, let's begin by understanding what the fantastic in fiction is and then define Romantic irony. The fantastic is a literary mode characterized by a group of attributes: the bizarre, the strange, the wondrous, the unreal, the illusory, the capricious, the uncanny, the incredible, the grotesque, the extravagantly fanciful, the odd and irrational, the eccentric. To be characterized as fantastic, a work does not necessarily contain all these attributes. It suffices that it has a number of the them and they are used continually throughout the story. The fantastic may be further characterized by its use of Romantic irony, the grotesque, and ambiguity. These three elements, which will be discussed in turn below, tend to overlap and intertwine. However, all of them do not have to be present in a literary work for it to be classified as fantastic. For example, a fantastic work may be simply ambiguous, or ambiguous with overtones of Romantic irony, or ambiguous and grotesque, or grotesque and ironic, or any possible combination of these elements in varying degrees. However, a work that contains Romantic irony will inherently tend to be both ambiguous and ambivalent because Romantic irony typically encompasses both of these qualities. The fantastic narrative may lend itself to a symbolic interpretation. The fantasist often uses dreams, strange phenomena, and altered states of consciousness to create his estranged world.

Romantic irony is a term which is not easy to comprehend or to define. It is useless to look for a coherent discussion of the concept of Romantic irony in the writings of the Romanticists. Even Søren Kierkegaard (1813–1855), Danish religious philosopher and author of *The Concept of Irony with Constant Reference to Socrates*, lamented that although he found Romantic irony frequently mentioned in the early nineteenth-century literary works, he could not find a clear-cut discussion of this subject (260–261). Many literary critics, including Georg Wilhelm Friedrich Hegel, German philosopher (1770–1831), consider Friedrich Schlegel to be the originator of the precise concept of Romantic irony, although various elements of Romantic irony can be observed in literature at least since the period. Schlegel, the major literary critic of the Romantic movement in Germany and "one of the greatest critics in history" (in the words of René Wellek), introduced the term *irony* into modern literary discussion (Wellek, *History* 3). His theory of Romantic irony, in turn, is based on the philosophy of Friedrich Wilhelm Joseph Schelling (1775–1854).

The aesthetic vision of Schelling, the philosopher of the German Romantic Movement, became the essential expression of the Romantic spirit. Schelling regarded art as the result of inspiration. In an act corresponding to God's act of creating the universe and analogous to it, the artist creates his work. In his *System des transcendentalen Idealismus*, he elaborated on his ideas of creative intuition, insisting that man can know absolute reality by means of aesthetic intuition, or artistic consciousness.

Inspired and bringing forth a divine revelation, the artist becomes a prophet of God. In the artistic experience, the phenomenal world (the world as revealed to us by sense impressions) converges with the noumenal world (the world of absolute reality) by means of a dialectic process of thesis, antithesis, and synthesis. The aesthetic experience becomes the apogee of human life. The aesthetic act was the cornerstone of Schelling's thought, since to him the universe itself was a work of art created by God, the supreme artist. Schelling's influence led Romantic authors to view their creativity as analogous to God's creativity. Since the universe was an organic whole, they regarded the works they created as organic wholes. Mimesis, which had been the ideal of artists and writers since Aristotle, was rejected by the Romanticists. Instead of mirroring nature, they considered themselves as inspired creators whose inspiration burned like a lamp within them.

Because they believed the aesthetic experience was the culmination of life, their literary works often dealt with artists, musicians, authors, and their creations.

Friedrich Schlegel, influenced by the philosopher Schelling, conceptualized a paradoxical and chaotic approach to both life and literature. He wrote in *Das Athenaeum,* the literary journal of the Romantic movement which he published together with his brother and fellow literary critic August Wilhelm Schlegel, "Irony is the form of paradox. Paradox is everything that is simultaneously good and great" (Friedrich Schlegel 12). At another point he declares, "Irony is the clear consciousness of the eternal agility and unending chaos" (97). By employing Romantic irony, the author intended both to assert what he was ostensibly saying and its opposite at the same time, clearly reflecting the paradox and chaos of life. By synthesizing the antithetical elements, one transcended the paradoxes. Reality, to the Romantic ironist, was almost entirely created by the human mind, which was able to transcend its creation. The Romantic ironist let his mind play with everything freely and without limits. Life was a play, a novel, or even a puppet show. By deliberately playing with the form of his story, the author showed that he transcended his literary creation. A good example of this can be found in the fiction of Ludwig Tieck, a friend of Schlegel. He often interrupted the flow of his fiction to demonstrate the haphazard nature of his plot, and belittled himself as a literary person within his own story. By directly speaking to the reader, or by speaking of the writing of the work itself, he broke the dramatic illusion that he had created.

Although the German Romanticists used Romantic irony extravagantly, English writers did not use it at all. According to René Wellek, "Romantic irony is completely absent from the English Romantic writers, even when they laugh or joke or parody" (Wellek, *Confrontations* 22). However, the American Romantics Nathaniel Hawthorne and Edgar Allan Poe did not follow the English tradition of Romantic prose, established by Sir Walter Scott in the historical romance, but rather wrote stories that were strongly influenced by the German Romanticists, and they both employed Romantic irony.

Long before Schlegel began to theorize about irony, the practice of synthesizing antithetical elements and holding an ambivalent attitude toward a literary work had been associated with the word *romantic.* The German literary critic Raymond Immerwahr comments, "In the Middle Ages the narrative form of Romance was arbitrary and capricious as well as involved and grotesquely paradoxical" (672). Wolfram von Eschenbach's Parzival is an example of such a work, since, according to Immerwahr, both Wolfram and his reader were cognizant of the contradictions, the playful form of the literary creation, and the irony of Parzival (683).

The chivalric romances of the sixteenth century, such as those by Ariosto, the Italian poet and author of *Orlando Furioso*, were also written in an ironic spirit. In describing Ariosto's work, Sir Walter Scott wrote that the author "in some passages at least, lifts his knightly vizor so far as to give a momentary glimpse of the smile which mantles upon his countenance" (276). The smile behind the vizor, or mask, was, in fact, one of the favorite topoi of the Romantic ironist.

Cervantes, highly admired by Andrew Greeley, played with the form of the romance more than did any other Renaissance writer. In *Don Quixote*, his burlesque parody on *Amadis of Gaul* and other chivalric romances, he spoke directly to the reader, made mock references to his own literary creations, and let the ironic spirit have free reign. Of course, *Don Quixote*, as translated into German by Ludwig Tieck, was widely acclaimed by the German Romanticists.

Among the Germans, Johann Wolfgang von Goethe, in his novel *Wilhelm Meister*, used Romantic irony by addressing the reader directly, mentioning the novel in the text, and mocking it and the reader. The Pre-Romantic author Jean Paul Friedrich Richter made extensive use of irony in his works, which were praised by Friedrich Schlegel in the "Letter on the Novel" which Schelgel ironically inserted into his *Gespräch über die Poesie* (*Conversation on Poetry*). Schlegel praised Jean Paul's arabesques as being the only romantic fiction in an unromantic age (509). In the arabesque, a manifestation of Romantic irony, the author plays with the form of the narrative, breaking it into segments to portray multiple points of view. An excellent example of this kind of writing is E. T. A. Hoffmann's "Der Sandmann," ("The Sandman"), in which, "as in a series of mirrors, there is endless romantic ironic reflection" (Walzel 226).

An ironic story may be written in such a way that irony is a principle of structure with the surface meaning saying one thing and the deep meaning conveying the exact opposite. A clever reader will often discern a hidden symbolic meaning that conveys views that are contrary to the literal ones.

A relationship between irony and ambivalence is noted by Angus Fletcher for whom irony is "the extreme degree of ambivalence" (230). Ambivalence, not to be confused with ambiguity, signifies, when applied to a literary work, that the work exhibits the presence of reciprocally contradictory emotions, thoughts, or attitudes.

In sum, the following definition of the term *Romantic irony* is proposed: Romantic irony is the deliberate toying with the form of a literary work, and/or the use of paradox and ambivalence to create its structure. The Romantic ironist enjoys employing antithetical and parallel ideas and situations, the arabesque, doubles (Doppelgänger), reflections in mirrors, in water, and in other surfaces. His literary creations can often be interpreted as having more than one meaning.

Closely associated with Romantic irony is the grotesque, which the German Romanticists employed to portray the ominous forces that assault people. In using the grotesque, German Romantic writers were following a tradition that Wolfgang Kayser, in his book *The Grotesque in Art and Literature*, traces back to the Middle Ages, when the word *grotesque* signified a particular decorative style, inspired by Antiquity; it was "playfully gay and carelessly fantastic" while being simultaneously "ominous" and "sinister" (Kayser 21). It depicted a world entirely different from the one with which we are familiar. Excellent examples of the grotesque are observed in the artwork of Hieronymous Bosch and in the theater of the *commedia dell'arte*. Pantomime, soliloquy, acrobatics, romance, buffoonery, jokes, tirades, slapstick, dance, and music comprised the usual repertory of the *commedia dell'arte*. With just a basic background to suggest the setting, stock characters, recognized by their masks and costumes, depicted the behavioral characteristics and peculiarities of humanity. Under a cloak of the absurd Callot's grotesqueries are highly ironic and the work of a great mind. They reveal hidden meanings to the clever observer who can perceive them beneath their preposterous appearances.

The use of caricature, also employed by the German Romantics, links Greeley to the *commedia dell'arte*. The Romantic ironist play with his characters making caricatures of them rather than trying to make them credible; Romantic irony hides behind the grotesque. Viewed as caricature, the grotesque provides a vision that is chaotic, ludicrous, and frightening. The grotesque seen as caricature provides a vision of the absurd, the ominous, and the chaotic. Since the grotesque and the ironic have a tendency to converge, the dual vision of the absurd and the ominous is very close to the paradoxical vision of Romantic irony. It is possible for a literary work to be fantastic without also being grotesque, but the grotesque always has elements of the fantastic.

Since the grotesque has elements that are ominous, it does not occur in all fantastic literature. The grotesque can also be an element of humor, as it is with Greeley in *God Game* and as with Jean Paul, who regarded it as a *vernichtende Idee* (an annihilating idea) and a stepping stone to skepticism (Richter 129-132). Jean Paul, as well as Schlegel, and Victor Hugo, saw the demonic as a secondary element of the grotesque (Kayser 58).

To be genuine, the grotesque, according to Wolfgang Kayser, must ensue from deeds, not from discourse; it should be simultaneously both atrocious and funny. Although the grotesque can be paramount in a short work of fiction, it cannot be predominant in a longer work, but will appear only in episodes and scenes; it cannot be the principle of structure for an entire work The grotesque is, in Kayser's opinion, an "estranged world," an absurd world and for it to be truly grotesque the author must not make any attempt to minimize its absurdity or seek to establish its meaning (184). In the grotesque vision, life is an "empty meaningless puppet play" (186). At this point the grotesque perception closely borders on the ambivalent regard of the Romantic ironist with his multifaceted perspective on life.

Another characteristic of the fantastic, and one that occurs in almost all fantastic fiction, is the use of ambiguity. Often the text of a story will be unclear as to its meaning and open to more than one interpretation—in short, ambiguous—thereby creating the effect of being fantastic. Deliberately trying to suggest more than one interpretation of a statement, the text is equivocal, ambiguous, and perhaps ambivalent. By constructing a paradox into a story so that it conveys two or more contradictory things, Romantic irony can also create ambiguity. A literary work that exhibits the chaotic Weltanschauung of the Romantic ironist is highly ambiguous and therefore fantastic because it expresses no clear and explicit meaning for the events it portrays. Good terms to describe it are bizarre, strange, wondrous, unreal, capricious, or uncanny.

The use of ambiguity is a technique that Greeley employs in *God Game* for creating the fantastic. Often one cannot tell what is reality or an alternate reality. Ambiguity exists as to whether the narrator is dreaming or awake or in a hypnotic state. One cannot tell at times whether the narrator has had too much of the creature taken, to use a Greeley expression, and is therefore an unreliable witness. Much ambiguity is found throughout *God Game*, as we shall see as we examine the story.

It must, of course, be acknowledged that the reader's role in the evocation of the fantastic is very important. Greeley wrote *God Game* for the urbane and sophisticated reader who is clever enough to grasp the exquisite subtleties and secret hidden irony of his fiction. Unable to penetrate the various meanings of the story, the pedestrian reader will enjoy only partially what Greeley presents. Furthermore, Greeley's reader must be willing to let the author permeate his consciousness so that he can experience with Greeley the chaotic and paradoxical *Weltanschauung* of the Romantic ironist with all its ambiguities and grotesqueries. The reader must feel the confusion which an ambiguous text like *God Game* strives to evoke in order to perceive the story as the author intended. Romantic irony, the grotesque, and ambiguity must be understood in terms of the reader's experience in relation to the author's purposes implicit in the formal techniques of the work. Although each reader brings his own experience to the reading of the text, the cosmopolitan and sophisticated reader who participates in the illusion that the author has created finds a richly polysemous narrative.

The reader of *God Game* notices at the very beginning of the story he has stumbled into a strange world when the narrator begins by saying: "It was Nathan's fault that I became God. It is, as I would learn, hell to be God" (1). The reader considers the possibility that the narrator is unreliable, that he cannot be believed. Confronted by the paradox that "it is hell to be God," the reader might begin to suspect that the author was creating a work of speculative fiction.

Soon the narrator reveals that a friend of his, a fellow academic, Nathan, a Jewish political scientist, has given him a game titled "Duke and Duchess" to play on his computer. The paradox and irony continue. There is a picture of a dragon on the cover of the game, but there is no dragon in the game itself. The setting for the game is medieval/futuristic—more paradox. Wearing a loin cloth like a primitive man, Duke Lenrau, a knight carrying a large sword, sometimes wears weird red armor or a purple jockstrap. His warriors carry both spears and ray guns.

When lightening strikes the narrator's satellite receiver dish, the game on his computer and TV screen changes and instead of the animated figures of a video game, the characters are suddenly real people who regard the narrator as "the Lord Our God." Who is the narrator? He is a priest, a social scientist, an author of fiction and the creator of Blackie Ryan and Eileen Kane, among other fictional characters. Just when the reader decides that the narrator is Greeley, Greeley intrudes into the novel, in the manner of the Romantic ironist, playfully employing the arabesque form with an authors note on page 53 and subsequently three more times in the course of the book on pages 179, 241, and 307. In his first arabesque intrusion he attacks his narrator accusing him of "making sly hints" that he is Greeley and of trying "with his clever schemes" to take the story away from him, the author (53). The narrator, it turns out, is a Doppelgänger—a double of the author. But that is not all he is. In his role of the Lord Our God to the strange people of the game, he is a double for the "Other Person," the narrator's own God. Soon the reader has the feeling of having stumbled into a hall of mirrors in which "the Land" —that is the only name it is given—is a mirror of the narrator's world and some of the characters in it are doubles of people who live in the narrator's neighborhood. For example Malvau and N'Rasia, a married couple trying to save their marriage, are doubles of the Hagans who also have marital problems and with whom they seem to communicate in dreams. Ranora, the strange elf child of "the Land" is a double of Michele, the narrator's friend who resembles Noele Farrell in *Lord of the Dance*. Very strangely Ranora is able to communicate with the narrator through Michele.

The narrator engages in the self-deprecation and self-denigration that one expects in a story in which Romantic irony is in full sway. When speaking of his friend Nathan, the narrator comments that Nathan is "far more a God-haunted character than I am (you don't have to be very religious at all to be a priest)" (6). When his satellite dish is struck by lightening, he comments "Wow, I said with dismaying lack of originality" (19). With the typical ambiguity of the Romantic ironist, he asks, "How do I know that the lightening didn't strike me instead of the dish and that I was not temporarily round the bend, or more so than usual?" (28). His computer and monitor are "all messed up in the crazy system of connections that an electronic illiterate" like him can "put together without half trying." He even admits to being "a blithering basket case" (140). The best example of his ironic mocking of his abilities is this:

SF writers, of course, men and women with much larger and more generous imaginations than I have, take such exchanges between alternative cosmoi for granted.

But this is not Speculative Fiction. This is an attempt at a sober report by a social scientist of what happened when he began to play an interactive fiction game of which he ought to have been more suspicious. I don't have the imagination to do Speculative Fiction. (46)

What irony! He is really putting the reader on with this, because this very story is an admirable piece of speculative fiction.

Greeley, in his intrusion into the story in his author's note, also maligns his narrator by asking "Could anyone with a Ph. D. be that dumb?" (54). He refers to him scornfully as "our bumptious narrator" (179). Not only is he mocking his narrator but he is being scornful of academe itself and through his narrator continues to show ironic disdain for the academy throughout the story. Nathan is a full professor "(thus an academic immortal)" (1). Mockingly the narrator refers to himself, an academic, as "the old suggestible kid" (222). He even comments on his use of the word *cosmoi* by tossing in the following: "(Greek plural, note what even a bad classical education can do for you)" (43). When he makes a seemingly intelligent remark about how the two cosmoi of the novel might possibly be connected he undercuts his statement saying, "I wasn't sure what that explanation meant since it was mostly academic happy talk. . . " (264). Later when he is trying to explain the connection between the two worlds, he makes some rather hazy statements and then comments on what he has said. "Consider that last sentence: it's a masterpiece of academic scholarship. What does it really say? Not a hell of a lot" (154).

His mocking of academia is quite satirical. A group of academics get together to hold a seminar on the tapes that had been made when the narrator played the God game. Pedantically they give their opinions about the strange world with its purple sun and its pigs that lay eggs. Scholarly discussions are held as to whether the people of "the Land"are truly hominids. To give credibility to his narrative, the narrator will even supply the reader with the names of a couple scientists who saw the tapes and can vouch for them.

The crowning satiric comment on academia comes at the end of the book when the narrator states his intention to get even with Nathan for involving him in the God game. " I am part of a conspiracy to teach him what it is like to have to play God to a group of fractious humans, to have far more responsibility that you have power. We're going to make him departmental chairman" (305).

Only a fellow academic can understand the full impact of this stratagem. Department chair is the last job most academics want. Yet many people who do assume the position tend to think they are God with the right to determine the lives of the contentious members of the department. It is highly ironic for Nathan with all his accomplishments to be rewarded, even in jesting, with the department chairmanship.

Not only does the narrator mock himself and academia, he attacks the characters of the story. He describes Malvau as "a pompous bastard" (72), "insensitive dummy" (79) "a complainer, a nagger" (80). His wife N'rasia "whines and bitches"(80). In addressing Malvau, he calls him "you stupid idjit" (84). G'Ranne, another female character, is "the ice maiden" (93). Duke Lenau, the supposed protagonist of the story, is "Harry Hangdog, king of the wimps" (217), Sammy Sad Sack" (218), "Willy Weakling" (271), "Terry Timid" (273), "Marty Macho" (275),and other things equally denigrating. The Duchess is a "stupid little bitch" (148) and a "vain little chit" (200).

As one would expect in a novel in which Romantic irony is the most constantly used literary device, the narrator adds a lot of extraneous and intrusive material into the story. He tells of an incident in the life of his sister; makes extraneous comments on his friend Kenny; includes gratuitous information about a town called La Porte; relates what his mass homily for the week was; and includes some of the text of "At Swim Two Bird," a poem on marriage, and many other things.

Another manifestation of Romantic irony is having the characters of the story visit the narrator and discuss their roles in the story with him. They appear to encounter him in his dreams, yet often the next day a telltale souvenir of the meeting is found in his room, giving the impression that the character was actually present there. It is difficult to determine what is dream and what is reality. The narrator and the characters even discuss who is doing the dreaming—the characters or the narrator. One wonders about the reliability of the narrator who likes to enter self-induced hypnosis and let his mind flow freely where it will. He has also been known to drink four glasses of Bailey's Irish Creme, which might have influenced his perceptions of reality.

Parallel events occur in each world to add to the confusion and ambiguity of the story. There also is much hesitation as to whether an event is really as it appears to be.

The grotesque comes into play in the book through the activities of the mad scientists and the clergy, who are caricatures that enable the narrator and Greeley to make a number of barbed onslaughts on the Catholic clergy—a favorite target for Greeley's satire. In this story the clergy are the bad guys. The reader is introduced to them when the narrator comments that he "saw some clergy conniving in the darkness" (45). Both principalities in the "Land" have a clergy, a pagan priesthood; the two clergies unite in order to try to overthrow the Duke and the Duchess in a coup and take over the government. It is clear that Greeley is commenting on Catholic churchmen when he describes the antics of the clergy of "the Land."

A cardinal and a mother superior discuss what to do with Ranora, the ilel double of the vibrant teen Michele and how they can eliminate her so as to seize power. Speaking of the cardinal, the narrator comments, "I said Cardinals were prudent, not necessarily virtuous" (90). Even when discussing murder, the cardinal does so "in his usual richly pious voice" (186). At other times "The oil from the Cardinal's voice was pure slime" (276). When the mother Superior calls for killing Ranora "for her own good," the narrator tries to intervene by pushing his ABORT PLANS button and comments. "No wonder the Other Person [God] has so much trouble with the Curia Romana." (90)

On another occasion when the narrator checks on the clergy, he finds the cardinal, two witches and a high priest staring into a huge kettle. "Eating a missionary?" quips the narrator. When the one priest whom the narrator dubbed the Admiral, stirs the pot vigorously, it eventually turns over, shatters and spill its contents. "Too many witches," he [the cardinal] sobbed "spoil the brew." This kind of punning remark is typical for a Romantic ironist as is the one the narrator makes when he hears that the way priests dispose of their enemies is by sticking a knife in their backs: "*Stylus curiae*" (167).

The narrator drafts the mad scientists whom he dubs theThree Stooges—Larry, Curly, and Moe—as allies in doing away with the clergy. However, everything they attempt turns out to be a failure. The cardinal is described as "part troll, and part small-time Mafia hit man or as a crooked southeast-side Irish precinct captain" (271). For this reason the narrator refers to the cardinal as "Troll." While Troll, with a heavy sword in hand, stands over Lenau, who is a prisoner stretched out on a sacrificial altar, the following occurs:

ZAP PRIESTS, I assaulted my keyboard with frantic fingers.
WHICH PRIESTS?
Delete Cardinal Krol.
I DO NOT KNOW CARDINAL KROL.
Lucky you. (295)

To conclude, *God Game*, a comedy in which some of the characters make love matches, is a highly sophisticated story with much urbane good humor, a lot of Romantic irony, touches of the grotesque, and considerable ambivalence and ambiguity. Written by a savant for other savants, by a literary man for other belletristic people, by an academic for other members of academe, it is a fascinating piece of fiction and contains some of the best of Greeley's divine and human comedy in which all ends well. The story demonstrates that Greeley is an accomplished writer who knows his craft and how to employ it.

Also in a humorous speculative vein is the Angel trilogy, which begins with *Angel Fire* (1988), a provocative romantic fantasy, is continued in *Angel Light* (1995), a captivating modern version of the biblical love story of Tobit and Sarah, and concludes with *Contract with an Angel* (1998), a thought-provoking piece of speculative religious imagination that has certain similarities to Goethe's *Faust*. The three stories are based on the premises that evolution is directed toward mind and that, according to St. Augustine and St. Bernard, angels have spiritual bodies. Angels are important characters in all three stories. In *Angel Fire*, the lovely Gabriella Light, comes to the aid of Sean Desmond, an agnostic Nobel Prize laureate, who battles with the forces of evil on his trip to accept the honor that has been bestowed on him. Her daughter Raphaella Light, in the story *Angel Light*, helps two young lovers to defeat the evil powers that threaten their happiness, and finally in *Contract with an Angel*, Michael the Archangel signs a contract with Raymond Anthony Neenan for his immortal soul. All three stories are powerful parables of divine love and grace, but it is the final story of the trilogy that most stirs the heart of the reader because of the excellent psychological depiction of the protagonist and his very positive response to the angel's call for his transformation. *Contract with an Angel* is one of Greeley's masterpieces and the fitting crown of the trilogy.

A powerful story of grace and love, *Angel Fire*, speculative fiction at its very best, is a witty, humorous, and scintillating comedy in which Sean Desmond encounters the lovely feminine Gabriella Light, his guardian angel and the angel who sang at Bethlehem. So that Desmond can see her, Gabriella Light—"any similarity between her and any angel (or seraph) living or dead is purely coincidental"—assumes an analog body which is dazzlingly beautiful and voluptuous. From his experiences with her which restore and revitalize his faith, the agnostic professor of biology and Nobel Prize Laureate, Sean Desmond learns to love again. His fear of women vanishes in the healing warmth that radiates from Gabriella, as he recuperates from his failed, and soon to be annulled marriage with Moanin' Mona, who walked out on him and their two teenaged daughters, Fionna and Deirdre.

Delightful with its charming banter and blarney, *Angel Fire* is a beguiling fantasy romance with a capacious measure of suspense and intrigue. Left over from the Hitler regime—known for its occult practices—some modern-day sorcerers, surviving and prospering in the former German Democratic Republic, want to kill Desmond and capture his angel to further their Nazi plans to conquer and rule. However, every time someone makes an attempt on his life, as Desmond and Gabriella journey to Stockholm and beyond, Gabriella destroys them with colossal power and energy.

In this captivating story which is highly refreshing and a sheer pleasure to read, Greeley has incorporated some of his most significant theological observations. It is not a coincidence that the angel in the story is female. Sexual differentiation, as was discussed in an earlier chapter, is very important in Greeley's theology. In *Angel Fire* the feminine qualities of God are expressed in an especially powerful manner through the charmingly feminine angel Gabriella Light. Since God has both masculine and feminine qualities and has used sexual differentiation in human beings to reflect this, it would be only logical to assume that the angels who are superior beings would also reflect the androgyny of God if they have bodies—as St. Augustine affirms they do—and that both male and female angels exist. To illustrate this concept, the angel in *Angel Fire* is feminine, wonderfully loving, and maternal, radiating God's maternal love—Madonna love.

The greatest metaphor of God's maternal love is to be found in Mary, the Mother of Jesus. This needs to be understood before we can understand how Greeley uses feminine characters as metaphors for the love of God. Speaking of Mary as the *imago dei*, Greeley says:

> However to say that Mary is 'the mysterion," the *imago dei*, is not to give her a lesser title than *theotoxos* but a greater one. To put the matter differently Mary is the *imago dei* because of her maternity. As Jesus himself said in response to praise of his mother, "rather blessed are those who hear the word of God and keep it." In other words, blessed are those who reveal and reflect the goodness and love of God. (*Myths 360*)

To Greeley, Mary must be seen as "a sacrament of Yahweh our loving Mother," the sacrament of God "who is as tender and gentle, as passionate and as generous at the Madonna" (*Myths* 444, 454). If one accepts that Mary reflects the mother love of God, then, as a corollary, all Christian women can be seen as metaphors of that love. As Greeley says, "Women, then, seem to mediate on the womanliness of God for men; they are sacraments of God's womanly love for their men" (*Catholic Myth* 251). Furthermore "they spread the story of God's womanly love by their own behavior as sacraments, by the revelatory power of their own passion that tells the story of God's passion for us" (*A Piece of My Mind* 18).

The heroine in *Angel Fire*, Gabriella Light especially reveals God's womanly love. She is a seraph—one of the beings who stand before the face of God— a veritable fireball of love, whose mere touch fills Desmond "with all the peace and goodness and beauty of the universe" (65).

When someone tries to kill Desmond in the shower, she disposes of the man by splitting his head in half and then causing his remains to vanish almost instantly. Enfolding Sean in her arms "like he was a boy child with a scraped knee" (144), she soothes away his injuries and pains.

The brilliant and glorious epiphany in the railroad carriage, in which Gaby reveals herself to Sean as she really is, overwhelms him with her beauty and the certainty that God exists. "No longer, in the face of so much beauty, could he doubt" (152). So overcome by this limit experience, he lies "sobbing in his guardian angel's arms" (152).

Another beautiful and glorious experience which brings Sean "total illumination" is Gaby's dancing for and with him. The pure beauty and symbolism of the passage, a delightful bit of fantasy prose, makes it noteworthy: "They whirled off into space, dancing across the cosmos, sliding down the tails of comets, tapping on asteroids, skipping from spoke to spoke of galaxy wheels, drinking in the Milky Way, doing the polka on the moon, riding up on solar winds, frolicking on the rings of Saturn, waltzing across the canals of Mars, jitterbugging in the fog of Venus" (202–03).

The power of Gaby's maternal love transforms Sean slowly step by step. When she finally lets him make love to her, her love is so overpowering that it almost destroys him. The description of this event is filled with beauty.

Gaby's love for Sean is so great that not only does she save him from every danger that threatens, but she also provides for all his needs— including clothing, money, an annulment from Moanin' Mona, and most of all, when she disappears at the end of the story, a new wife who looks exactly like her analog body.

Gaby is a beautiful metaphor for the love of God in this charming fantasy romance. With extreme skill and expert craftsmanship Greeley has created in *Angel Fire* a fantastic tale of rare beauty and charm, employing the techniques of the fantastic as an accomplished artist. As customary in fantastic fiction, Sean is constantly hesitating throughout much of the book as to whether or not Gabriella is real. Sometimes he thinks he must be dreaming, or imagining, the things that happen to him, for altered states of conscious almost always play a part in the creation of the fantastic. When Gaby provides him with a telltale souvenir, he can no longer doubt her reality. There is a touch of the grotesque in the modern-day sorcerers who try to capture Gaby. Above all, the book is pure comedy from beginning to end with joyful good humor on almost every page. As is to be expected in Greeley's fiction, love and life triumph and the happy ending comes when Sean meets the woman Gaby has arranged for him. The feminine traits of Gabriella which reflect the feminine qualities of God provide renewal experiences for Sean. In his numinous encounters with the angel he perceives the purposes of God and his own place in the universe.

Angel Light, the second volume of the Angel trilogy, is a humorous modern version of the biblical love story of Tobias and Sarah. In Greeley's version of this ancient love story, the young lover is G. Patrick "Toby" Tobin of Chicago and his distant cousin is Sara Anne Elizabeth Tobin of Galway in Ireland. Instead of the biblical ten talents of silver, the money that Greeley's protagonist is to garner is ten million dollars, bequeathed to him by Great Uncle Gerry Tobin's will. However, there are some conditions he must satisfy before he can collect his fortune. He must carry a letter to his distant cousin Ronan Tobin and end a long standing family feud, by marrying Ronan's daughter, the lovely Sara, within the month. He is also forbidden from discussing the inheritance with her until after the wedding.

Looking for a travel agent on the Internet, Toby encounters Rafe, who turns out to be the Angel Raphaella—the charming, delightful, very feminine, daughter of Gabriella Light, from the book *Angel Fire*. Together they travel to Ireland to the home of Ronan Tobin and the delightful Sara Anne. However, Toby soon learns that the woman he hopes will be his holy grail has black moods, which are the work of the demon Asmodeus in the person of one Oisin O'Riordan who, before Toby arrives on the scene, raped her and sold her to one of his buddies to be raped by him. When Toby learns the secret of her moodiness, he is able to help her by getting her to see a psychiatrist. The Angel Raphaella, famous for her healing touch, completes Sara Anne's healing and saves the young couple from the horrible wrath, murderous rage, and destructive fury of O'Riordan. The story climaxes when Bishop Blackie Ryan officiates at the marriage of the young couple, who with ten million dollars in the bank should be able to find a modicum of happiness and peace.

This book, a pleasant story of young love, is a fantasy romance, "a great, romantic adventure" "with a pot of gold" (25). Resembling earlier Greeley fiction, it is a quester story in which the young hero, who thinks of himself as Lancelot, Galahad, or Art MacConn, seeks his holy grail, Sara Anne, and a pot of gold at the end of the leprechaun's rainbow. The fantastic is created with the same techniques employed in *Angel Fire*. The protagonist is frequently confused as to whether the events that he experiences are real or imaginary. His altered states of consciousness are caused by dreams and even by his being knocked out when the angel saves his life by pushing him out of the way of a double-deck Dublin bus. When he is unconscious following the bus episode, he thinks that he is dead, dying, or in purgatory. Actually he finds himself in an out-of-the-body experience in Sara Anne's bedroom where the young lady, like Sarah in the biblical account, is thinking of taking her own life. Unable to touch anything or speak, he saves her by using the power of his mind to spill the glass of water she plans to drink to swallow the fatal pills. When his consciousness returns, Raphaella is ministering healing to him.

Dreams are also important in the story in creating an alternate reality and in providing an occasion for the grotesque. Touches of the grotesque can be found especially in the dream in which the demon Asmodeus, a huge black shape "like the vampire in the film Bram Stoker's "Dracula" hovers over Toby (*Angel Light* 34).

The Angel Raphaella is very talented at assuming identities at will. When Toby needs tickets and a passport, she provides them. Later she appears on his flight to Ireland as the flight attendant whose maternal arms enfold and soothe him when he has motion sickness. Still later she is Commander Warde, the uniformed woman, who saves Toby from the British immigration officials—satiric caricatures who think he is an Irish terrorist. Throughout the story, Raphaella continues to appear in various disguises.

One especially fantastic element in the story is the manner in which Toby communicates with Rae, his nickname for the angel. He talks to her on a computer that is not hooked up in any way with the internet. Since he is a computer specialist who plans to become the Bill Gates of the coming millennium, he is especially baffled as to how the communication takes place. If he wants Rae, all he has to do is type in "Go Rafe" and she is instantly there.

With picturesque local color, the atmosphere and charm of Ireland is captured as Toby experiences the various sights and engages in dalliance in the dales with Sara. Even the Angel Raphaella gets caught up in the Irish atmosphere and assumes a quaint Irish accent at times. Humorous are the various colorful idioms of the Irish which are employed in the book. One cannot help but laugh, or at least smile, at Irish expressions like "gobshite," "onchuck," "amadan," "shite house," "nine-fingered shite hawk," "dead frigging brill," or "a dead frigging grand nun" (137, 138, 134, 154, 190, 256). In a note, Toby explains that the Irish language lacks "any truly obscene words" (77). For this reason they took to Anglo-Saxon obscene and scatological words "with unrestrained glee" (77).

Besides being a comedy, *Angel Light* is definitely a parable of love and grace. At the beginning of the story, Toby is gauche and does not know how to talk to women or how to act with them. Sara brings out the best that is in him and he becomes tender and loving. In his association with Rae, he learns even more about love and also about sex, because she gives him instruction to prepare him for marriage. Sometimes she whispers in his ear what he should say to Sara, but most importantly she teaches him about love. When Toby, also called Paddy in the story, says he does not understand why the Angel Raphaella spends so much time worrying about him and Sara, she explains that is because of love. "It's called love, a love far more intense for us, and infinitely more intense for him, than the passion you feel for the young Sara Anne" (223). In these discussion about love and the Other, Rae's word for God, she explains to him why she refers to God sometimes as he and at other times she. "She is both and neither. But she is certainly the life bearer of us all, is she not?" (223). But Raphaella does not just talk to Toby about love, she demonstrates her love and the love of God by delivering Toby and Sara from Oisin O'Riordan and by healing them both of any ill effects that O'Riordan might have caused them. Then, by revealing herself to them, she provides them with a tremendous limit experience, similar to the experiences that Gabriella bestows on Sean Desmond.

When Raphaella identifies herself to Sara as a seraph, the reader chuckles when Sara in astonishment cries out, "You're no frigging seraph!" to which the angel replies, "Oh yes, my dear. I am a frigging seraph. . . . For sweet charity's sake, come dance with me in Ireland." A beautiful and ecstatic mystical experience follows in which Sara and Toby acquire knowledge—she of the music she will later write, he of computers to make it possible for him to be highly successful in business. This aspect of their experience illustrates Greeley's belief that ecstasy is a way of knowing, of obtaining information that one cannot obtain in any other manner.

In conclusion, *Angel Light* is a charming comedy of young lovers who with the help of an angel overcome the obstacles to their love and find happiness together. Above all, it is the story of the Love that pervades the universe with ineffable radiant joy. It is a delightful addition to Greeley's comedy.

With its penetrating psychological insights into the human psyche *Contract with an Angel*, the third story of the trilogy, is a masterpiece of speculative religious thought. It is the story of Raymond Anthony Neenan, whose life is in shambles—his parents hate him, his ex-wife from an annulled marriage detests him, only one of his children is on speaking terms with him, his employees fear him, and he has never really taken the time to know his new wife. On an airplane flight, he finds himself sitting beside a large black man who introduces himself as Michael, saying, "I'm a seraph. . . . In fact as you will remember from Sister John Mark's class in grammar school, Raymond Anthony Neenan, I am the boss seraph" (13). Raymond soon learns that Michael, a comic figure, visible and audible only to those he chooses, wants to make a deal with him for his soul by informing him that he has only three months at the most to live. To persuade him, Michael touches him and he experiences an overwhelming ecstatic experience of love, which love Michael assures him he will lose if he loses his soul.

When Neenan signs the contract agreeing to follow Michael's instructions, he begins to hear the music of the angelic hosts, who are celebrating the occasion, and whose songs of joy he will continue to hear whenever he does something good. Once Neenan has signed the legal-looking document, Michael tells him the terms of the agreement—he is required to amend his life by attempting to reconcile with everyone that he has injured or alienated. As he tries to make amends with his former wife Donna, his parents, his children, business associates, and the many women with whom he has had extramarital affairs and whom he has treated merely as sex objects, the story of his life is revealed and his very soul is laid bare. Greeley offers insights into the human heart and traces the convolutions of Neenan's twisted psyche as he develops this character.

Neenan feels that he is falling apart, a feeling which intensifies as the encounters with Michael continue. Since only Neenan can see or hear Michael, the angel instructs him on what to say and do in his interchanges with others who are often startled by what Neenan says, since it is not in keeping with his character as they have known it in the past. Whenever Neenan tries to rebel, Michael taps the contract, insists that he do as told, and Neenan submits.

When Michael inquires about his wife of eight years, Neenan tells the angel that she is "not much" (52). Annoyed by this attitude, and categorizing Neenan as "perhaps the greatest all-time asshole of the Western world," he indignantly informs him that the angels arranged his marriage with Anna Maria, one of Greeley's typical Sicilian woman characters like Maria Manfredy in *Ascent into Hell* or Maria Lyons, the mother of Diana, in *Love Song* (52).

A warm, sensuous, passionate woman, deeply in love with God, Anna Maria laughed at the toughly worded prenuptial agreements that Neenan made her sign before he would marry her. Since Neenan had quit playing golf with her because she always beat him, one of the first things that Michael requires of Raymond is to take his wife to mass and then play golf with her, because his salvation depends on how he treats his wife.

Raymond, an agnostic who quit the practice of Catholicism some years past, does not yet realize that Anna Maria is a metaphor of God for him. However, upon his return home after his meeting with Michael, he can hear the singing of the angels as they begin to make love and he experiences a very moving limit experience at the same time.

Afterwards as Anna Maria sleeps peacefully in his arms, Michael appears to him and tells him that finally he is beginning to realize who his wife is and that he is doing well. Michael is turning a bad man into a good one with a licit love, exactly opposite from the way Mefistopheles turned Faust into an evil man with an illicit love. As he makes progress in trying to make up for his past neglect of his wife, he can hear the angelic choir humming their approval and Michael congratulates him on his improvement. The angel chorus sings an elegaic melody of new life and springtime when Anna Maria moves into his bedroom with him, and Ray has the most wonderful sex of his entire life at least once a day.

Michael prods Neenan into attempting reconciliation with all those in his life that are alienated from him. The first is Donna, the mother of his children, who refuses to forgive him when he apologizes for the failures of their marriage, which she had annulled, and blames him for the failings of their children, calling Anna Maria "a cheap dago whore" (99).

Realizing that he is a deeply flawed human being, Neenan grieves over his approaching death and the thought that his wife would be a widow before she is forty. He weeps for them both. As he grows closer to his wife and to God, the feelings of ecstasy come to him like hugs, but still Neenan feels he is falling apart. Rewriting his will to give his son Vincent control of the company, to provide a large trust fund for Anna Maria and smaller trusts for his children and his parents, to arrange gifts to charity and others, as well as money for chairs at Loyola Univeristy, Neenan hears Michael congratulate him for the good he is doing.

Clearer revelations about himself and insights about others brings Neenan to the realization that to avenge himself the women he had pursued were cruel and angry like his mother. Such soul searching is unusual in speculative fiction in which the story line is usually all important and character development nonexistent. For this reason Greeley's speculative fiction is unusual, for Neenan is changing and the author notes the changes as they occur.

When he discusses his new discoveries about himself with Michael, the angel tells him that his insights are good but not perfectly accurate, that he has more to discern. Neenan's soul is laid bare in his prayer which he begins by addressing "occupant or Occupant if You prefer" (229). Let's look at what he says.

You seem to want me to think that You touch me and I touch You through her [his wife]. If that is true, it is a very clever scheme and I certainly won't complain.

If You are really, the Third that explodes in my life through my wife, then You are not only the Other, but Something Else Altogether and I'm afraid of You and deeply in love with You. (162)

Later when Gaby—Gabriella Light of the story *Angel Fire*—appears to Neenan, their conversation about God is very enlightening. Even though her companion, the angel Lucifer, lost his life—angels have ethereal bodies and are subject to death—she is firmly convinced that she will see him again. She assures him that he, too, will see Anna Maria again in the next life because of the Other.

To reconcile with his parents who live in the expensive home he provides for them, Ray and Anna Maria, accompanied by Michael and Gaby, fly to Florida in Ray's private plane. Michael instructs Ray to forgive his parents, put aside his feelings of resentment, and be charming and gracious no matter what they say or do.

The scene at the home of Ray's father and mother is a dismal one. His mother denies that she has a son and his father insists that he is not Ray's father while accusing Ray of swindling him out of all his money and refusing to forgive him even to save his soul. Apparently in the last stages of Alzheimer's disease, Ray's mother wails disconsolately instead of fighting with her husband and son as she had always done in the past. Having done everything he can to insult Ray, the old man finally orders him to leave his house which Ray bought and paid for.

Controlling his anger, Ray kisses his mother and says good-bye to his dad. The angels are pleased at Ray's self-control and assure him that the man really is his father. The angels have done all they can for his parents; now they are "the Other's problem" (190). They assure Ray, "The Other dislikes losing even more than we do" (190).

The visit with his parents brings Ray more insights into his psyche, making him realize that he has been chasing women who were like his mother in order to take them all away from his father just as he wanted to take his mother away from him, because of their endless fighting.

Almost as if it were a reward for his self-control and growth, Ray has a beautiful limit experience with Anna Maria as they swim in the Gulf.

It was like a ride through a mind-bending computer game or an LSD trip, with which he had once experimented back in the sixties at the university.

Anna Maria and he were skipping over the water, almost skating on it. The angel choristers were singing psychedelic songs. Gaby and Michael were dancing with them.

Suddenly they plunge on dolphins' backs deep into the sea.

They breathed under the water without difficulty. Their plunge into the darkness had been a pleasant ride, not the battering and dangerous collision it ought to have been. This had to be some sort of dream, induced by seraphic dust or maybe a delayed effect of the Seraphic Vineyards Chianti. (203)

Together with the angels they dance over the seas and rivers of the world and finally return to the beach where it started. The next day when they discuss what happened, they decide that it must have been a dream.

Tremendous changes are taking place in Neenan. He has gone from being an agnostic to a man of virile faith. When Estelle Sloane tries to seduce him, Ray wins a great victory over himself, politely declining and begging her forgiveness for any injury he might have caused her in the past, he notes the cynicism in her eyes. When she breaks down, cries, and apologizes for trying to seduce him, he comforts her, saying that her husband is a special gift she should receive and treasure. As Ray helps the woman into her car, he feels great love for her, love without lust. To her comment, "I think you just saved my soul," Ray replies, "God and her angels do that" (217).

Gradually Ray becomes friends with his children. He attends mass daily at Old St. Patrick's Church. He even starts to worry that it might be possible to be too good. Suddenly his world seems to collapse when, for various little reasons, the people that he loves leave him. His wife moves out of the house and his son out of the firm. All seems lost when something highly unusual and very beautiful happens.

As he leaves Old St. Patrick's after his daily noon mass he spots a young woman sitting at the window in a Starbuck's coffee shop who motions for him to come in. She has black hair, olive skin, brown eyes, is very pretty, and looks like a young Palestinian. She is wearing a blue suit and a light blue blouse. As he sits down at the table, he knows who she is. He says to her, "They've sent in the first team" (259).

Ray feels he has entered an alternate reality, as the Mother of Jesus pours him tea, which is an impossibility because the Starbucks coffee shop doesn't sell tea. After she serves him the best tasting chocolate chip cookies he has ever eaten, Neenan thinks perhaps it is an illusion, a dream, or an hallucination, even though it seems very real. The scene that follows is beautifully and delicately drawn and needs to be read in its entirety to be truly appreciated. However, as the conversation with Miriam, as she instructs him to call her, is ending, she tells him that from time to time, she will send him cookies, which, she assures him, she makes herself, so that he will know that their conversation was real. She gently sings him a lullaby which he will hear in his head in the future and recognize and know that something very important happened between them. Most important, before they separate she tells him that everything will be all right for him.

Not long after his wife moves back in the house and his son returns to the firm, both of Ray's parents die. A week after his parents' funerals, Neenan drives his car into a scene in which gunmen are targeting each other and two young Mexican children are caught in the middle. Trying to rescue the children, Neenan is hit by a bullet just as he is putting the kids in his car. His death hour has arrived.

In an out of the body experience in the hospital intensive care unit, he sees Anna Maria and his children gathered around him. Michael and Gabriella are also there, as is Estelle, the woman who had tried to seduce him and failed, and her husband. Behind Anna Maria are two girls in their early teens that he does not recognize.

After hearing the pronouncement of his death, Neenan passes through a long tunnel to emerge in a radiant city where he recognizes people who had previously died. Everyone here is young and happy, including his parents looking like they did in their wedding picture. Both are grinning at him, as he thinks that perhaps now he will be able to straighten things out with them. Later he learns that purgatory is not a place, but an activity and that his parents are struggling through it. The tunnel ends at a sphere of light from which flow rivers of passionate love.

"Occupant," he whispered.

"Someone-Else-altogether. . . . Welcome, Raymond Anthony," a rich alto voice said with an amused laugh. "You never thought you would enter this place as a hero, even as a martyr, did you?"

"I'm not a martyr."

The Voice laughed again in gentle amusement.

"Perhaps not by the Church's definition, but here I make the rules."

The Voice was thunder, but tender thunder; roaring waves, but waves that touched the beach softly; wild waterfalls, but falls that also bubbled like a brook; screaming winds, but winds that were as slight as the first zephyr of spring.

"Are you really a woman?" he asked.

. . .

"Both men and women in your world are metaphors for me. In your case it seemed better to disclose at this time the womanly metaphor since so much of your life and your salvation has been related to women." (297)

There follows a beautiful conversation in which God reveals to Ray that s/he empathizes with all her/his beloved children and says, "I create because I love stories, especially love stories. Like all romantics I delight in happy endings." In this statement we can understand why Greeley calls the writing of stories his most priestly activity. In writing stories, he is imitating God who creates stories with human lives. He is a storyteller not unlike the Original Storyteller. He also favors happy endings and is a great romantic. And not unlike the Original Storyteller, he often writes straight with crooked lines.

Ray then learns that in time he will be reconciled with his parents. He also learns that he died too soon. The Voice of the Other explains:

Like all storytellers, you see, I am an empiricist, a pragmatist, I play it by ear as I tell my stories. Since I deprive no one of their freedom, my characters and the forces of nature in which they live may choose not to follow my most preferred scenario. Therefore I must fall back on other and less preferred scenarios. In the end I see that their freedom leads to my happy endings, but it often requires, how shall I say it, considerable dexterity on my part. (300)

Ray, when given the opportunity to return to Anna Maria, wishes to stay where he is, insisting that no one back on earth really needs him. The Voice speaks of the two teenaged women at his death bed. They are the twin daughters that Anna Maria conceived during the beautiful interlude they had on the beach in Florida. Because of love, Ray decides to return—God's love for him and his for God. Realizing that it would be pleasing to God for him to return to earth, he agrees.

When he returns it is Christmastime. Madonna love envelops the universe as he sees his wife's smiling, tear-stained face, knowing now ever more clearly that Anna Maria is a metaphor of God for him.

This story deals with themes and concerns that are very significant and quite serious, but the tone of the book is one of comedy. How has Greeley managed to make such topics humorous? The angels set the tone for the entire story. Their joyfulness and humor serve as a counterbalance to the serious problems that confront Raymond. From the very beginning when Michael introduces himself as "the boss seraph" (13), the humorous tone is established. Michael is good at whipping up out of thin air special alcoholic beverages that have the label "Seraphic Vineyards." When Gaby offers him some Seraphic Single Malt, Raymond sips it and coughs. "Seraphic Irish whisky, Neenan thought, might also be marketed as a cure for postnasal drip."

Much of the conversation between Ray and the angels is humorous. For example, to Ray's question "Do you, ah, screw?" Michael replies, "Naturally and to respond to your prurient questions before you ask them, it takes days. . . " (37).

The clothing that the angels wear and keep changing for every different occasion is really quite interesting and reflects their vanity and sense of humor. Michael appears in jeans and a crimson sport shirt at Ray's computer station. He materializes in Ray's car wearing designer jeans, a powder blue turtle neck, a tan windbreaker, and a jewel in his ear. At Ray's office Michael appears all in black. His black shirt sports a silver collar which goes well with his black and silver tie. His cuff links look like they have a flame inside them because they flicker on and off. It is especially amusing when Michael shows up in the men's locker room wearing purple undershorts. As he dresses, he pulls on purple socks, a knit purple shirt, and other purple garments, causing Ray to think of him as "the purple crusader" (210). Shortly afterward Gaby materializes wearing a purple outfit that matches Michael's. Gaby also likes white shorts and red halters and two-piece swim suits. As part of his knowledge of popular culture, Greeley is always able to dress his characters according to the fashions of the day.

In conclusion, *Contract with an Angel* contains Greeley's main literary themes. Ray Neenan is a resurrection person par excellent, since he literally returns from death. His wife, Anna Maria, is a metaphor of God for him. At the end of the book, they are united in a strong and happy marriage. The story holds a promise of hope. Once again, Greeley demonstrates that love prevails over hatred, and life triumphs over death in this divine comedy in which God plays an important role and brings about the happy ending. Greeley is to be applauded for his inspiring use of the genre.

There is a particular technique that Greeley employs in this story which should be mentioned. The French structuralist critic, Jean Bellemin-Noël has labeled this phantasmagorical technique *l'effet de mirroir,* or mirror effect ("Notes"19). By this designation, Bellemin-Noël signifies that a second story, in reduced proportions, is embedded in the narrative and reflects the main plot. The story of Patricia the Penny Planter is presented at the beginning of Chapter 7. This story reflects the plot of *Contract with an Angel.* Penny conducts a treasure hunt and in so doing reflects what God is like and how life is a hunt for the treasures God has placed in hiding for us to discover.

To conclude this chapter, with the writing of these four stories in the speculative fiction genre, Greeley reveals his virtuosity as an author. He skillfully employs the techniques of the fantastic with aplomb. Dreams, alternate universes, and altered mental states give rise to the creation of fantastic elements. Often the characters and even the reader must hesitate between deciding whether something supernatural takes place or not. This is in conformance with the literary theories of Tzetvan Todorov (37–38) and most of the other French critics who pioneered theorizing on the genre and see this element of hesitation as necessary to the fantastic.

Setting his fantastic stories firmly in everyday reality, as did E. T. A. Hoffmann, the first master of the genre, Greeley suddenly violates the basic ground rules of his narrative, as did Hoffmann, and spins the reader around about 180 degrees and presents her with some incredible event that causes the characters and perhaps the reader to hesitate between a natural or supernatural explanation. This is in keeping with the theory of Eric Rabkin who writes, "The fantastic is a quality of astonishment that we feel when the ground rules of a narrative world are suddenly made to turn about 180 degrees" (41).

The unexpected elements of the narrative add to its fantastic quality. Nobody would expect to find St. Michael the Archangel as a large black man wearing purple shorts in the men's locker room. These fantastic unexpected elements also contribute to the humor of stories.

As for Greeley's using the genre to probe the philosophical and theological issues of life, this is quite consistent with the theory of Roger C. Schlobin who defines the fantastic as "a mythopoetic force" which leads man into an examination of truth and of his own nature, and in an expansion of his frontiers, as it "confronts, materializes, and unifies the paradoxical, the ambiguous, and the non-effectable common to the human condition" (xx).

What is unusual about Greeley's use of the speculative genre is the way he adapts it to his purposes of showing character transformation. Sean Desmond, Toby Tobin, and Ray Neenan are not the same at the end of the story as they were at the beginning. They are all transformed, resurrection people who have gone from little or no faith to confidence in God's love and understanding of their place in the cosmos.

In addition to *l'effet de miroir*, or "mirror effect," Greeley employs, another special technique referred to by Bellemin-Noël as the *mis en abîme* or phantasmagorical effect ("Notes" 22). In the use of this technique, the fantastic narrative speaks of its own writing and of writing in general. In *God Game*, as was previously noted, Greeley makes frequent reference to the writing of the story itself and to the writing of other authors.

Finally, the speculative fiction in this chapter demonstrates that Greeley is a versatile author who is not limited to any one genre, but is able to master any genre he attempts. Of course, this does not come as a surprise to those who know Greeley and are aware that he is also a talented writer of detective fiction, poetry, and of discursive and analytical prose.[1]

NOTE

1. For further commentary on the fantastic see Allienne R. Becker, "Introduction" in *Visions of the Fantastic: Selected Essays from the Fifteenth International Conference on the Fantastic in the Arts*. Ed. Allienne R. Becker. Westport: Greenwood, 1996.

WORKS CITED

Bellemin-Noël, Jean. "Notes sur le fantastique (Textes de Théophile Gautier)," *Littérature* 8 (1972): 3–23.

Greeley, Andrew M. *Angel Fire*. New York: Warner, 1988.

———. *Angel Light*. New York: Tom Doherty, 1995.

———. *Contract with an Angel*. New York: Tom Doherty, 1998.

———. *God Game*. New York: Warner, 1986.

———. *The Myths of Religion*. New York: Warner, 1989.

———. *A Piece of My Mind . . . on Just about everything*. Garden City: Doubleday, 1983.

Immerwahr, Raymond. "Romantic Irony and Romantic Arabesque Prior to Romanticism," *German Quarterly* 42 (1969: 665–85.

The Jerusalem Bible. Garden City: Doubleday, 1966.

Kayser, Wolfgang. *The Grotesque in Art and Literature*. Trans. Ulrich Weisstein. Bloomington: Indiana UP, 1963.

Kierkegaard, Søren. *The Concept of Irony with Constant Reference to Socrates*. Trans. Lee M. Capel. London: Collins, 1966.

Richter, Jean Paul Friedrich. "Vorschule der Aesthetik," in *Werke*. Ed. Norbert Miller. Munich, Hanser, 1963).

Schlegel, Friedrich. *Kritische Schriften*. Munich: Hanser, 1964. (Translation mine).

Schlobin, Roger C. *The Literature of Fantasy: A Comprehensive, Annotated Bibliography of Modern Fantasy Fiction*. New York: Garland, 1979.

Scott, Sir Walter. "On the Supernatural in Fictitious Composition," in *Essays on Chivalry,*

Romance, and the Drama. London: Frederick Warne, 1887.

Todorov, Tzetvan. *Introduction à la littérature fantastique*. Paris: Editions du Seuil, 1970.

Walzel, Oskar. *German Romanticism*. Trans. Alma Elise Lussky. New York: Putnam, 1932.

Wellek, René. *Confrontations: Studies in the Intellectual and Literary Relations between Germany, England, and the United States during the Nineteenth Century*. Princeton: Princeton UP, 1965.

——. *A History of Modern Criticism, 1750–1950*. Vol 2. New Haven: Yale UP, 1955.

7

White Smoke

Theoretically *White Smoke* could be classified as speculative fiction, since in it Greeley depicts and analyzes the various forces, ideas, factions, and intrigues that exist in the Church today and extrapolates what will occur at the next papal conclave. However, since there is nothing fantastic—rationally inexplicable—in the book, and since Greeley does not use the conventions or the linguistic patterns of fantastic fiction—it would be inappropriate to classify the book as speculative fiction. Rather Greeley has created a new genre—the apocalyptic sociological novel—based on the idea of the sociological model. *White Smoke* is not a sociological model per se; the book does not contain the empirical data to support it as a model. It is rather a simulation. The book develops a theoretical perspective from which the various components working to elect a new pope, and often at war with one another in a struggle for power, might be viewed. The main factions delineated in the book are (1) the curia, which wants to keep its power; (2) conservative old-guard cardinals who wish to maintain the status quo but do not want to vote for the losing candidate; (3) cardinals who, in the spirit of Vatican II, believe in democracy and human rights and want to see decentralization of authority and pluralism augmented in the Church; (4) the authoritarian papacy, which is attempting to survive through the controversial activity of the various institutes that have flourished and have been strongly supported by the papacy during the pontificate of John Paul II; (5) the media and the worldwide attention it provides with the resulting pressure of public scrutiny being more powerful than at past conclaves due to increased technology. All of these groups have much to gain, or lose, in the coming election. The depiction of corrupt Italian journalists trying to shape the conclave is based on Greeley's observations at the second conclave of 1978.

White Smoke is apocalyptic in that it predicts the outcome of the next papal election. Interestingly, Cardinal Bernardin, archbishop of Cincinnati at the time, once introduced Greeley at the University of Dayton in 1976 as "a friend, a scholar, and a prophet" (*Confessions* 290). Greeley is on record as having predicted the outcome of both papal elections in 1978. By a process of sociological analysis using a computer decision-making program, which had been developed by James S. Coleman and applied by Coleman and Greeley to data collected by Jim Andrews, Greeley determined that Luciani would be elected. After the short reign of Luciani as Pope John Paul I, Greeley again applied the computer program to his data and determined that Wojtyla would be the one chosen.

Overarching the political aspects of the conclave in *White Smoke* is the love story of Dinny Mulloy, *New York Times* correspondent, who falls in love again with his wife, Patty, anchor for CNN; both of them represent the American media in Rome at the conclave. Being Americans from Chicago, they are supporters of their cardinal, Sean Cronin, who with his auxiliary, Bishop Blackie Ryan, stands firmly behind the candidacy of Luis Cardinal Menendez of Valencia in Spain, who is imbued with the spirit of Pope John XXIII. The love story of Dinny and Patty illustrates Greeley's religious and sociological thought on love and marriage, which we have already discussed at some length in previous chapters. Patty is also the target of a woman-hating psychopath who is bent on assassinating both the newly elected pope and her. By kidnaping Patty, a faction entangled in a new Vatican financial scandal intends to prevent Dinny, until after the new pope is elected, from submitting his column to the *New York Times* revealing their plot.

Most of the intrigue surrounding the coming papal election in *White Smoke* is attributed to Corpus Christi, a fictitious institute that wants to continue the authoritarian type of administration which has characterized the papacy of John Paul II. Greeley first introduced his readers to Corpus Christi in *The Cardinal Virtues* in the person of Father Louis Almaviva, the local superior of Corpus Christi and a modern Torquemada type who tries to get rid of Father Lar and take over St. Finian's parish.

Although Corpus Christi is a fictitious institute, there are in fact secular institutes in the Church today that are trying to take over the Church. Three of these institutes have a world membership of around thirty million adherents and count cardinals, bishops, and priests among their members, making them totally self-sufficient. They answer to no one. Anyone who is not familiar with them and their totalitarian approach to religion may consult *The Pope's Armada* by Gordon Urquhart, who was for nine years a leader in one of these institutes and was even editor of one of their official magazines. Urquhart has written a well-documented account of the secular institutes and gives an extensive bibliography for anyone wishing to pursue the study. He explains that they take the socialist's "cell" structure and combine it with their idea of the religious life. "But, above all, the movements share the socialist view of the individual's role in society: he or she has meaning only in terms of the collective, in the context of 'the history of the party' or 'history of the movement' " (360). According to Urquhart, these movements operate as cults which brainwash their members in order to control them. "The sloganeering and repetition practiced by the movements are devices borrowed from secular totalitarianism designed to effect changes in peoples lives" (434). The institutes have amassed great wealth from the contributions they require of their members. Urquhart who was under vows of poverty, chastity and obedience was required to give his entire wealth to the movement upon joining, but nothing was returned to him when he left. Patently the time when the members of these secular institutes are most visible is when they attend the World Youth Day celebrations and demonstrate their enthusiasm for the pope. One institute alone spent in excess of thirty million pounds sterling on World Youth Day in Denver 1993 (386). In *White Smoke* Corpus Christi, compared to the Unification Church of Sun Myung Moon, is shown to base its casuistry on what is for the good of their institute.

Corpus Christi members are not the only ones who engage in smoke and mirrors politics in *White Smoke*. "The vicious backbiting and defamation in the Vatican is known to anyone who has dealings with the Curia" (374). In view of the Michele Sindona financial mess a few decades ago, it is not hard to visualize the new money scandal that occurs during the scope of the novel. Humorously it is noted that St. Peter's Basilica itself is the product of still another financial scandal—the selling of indulgences to raise the money to build it in the sixteenth century.

Since *White Smoke* is an apocalyptic sociological novel, the question arises, What does the novel predict as the outcome of the next conclave? The answer quite simply is this: the cardinal electors will elect as pope the candidate who will reverse the uncompromising authoritarianism and legalism of the past two papacies. The new pope will recapture the enthusiasm for renewal that is the legacy of Vatican II, and which was curtailed by power hungry men in the Vatican.

Many of the council reforms have taken place and continue—the Mass in English, for example. But reform of the institutional structure itself, which the council called for, never occurred, because the proposed decentralization of power frightened Pope Paul VI.

In calling for a reform in the institutional structure of the Church, Greeley does not question any Catholic doctrine. He simply wants to change the style of insti - tutional leadership.

I question no Catholic doctrines in this story (and refute as false any charges that I do). Rather I question organizational style from the perspective of one who can claim to be an expert on that subject. I deny that criticism is either disloyal or disrespectful. On the contrary, to remain silent after my long years of studying the sociology of the Church as an organization would be disloyal.

In effect, I am arguing on grounds of sociological and organizational analysis the Church should return to the style of the late Pope John XXIII. (376)

White Smoke projects a change in the style of ecclesiastical leadership—a change from secrecy-obsessed authoritarianism to an open and decentralized pluralism in which true collegiality exists among the bishops.

Those who are ignorant of Church history imagine that the polity of the Church has always been as it is today. That is simply not true. We are a long way from Galilee. We have also come a long way from the undivided Universal Church which endured a thousand years before it split into the Latin Church in the West and the Greek or Orthodox Church in the East. In those days the Roman pontiff was known simply as the vicar of Peter. Furthermore, as the book explains, "For the first thousand years a papal decree was considered to be valid only when it was accepted by the whole Christian people" (69).

Pluralism, collegiality, and decentralization continue in the Eastern Orthodox Church today which is made up of autocephalous churches which have never deviated from teaching the orthodox faith as it comes down from the apostles; their sacraments are held to be valid by Rome. Hundreds of millions of Christians have lived and died in the Orthodox faith. Today the Orthodox estimate having about three hundred million members.

Tragically the Latin Church separated from the Greek Church on July 16, 1054, when Humbert of Silva Cardinal Candida and two other papal legates entered the ancient Church of the Holy Wisdom in Constantinople just as a service was about to begin. They made their way to the sanctuary and placed a Bull of Excommunication on the altar and swiftly departed. The patriarch of Constantinople, Michael Cerularius, a few days later excommunicated the pope, the patriarch of the West. Finally after nine hundred years, the mutual excommunications were rescinded by Pope Paul VI and Patriarch Athenagorus I on December 7, 1965.

After the separation of the Universal Church into East and West, the papacy, to exert power and dominion in western Europe, took on the characteristics of the emperors of the Holy Roman Empire. Perhaps the medieval trappings of monarchy were needed for the papacy to survive in a world of princes and emperors, but that world is gone. Nevertheless the papacy of the twentieth century has been marked by medieval absolutism.

The bishops of the world, even the conservative men that he [the previous pope] had appointed, found that instead of the freedom to govern their own dioceses as successors to the apostles, indeed in union with the pope, but mostly without his interference, they had become low-level civil servants under the constant supervision of the Roman Curia and their spies. The reform of the Vatican council, which implied more day-to-day power for the residential bishops, had not only been aborted. It had been reversed. The bishops have been subject to constant harassment. The pope and the Curia, it seemed, trusted their own appointees less than they trusted the writers of crank letters or spies from Corpus or the Opus Dei or other of such groups. The word "pluralism," which you will hear often during the next week, is the buzzword of bishops who would like to be left alone to run their own ship without constant interference from Rome. (66–67)

Furthermore, according to Blackie Ryan, the election of the pope in the earlier ages was a democratic process in that the parish priests of Rome chose one of their number and brought him forth to the balcony. If the waiting crowds cheered him, he was made pope; if they showed their displeasure, the cardinals would make a new selection.

In *White Smoke*, Luis Cardinal Menendez of Valencia in Spain, the favored candidate of Sean Cronin, expresses his belief in collegiality. Shortly before the voting takes place he explains very clearly how his new style of administration will work.

The pope must listen to his brother bishops, the bishops must listen to their brother priests, and the priests must listen to their people. Only when we are ready to admit the possibility that the Spirit speaks wherever She wishes to speak, and that therefore we must listen always and everywhere, will we be able to discern the work of the Spirit in the world. (140)

Menendez outlines his program in some detail. Striving for global justice, the Church will preach the truth by using a new style of communication that will seek to persuade, not to intimidate or compel. Isolation from the people will not be acceptable. A Church of love will replace the legalistic Church of the past two papacies. We must be ready to change. "We must not confuse what is essential in the Church with that which is mutable, no matter how ancient it may be" (141). Furthermore, the Church must not be regarded as an end in itself. "We have often seemed to worship not the Father in heaven but our own institutional being. We should not, my fellow Catholics, worship the Church. . . " (141). The Church must be seen merely as a means. "More important for us today, however, is the reaffirmation that we exist to preach a God of love, we try to be people of love, and we want our Church to be, insofar as we poor humans can make it, a Church of radiant love" (143).

White Smoke also has a few more projections concerning the next pontificate. The new pope who takes the name of John XXIV will not have a coronation but instead an inaugural. He will wear a Roman collar and a black suit, reserving white robes for liturgical events. He will work for the elimination of secrecy in Church affairs and to straighten out Vatican finances. He will invite the arch-bishop of Canterbury and the patriarchs of Constantinople and Moscow to visit him as soon as is convenient for them, promising that he will make return visits to them. He also will update and simplify papal elections. And finally, since all the other bishops are required to retire at seventy-five, he will do likewise.

In this apocalyptic sociological novel, Greeley as a sociologist, projects a new model for Church administration—one that is characterized by openness, truth, freedom, and respect for the individual. The curia will work for the residential bishops instead of the bishops working for the curia. Major decisions will be made only in consultation with the bishops. "Thus unilateral decisions like the late pope's letter on the ordination of women would be rare—if they happened at all" (29). Bishops will have the freedom to administer their local affairs without constant intervention from Rome. It will be a Church in which the local bishop will represent his priests and people to the universal Church. Priests will be encouraged to use the talents God has given them, rather that to be forced into lives of mediocrity by clerical envy and repression. It will be a Church in which the opinions of the laity are heard and valued since they too are chosen vessels of the Holy Spirit. According to the Catholic teaching that Greeley received in the seminary, "the learning church (the laity and their experience) is as infallible as the teaching church (the pope and the bishops); that the Catholic people cannot make a mistake in their belief and practice any more than the official authority; and the 'sense of the faithful' is a proper place to discover sound Catholic doctrine" (*Making of the Popes* 47.) Above all else, the new Church will be a Church of love.

White Smoke is more than a prophecy of what the Church of the future will be, it is also a comedy. When he observed the conclaves in 1978, Greeley wrote, "The best way to treat this whole show is as comedy" (*Making of the Popes* 36). And treat it as comedy, he does, by making *White Smoke* a love story and an adventure tale with a happy ending. Dinny Mulloy and his wife Patty are separated at the beginning of the novel, having decided that their marriage just cannot work. In the course of the conclave which they are covering for the *New York Times* and CNN, respectively, they fall in love again and rekindle their marriage. Dinny, who is an agnostic and a nonpracticing Catholic at the beginning of the story, returns to the practice of his religion when he reestablishes his relationship with his wife, who, like all Greeley heroines, is a metaphor of God for him. The two of them get caught up in the adventure of the Vatican banking scandals, when some of the players in the affair kidnap Patty to keep her husband from reporting the information he has collected on them to the *New York Times*. Patty's rescue makes for exciting reading and is a typical Greeley adventure. Despite the seriousness of the conclave and the banking scandal, much good Greeley humor pervades the entire story. The happy ending for the Church and for Dinny and Patty, makes an enjoyable experience for the reader.

White Smoke is a well-plotted novel by an author who writes convincingly about the coming papal conclave and election. Having attended two conclaves in 1978 as the head of a task force covering the elections for Universal Press Syndicate, Greeley is very familiar with what goes on behind the scenes in the corridors of power in the Vatican. For his nonfiction work *The Making of the Popes 1978: The Politics of Intrigue in the Vatican*, he interviewed a tremendous number of men involved in the conclaves. One of his sources was the anonymous "Deep Crimson" who provided him with a great amount of valuable information. Much of the factual information in *White Smoke* is based on Greeley's experiences in Rome before, during, and after the 1978 conclaves and is drawn from the large numbers of audio tapes and notes that he made then. Patently, it will be very interesting to see what the future holds at the next conclave and how it compares with Greeley's projections in *White Smoke*.

WORKS CITED

Greeley, Andrew M. *The Cardinal Virtues*. New York: Warner, 1990.

———. *Confessions of a Parish Priest: An Autobiography.* Simon and Schuster, 1986.
———. *Making of the Popes 1978: The Politics of Intrigue in the Vatican.* Kansas City: Andrews and McMeel, 1978.
———. *White Smoke.* New York: Tom Doherty, 1994.
Urquhart, Gordon. *The Pope's Armada.* London: Corgi, 1996.

8

Star Bright! and Other Short Fiction

Andrew Greeley has a special love for Christmas. In December his apartment abounds in lights, ornaments, crib scenes, Santas, and piles of Christmas presents ready to be given to others. In his meditations on Christmas we read, "The light penetrates the darkness and the darkness cannot put it out. The warmth breaks through into the cold and the cold cannot dim its fire. Love fractures death and death cannot be put back together again" (*Year of Grace* 170).

In *Star Bright!* Greeley has touched upon the deepest experiences all of us have had of Christmas and confirms our deepest hopes. In this beautiful Christmas story, he has given us new perspectives and shattered some of our old ones. Tatiana Alekseevna Shuskulya, a joyous Russian girl, brings the wonder and mystery of Christmas to the Flanigan family of Chicago. She is one of the most superb metaphors of God that Greeley has ever portrayed.

In the prelude to the story, Tatiana recounts an ancient legend of Russia about the twelve wise men that find Mary, Joseph, and the Holy Child on one of their special visits back to earth on Christmas night. According to Tatiana, when people of faith find and enter the cave where the Holy Family rests, something truly astonishing happens. "They see that the face of the Child is their own face" (9). This Russian mystical vision of Christmas is a leitmotiv of *Star Bright!* One must find one's self in Christ to know the true joys and glory of Christmas.

Tatiana is a mystic in the Russian tradition. Ablaze with the love of God, she brings faith and joy to everyone she encounters. Although both of her grandfathers were secret priests in the Orthodox Church and they celebrated the Divine Liturgy of St. John Chrysostom in their homes, it was not until Easter of 1989 after the fall of communism that her soul experienced the torrent of God's love for the first time. Now everything she does is suffused with grace which flows from her to all she encounters.

When Jack Flanigan first meets Tatiana at Harvard University, where she is a student and works at the Russian Center, he quickly learns that she is a mystic. He is surprised that she is not planning to enter a monastery, but is thinking of marriage. Since many Russian mystics are married, she thinks it is natural to marry since, as she explains, "God considers a spouse to be an ally rather than a rival" (52). When Jack asks her if sex "gets in the way of God"(55), she expands on her tradition's views on sexuality. "Anything can get in the way of God, greed, lust, envy, pride. But sexual love, if it's really love tells us what God is like. God, you see, is an aroused lover. All the time. Also a very patient lover with a wonderful sense of humor, as you Americans would say" (55–56).

Jack soon learns more about her Orthodox faith when she invites him to her apartment to celebrate her twenty-first birthday. To his surprise she has other guests: Peter, an Orthodox priest from St. Vladimir's Church, Annah, his wife, and Tim O'Brien, an Irish American priest from St. Paul's Catholic Church. Tatiana attends services at both their parishes and feels that the separation between the churches is "absurd" (20). Jack agrees. Obviously Greeley is of the same opinion. With gentleness and love, instead of the vitriolic satire he employs in other stories when he is striving to make changes in the status quo, Greeley hopes to help heal the breach.

Since July 16, 1054, when the Church split into East and West, there has never been any question as to the validity of the sacraments, there has only been an outward division. The Church in the East developed in a more mystical tradition than the Church in the West which has always been preoccupied with a legalistic approach to the faith. One of the main differences between East and West is that in the Orthodox Church married men are ordained priests. Priests are not allowed to marry. If a man wants to be ordained, he marries first and then is ordained a priest. If his wife dies, he cannot marry again, because priests do not marry. Married men are not consecrated bishops. All bishops are celibate and recruited from the monasteries. If a priest's wife dies, the priest can, if he wishes and only if he wises, enter a monastery. Otherwise he will continue in a parish as a celibate priest. If he chooses to enter a monastery, he can then later on be consecrated a bishop, if he meets the other criteria for the office.

One of the great obstacles to reuniting the Orthodox with the Catholic Church is over enforced celibacy of the clergy. The Orthodox also differ from Rome on the question of birth control. For the Orthodox, any form of birth control is permissible provided it does not harm an unborn child once it is conceived.

Pope John Paul II has been making a concerted effort to reunite Eastern Orthodoxy and the Church of Rome. On May 25, 1995, he promulgated a major encyclical titled *Ut Unum Sint* (*That They May Be One*), which seeks to encourage the efforts of all who work for the cause of unity (Intro 3). A large section of Chapter 2 of this encyclical is devoted specifically to bringing the Eastern Orthodox Churches and the Catholic Church, referred to throughout history and in this document as "Sister Churches," into full communion with each other.

In *Star Bright!* the beauty of Orthodox Christianity shines forth from the soul of Tatiana who is "a day star" for the Flanigan family when Jack takes her home to Chicago for Christmas. Her beautiful and simple way of speaking of God on all occasions surprises Jack and his family who are accustomed, as good Irish Catholics, to speak of God "only at wakes and then cautiously" (54). The Flanigan family, described by Jack as a "dysfunctional bunch" is touched by the spiritual beauty of Tatiana. Even Jack's father, an eminent and very arrogant Chicago surgeon, says that he thinks they could learn a lot from the Orthodox. The entire family is receptive to the charming Tatiana as she bakes Russian Christmas treats and serves them Russian tea in an elaborate ritual from her samovar. Peace descends on the entire family as they open their hearts to Tatiana and the love of God that flows from her joyful heart. They are all astounded when Tatiana, speaking of Christmas, tells them, "In my country husbands and wives say their best lovemaking comes on this holy night. They give themselves to each other with abandon in imitation of Jesus who empties himself totally for humankind, even though he was God, becoming like us in all things, save sin alone" (106). When one of the surprised members of the family asks "The church approves of this?" she replies, "The Church says nothing. Even the priests are married. How could the Church criticize the fullness of human love?" (106).

Obviously all the difficulties and problems of the Flanigans are not suddenly over, but they have experienced Grace. Their encounter with Tatiana has opened their hearts to further growth in God's love. Hopefully those of the West who read *Star Bright!* will open their hearts to the Orthodox and do what they can to speed reunion with them, for, no doubt, this is what this parable of grace suggests.

The future looks indeed bright for the entire family because they want Jack to bring Tatiana, their Christmas angel, to them every Christmas. The story ends with Jack saying: "With the grace of God and a little bit of luck and care with my loud mouth, I would have my own personal bright day star for the rest of my life" (126). Here we have the main elements of a comedy—a young couple in love and on the way to union in marriage.

Star Bright! is an exceedingly beautiful Christmas story. The lovely Tatiana conveys the real meaning of Christmas to the reader. The wonder of Christ's birth as reflected in the soul of this young woman glows throughout all the pages of this short book. Of all the stories of the Catholic faith, the Christmas story is the one that most stirs the religious imagination. In *Star Bright!*, Greeley has created a story that will take its place beside classics like Dicken's *Christmas Carol*. It is a story to be treasured and reread every Christmas. With the Flanigans we all say, "Bring Tatiana back to us again next year!" (At the present time Greeley is writing the libretto for an opera based on *Star Bright!* It will be produced in Chicago.)

Christmas is important to Greeley. He writes about it often in his fiction. Christmas music, "Silent Night" and *Adeste Fideles*, sanctuaries overflowing with poinsettias, midnight mass, the manger scene with Mary and the baby, trees shimmering with lights, tall candles, altar boys in red and white, and the wonder in children's eyes—all tell of the birth of Jesus and of his Mother Mary. God's love is incarnate in the crib scene in a way that is so moving that Greeley says "I believe that is the ultimate symbol of what the universe is all about" (*Love Affair*

66). It shows us that God loves us like a mother loves her little baby. Catholic devotion to the Mother of Jesus is at the heart of Catholicism. As Greeley says: "There is no better manifestation of the Catholic imagination than devotion to the Mother of Jesus' (*Catholic Myth* 62). Mary is the transparency through which we see God.

Greeley has several Christmas stories and one about the Mother of Jesus in his collection of short fiction entitled *All about Women.* The title signifies that all the stories are about women and not that the author is going to tell the reader all there is to know about women. Many of the stories in this collection are either the kernels from which novels sprouted or excerpts from Greeley's novels. For example, the story "Lisa" recounts Lisa Malone's visit home for Christmas 1970. Readers of Greeley's detective fiction will recognize the story as being very similar to Chapter 2 of *Happy Are the Clean of Heart.* There is also the 1947 Christmas story of a teenaged Mike Casey and his parents titled "Marge," which was published in *Ladies' Home Journal* in December 1984 as "A handful of Tinsel." Mike Casey relates this story at a time in his life after his wife died, leaving him with three children and three grandchildren; he has not yet found Annie Reilly. There are stories in the collection about Andrea, Cindasoo, and even Martina. "Martina," published in *The Literary Review: An International Journal of Contemporary Writing* in the spring of 1988 is almost the same as Chapter 4 of *The Cardinal Virtues,* which was published in 1990. Some of the women characters in the short fiction, such as April and Rosemarie, have yet to have their full stories published in the novels of the *O'Malley Saga,* which will be the subject of our next chapter, therefore let us turn our attention toward a jewel that is not related to the author's novels.

"Ms. Carpenter," first published in *U.S. Catholic* recounts how Ms. Mary Carpenter, a teenager with an olive complexion and dark hair and eyes, keeps a scheduled appointment with an archbishop to request a favor of him. He does not recognize the young woman smartly dressed in a gray suit and wearing a plaid scarf, until she bows and kisses his ring.

Greeley presents the reader with a portrait of the Mother of Jesus that is completely opposite from that of tradition. His Mary is not the lady dressed in blue with the saccharine smile on her face and who appears to children requesting churches to be built. She is a strong vital woman true to her ethnic origins—a mother whose love is ready to do what is necessary for the welfare of her children. The fact that she gives her name to the archbishop's secretary as "Ms. Carpenter," instead of Mrs. Carpenter, tells us a lot about her right from the start. She has an impish smile and laughing eyes and seems to be enjoying the game she is playing with the prelate and is obviously amused by him. When he asks what title she would like him to use in addressing her, she replies laughingly that she has quite a few but she thinks that "Ms. Carpenter" would be "fun," though she says he can address her as "Mary," if it doesn't "scare" him too much. To recover his balance, he immediately gets down to business and asks her what she wants of him. "A favor, Archbishop. What else have I ever wanted?" When he asks her if she wants a church to be built she replies, "Come now, Your Grace, you and I really ought to be beyond that sort of thing. Besides, they have already built one for me here in this country" (331). The archbishop is surprised by the "hoydenish quality" about her. Playfully she pursues the conversation while he presses to learn what it is she wants. "So businesslike—just when we were having such a nice conversation. Well, you don't need to look all that serious and solemn. I won't affect your budget at all." She was now a pretty fishwife in a marketplace, promising him a bargain. O Lord, he was in trouble. . . "(332).

These remarks make him believe she is reading his mind, which she denies, commenting that she is a shrewd bargainer and true to her ethnic origins. With the confidence of an accomplished negotiator, she asks him not to close down a certain convent in which there are only three old nuns and a single postulant, even though Rome is suppressing the entire congregation, because they have fewer than twenty members worldwide. When he protests by citing his orders from Rome, she tells him to ignore them, that she is accustomed to making up the rules as she goes along. When he tells her that her comment sounds seditious, she winks impishly at him and replies with much enjoyment that she is sure he won't tell on her. When he says she will have to go through channels and that he will arrange a meeting for her with the chairman of the priests' senate, she protests that they think she belongs "in a medieval monastery" (334). When he positively refuses to keep the convent open, she gets angry, stamps her feet impatiently and asks, "Why don't you wake up before you waste your whole life?"

Shock and dismay must have begun to show on his face. She smiled faintly.

"You're scandalized because I'm angry. I'm not supposed to get angry, right? Just a plaster statue to light candles for?"

"I'm a little surprised, " he mumbled.

"Sure, I should not have any human emotions at all, no strong feelings, no concern; you want to make me the kind of person who would be a good archbishop?"(335).

She explains to him that she would not have been given her job if she did not have powerful feelings. Finally, he capitulates completely and gives her what she wants. With more amusing and playful conversation she bows and kisses his ring and leaves. The humor is delightful in this comedic scene.

For this beautiful, realist, and untraditional portrait of Mary, the Mother of Jesus, Greeley won the Catholic Press Association award for the best short story of 1978.

"Ms. Carpenter"and *Star Bright!* reveal still another dimension of Greeley's versatility as a writer. Both stories have a luminous and numinous quality with many touches of comedy in them.

WORKS CITED

Greeley, Andrew M. *All about Women.* New York: TOR, 1990.

———. *The Catholic Myth*: *The Behavior and Beliefs of American Catholics.* New York: Scribners, 1990.

———. *Love Affair: A Prayer Journal.* New York: Crossroad, 1992.

———. *Star Bright! A Christmas Story.* New York: Doherty, 1997.

———. *Year of Grace: A Spiritual Journey.* Chicago: Thomas More Press, 1990.

John Paul II. *Ut Unum Sint.* *<http://vatican.va/holy_father/john_paul_ii/encyclicals>* May 25, 1995.

9

The O'Malley Saga

With the publication of *A Midwinter's Tale* in 1998, Greeley launched the first volume of *The O'Malley Saga* with two more novels of the *Saga* already written and awaiting revision before going to the publisher. The stories of the O'Malleys will no doubt extend through many more novels which are as yet only dreams in the mind of the author. For those unfamiliar with the term *saga* for a twentieth-century literary work, a word of explanation is in order. Originally the term was applied to the Old Norse stories of Icelandic heroes, which were told by word of mouth long before being put into written form. Nowadays, the term *saga* simply denotes a long narrative. The term *saga novel* can also be used. John Galsworthy used the term *saga* in conjunction with a series of five previously published novels which he published together in 1922 under the title of *The Forsyte Saga*. Three more volumes of Galsworthy's story continued in *A Modern Comedy* published in 1929. The final Forsyte novels were published after the death of the author in *End of the Chapter* (1934). Greeley's *O'Malley Saga* resembles Galsworthy's in that both trace the ups and downs of an upper-middle-class family and the society in which they live.

A better term for such long fictional narratives is perhaps *roman fleuve*, a term coined by Romain Rolland for his masterpiece *Jean-Christophe* comprising ten independent narratives. *Jean Christophe*, which led to Rolland's being awarded the Nobel Prize for Literature in 1915, is the story of Jean-Christophe Krafft, a musician, and those surrounding him. Another example of the *roman fleuve* is *A la recherche du temps perdu* by Marcel Proust to which Greeley alludes in the first chapter of his *Saga*. Proust's work comprises *Du côté de chez Swann* (1913), *A l'ombre des jeunes filles en fleur* (1919) *Le côté de Guermantes* I (1920), *Le côté de Guermantes II—Sodome et Gomorrhe* I (1921), and finally *Sodome et Gomorrhe II* (1922). After Proust's death, a number of novels which he had written for the *roman fleuve*, but had not yet revised, were published by his brother— *La Prisonnière* (1923), *Albertine disparue* (1925), and *Le Temps retrouvé* (1927). Similarly William Faulkner's Compson novels are examples of the *roman fleuve*.

The *roman fleuve* flows like a river for which it is named. Sometimes it meanders slowly; at other times it rushes forward on its course. Into it flow various plot streams and it often has many branching tributaries. Usually covering several generations of a family, the *roman fleuve* presents a vast picture of society and its mores. The Irish American family of Charles O'Malley binds together the various volumes of the *O'Malley Saga,* which begins with the story of young Chuck and then, in flashbacks, tells the story of his parents and others of their generation. The second volume is *Younger Than Springtime* (1999)and third, *Christmas Wedding* (2000).

The opening novel of *The O'Malley Saga, A Midwinter's Tale* (1998), bears a title which indicates that the story is a sad one, since, traditionally, winter tales are sorrowful. The book relates the events in the winter of Charles O'Malley's life when he was stationed in the military in Germany just after the end of World War II. Constant references to the cold and winter continue throughout the narrative.

The prologue also establishes what is to be the main element in the story plot. Chuck, in the First Constabulary Regiment, has assigned to him the task of rounding up a family of Nazis which is to be turned over to the Russians who want them as war criminals. When he finds the family—the father is already dead—Chuck falls in love with Trudi, one of the daughters, and decides that instead of turning them over to the Russians who will gang rape Trudi, her sister and their mother, he will arrange for them to escape into the freedom of the French zone of occupied Germany.

The love story of Trudi and Chuck is tender. Intending to marry her and bring her home to Chicago when his military term is completed, Chuck gives himself completely to her. As the book ends, Trudi and her family vanish into safety in Stuttgart, but the possibility that she is pregnant with Chuck's child lurks in the mind of the reader.

The novel is, in spite of its sadness, a comedy and Chuck is a comic character. The references to comedy in the book are many. In the first chapter, which flashes back to Chuck's childhood, he describes his parents as living *commedia dell'arte* and delineates the masks they assumed. This, of course, refers to the improvised comedy of the family's daily life, since in the *commedia dell'arte*, the dialogue is improvised in the skits of domestic life in which the characters wear masks to depict their roles. Chuck elaborates on his family's version of *commedia dell'arte* by saying that Jane, his thirteen-year-old year old sister knows "the lines in our improvised comedy," which she feeds to the other actors while Chuck plays the straight man and their sister Peg and her girlfriend Rosie Clancy are the audience who laugh at "the crazy O'Malleys" (40).

While he is still quite young, Chuck concludes that his life will be a "comedy of errors" (49–50, 54) Throughout the narrative he constantly denigrates himself. In school, he is the class clown, a small guy with scraggy red hair that resembles a wire brush. The kind of buffoonery that characterizes his life begins with the May crowning when Rosie Clancy who, when trying to crown the statue of the Mother of Jesus, falls off the wobbly ladder on top of Chuck who is trying to photograph the event and puts the crown on his head instead. The first of the major errors which make his life a comedy occurs when he receives an athletic scholarship to play football for his high school, simply because a congressman has the mistaken idea that Chuck is a good player, when actually all he does for the team is hold the ball for kickoffs. The comedy of errors continues when Chuck is actually forced to play football and bumbles his way into making the winning touchdown for the championship.

When he rescues Rosie Clancy from drowning in the lake in the middle of winter, Chuck becomes a hero for the second time that year. Some great hero! As he strides from the pier after the rescue, he trips and falls—a comic figure at whom the reader laughs.

While in Germany and while wearing the elaborate uniform assigned to the men of the Constabulary Regiment, Chuck and his "comic opera soldiers" break into a house of supposed Nazis to recover a cache of weapons while *Life* magazine photographers accompany them to get photos of "fanatical neo-Nazis" (146). After blundering into the home of some poor Germans, they find "only five terrified human beings" (146) and some nonoperational weapons and worthless ammunition. Nevertheless, *Life* publishes on its cover a photo of Chuck "standing triumphantly over a half dozen unworkable *Wehrmacht* rifles" with the frightened German civilians standing with their backs to the wall in terror (148). With one blunder following another, Chuck even describes the loss of his virginity to the German girl Trudi as one of the errors of his comedy. While dealing with some Russian black marketeers, he manages to fall flat on his face. When he picks up Trudi and her family to drive them to safety, he forgets to put gas in the car. Instead of a knight in shining armor, as he pictures himself, Chuck is a constant fumbler. Not only does he not know how to fix his flat tire, he even breaks the jack. After finally delivering Trudi and her family to Stuttgart, he has a horrible foggy drive back to Bamberg, causing him to vomit on the dashboard of the car. "Dear God, what a rotten hero I was" (412).

Later, when Chuck is instrumental in smashing the black market ring that some Americans are running by stealing the things they sell from the United States government, he blunders again. His flashlight won't work—dead batteries—and to top things off, he loses the key to his car in the dark and has to spend the night in the forest. Nevertheless, the black market people are rounded up and receive their due punishments and Chuck receives another stripe on his arm and a medal.

As the reader has come to expect, Greeley takes some satiric punches at the Catholic Church in the novel. Monsignor Meany, who lives up to his name, bears the brunt of Greeley's satire. He died after drinking his third Scotch to celebrate the death of Roosevelt.

As usual the nuns also are satirized. The mother superior in Meany's school was Sister Mary Admirabilis, nicknamed Sister Mary War Admiral by Chuck, who has to accompany his mother to the convent to discuss some school matters. Chuck writes humorously of the occasion, "The convent cookies and fudge—reserved for visitors of special importance—were beyond reproach. I will confess, however, that I was the one responsible for the story that, when the lemonade had been sent to a chemist for analysis, he had reported with great regret that our poor horse was dying of incurable kidney disease" (80).

The Roman clergy also feel the sting of Greeley's reproach. When Chuck spends Christmas in Rome he learns that "beneath the splendor and pomp of papal ceremonies there is hypocrisy and unbelief" (465). After returning home to Chicago and relating his experiences in Rome to his priest, Father John Raven at St. Ursula's comments: "Consider that Rome . . . is a proof that God protects Catholicism with Her special love. . . . We have been able to survive the corruption and the idiocy of the Romans" (365).

In this first book of his *O'Malley Saga*, Greeley introduces characters which will appear in subsequent volumes. The reader encounters Chuck's parents Vangie a.k.a. John the Evangelist O'Malley and April Cronin O'Malley as well as his siblings—Jane, Peg, and Michael. Jim Clancy, friend of the family, and his wife Clarice Powers Clancy, and daughter Rosemarie, among others, make their first appearances in the saga in this novel.

In a boating sequence with the children of the two families, Jim Clancy is shown to be a despicable character. The mysterious death of his wife, mentioned in passing in *A Midwinter's Tale,* will assume an important place in a subsequent novel as will the mean character of Jim Clancy. Rosie, to whom Chuck gave his first kiss, is depicted as having dark and painful secrets; Chuck becomes aware of this when he finds her in the church sobbing one night and again when she falls into the lake because of drinking too much alcohol. These are the threads of which subsequent stories will be woven.

A Midwinter's Tale is a bittersweet and often ironic comedy which does not end in the marriage of the two lovers Chuck and Trudi. It is a novel of beginnings which, though complete in itself, bears the promise of more stories to come. The novel is written against the backdrop of the great depression during the early years of the marriage of Chuck's parents; it includes Chuck's experiences at St. Ursula's growing up with Rosie Clancy, his military experiences, his return home to find that his parents are prosperous, and his growing understanding that his family is able to revert to the standard of living they had known before the depression. As usual Greeley the sociologist accurately portrays the society in which Chuck lives at each stage of his young life, giving a tinge of nostalgia to the book for those who have lived through the period of time covered in this story. The characters even use the slang that was popular in those days. Generously sprinkled with Greeley's humor, the novel is a joy to read, despite the fact that it is a winter's tale.

When someone in *A Midwinter's Tale* asks Chuck if Rosemarie Clancy is a young woman, he immediately replies, "Younger than springtime and older than the mountains" (211). Since Chuck identifies Rosie with this once popular song, it is very appropriate that *Younger Than Springtime* is the title of the second volume of *The O'Malley Saga*, since it deals primarily with Chuck's relationship with her, from the time he returns home after his tour of military duty in Germany up until he decides he wants to marry her. Embedded in this narrative is a second narrative, purportedly written by Chuck's father John O'Malley to help Chuck to understand Rosie better, by relating details about the friendships of John and April Cronin O'Malley with Jim Clancy and Clarice Powers Clancy during the days of their courtships.

In John's narrative, Jim Clancy is shown to be a miserable, perverse and despicable person. Extremely selfish, he has never really grown up and uses and abuses everyone he meets, trying afterward to make things right by using his wealth to placate them. A practical joker, he perpetrates cruel tricks on his friends. Clarice, the woman Clancy marries, drinks herself into a stupor and has to be put to bed by April. It is to be remembered that she died as the result of a fall down the stairs in her home when she was inebriated. Since mystery surrounds her death, the reader begins to wonder if it really was an accident.

In addition to developing the characters Jim and Clarice, John's narrative shows how Clancy wanted to marry April and never forgave John for winning her for his bride. Just as Clancy is the enemy in the courtship of John and April, he is also recognized as the enemy in the courtship of Chuck and Rosie. The third volume of *The O'Malley Saga* will expand and elaborate on the evil deeds of Jim Clancy and the suffering he causes many people.

Younger Than Springtime unfolds the character of Rosie Clancy, a beautiful vivacious young woman with a tragic flaw. When she is only eighteen years old, she is already on the way to becoming an alcoholic. Her family life with Jim and Clarice Clancy was so dismal that from her childhood she has made the O'Malley family hers. She is treated as a favorite child by John and April and their children regard her as a sister. Extremely astute and preceptive, Rosemarie does many things to make the life of the O'Malleys better. She leads Chuck, who wants to be an accountant, into being a photographer. She helps to mend family relationships so tactfully that no one notices she has done anything. Each member of the O'Malley family benefits from the relationship Rosie has with the O'Malleys. As the book ends, Rosie brings joy to the whole family at Christmas with her love and thoughtfulness.

Younger Than Springtime contains in Chapter 5, one of Greeley's grand comic scenes. Cordelia Lennon, a girl Chuck is dating while at Notre Dame, hopes to be a concert musician, but it is obvious to Chuck that she has no real talent, having acquired only well-practiced techniques. When Cordelia gives a concert performance at the rectory of Monsignor Sullivan in Lake Forest, everyone including the monsignor, his curates, Cordelia's parents, her Jesuit brother, and two Lake Forest couples pretend to be listening to a female Paderewksi. Only Chuck and Martin, an elderly Jesuit from England, recognize Cordelia's utter lack of talent. The colorful character descriptions and the pompous and phony elegant atmosphere of the monsignor's rectory are comic as is the situation. The scene is the kind of comedy readers have come to expect in a Greeley story. Embedded in the scene is Martin's explanation of love as the desire to be possessed totally by the one we love. The old Jesuit, a fascinating character based on the person of Martin Darcy, is actually presenting Darcy's ideas on love.

As the novel ends, one assumes that Chuck will marry Rosie but that there will be many problems that will confront them, because of her horrible father and her drinking. The reader looks forward avidly to the next novel to find out what happens to these memorable characters.

The third volume of *The O'Malley Saga, Christmas Wedding,* forthcoming from Tom Doherty, relates the doubts that Charles O'Malley experiences because of Rosemarie Clancy's drinking as his marriage to her draws near. When she confides in him, shortly before the wedding, that her father, Jim Clancy, had raped her and repeatedly forced her to have sex with him, Chuck feels that their marriage is doomed to failure. Since, he decides, it is too late to back out, he nevertheless goes forward with their marriage plans, feeling that he is trapped and cannot escape. *Christmas Wedding* is the story of the first ten years of the marriage of Chuck and Rosemarie O'Malley. The novel details the difficulties Chuck and Rosie experience because of her bouts with drunkenness, no doubt induced by the sufferings she endured because of her parents, especially Jim Clancy, whose revenge reaches from beyond the grave to torture his daughter and her husband. It also shows how Chuck truly falls in love with his wife and becomes determined to save her. More of the plot than this should not be disclosed before the book is even published. To reveal more—well, as Greeley would say, that would be telling, wouldn't it now?

Incest, alcoholism, murder, and psychological problems—all elements of Christmas Wedding —are very serious issues. Nevertheless, the book is a comedy. Chuck O'Malley, who narrates the story, constantly compares his marital life to the improvisations of the *commedia dell'arte* with him as Pierrot, his wife as Columbine, and Jim Clancy as Harlequin. The comedy of errors that began when he was a child continues with his life taking strange and unexpected turns which often seem to him like the wrong path to follow. Of course, the novel has a happy ending, as do all Greeley's comedies. The final line of the story is "*La commedia non e finita.*" The comedy is not finished. There will be, no doubt, many more volumes to come. The three volumes so far written hint at future events. The third volume, the most highly developed of the series to date, indicates that the subsequent novels will no doubt be some of Greeley's best.

In keeping with Greeley's having his characters reappear in many novels so that he, in effect, like Balzac, creates an entire society, Blackie Ryan appears in *The O'Malley Saga* in several veiled references pertaining to Chuck's life at the time of the writing of the books. The main characters Leo Kelly and Jane Devlin from *Summer at the Lake* make a brief appearance in *Christmas Wedding.* This is not surprising because Leo Kelly relates in *Summer at the Lake* that Chuck O'Malley and he and Jane went to school together. He also remarks that Chuck has become "one of the most famous photographers in the world" (66). It is also from Rosie that Patrick learns in 1977 that Leo is returning to Chicago to be provost of the university (*Summer* 292).

WORKS CITED

Greeley, Andrew M. *Christmas Wedding.* New York: Tom Doherty, 2000.

———. *A Midwinter's Tale.* New York: Tom Doherty, 1998.

———. *Summer at the Lake.* New York: Tom Doherty, 1997.

———. *Younger than Springtime.* New York: Tom Doherty, 1999.

10

L'Envoi

Certainly one of the most versatile of American authors, Andrew Greeley, having written over one hundred and thirty-five books and with more than twenty million copies of his fiction in print, is a master, both of creative writing and analytical discursive prose. His nonfiction writings, with the tremendous amount of data he has amassed as a social scientist and the wealth of knowledge and wisdom he has acquired as a priest, serve often as spring-boards or points of departure for his creative writing which is highly imaginative, innovative, and has the serious purpose of the illumination of his readers. His fictional works can be classified as novels of ideas, for he writes in the tradition of Honoré de Balzac (1799–1850) who is credited with being the originator of the genre. Other authors who have written in the same Balzacian tradition include, Léon Bloy (1846–1971), Georges Bernanos (1888–1948), François Mauriac (1885–1970), and Julien Green (1900–1998), to name a few who were favorites of Greeley in his early years. Many similarities exist between the fiction of Balzac and Greeley, as was observed in the introduction to this work. Points of comparison are also evident between the work of Greeley and others who have written in this same tradition. Since Greeley's fiction is thought provoking, intellectually stimulating, awash with his ideas about almost everything, and intended to illumine the reader, it cannot be classified as popular fiction. Popular fiction is written solely to entertain and amuse.

Andrew Greeley's divine and human comedy, while focusing on the Chicago Irish, the successful and upscale descendants of very poor immigrants, portrays the manners, ideas, and conflicts of society at large and of Catholic society in particular in twentieth-century America. In the next millennium, people will be able to read Greeley's fiction to obtain a well-informed depiction of life in the time period covered by the novels. Greeley's knowledge of popular culture is extensive and he displays it in every story. Deeply inspired and strongly motivated by a love for truth, he never hesitates to uncover the sins and failings of secular society as well as Catholic, not for the reader's amusement, but in hopes of sparking a reform and changing his world for the better. The sociohistorical dimension of the comedy, based on Greeley sociological expertise, adds to the literary value of the work, which is a serious, but at the same time a comical depiction of the world in which he lives. In all Greeley's fiction, life is a mixture of comedy and tragedy. Sometimes even violence snuffs out the lives of characters. However, in what Greeley terms "the great cosmic joke" life always triumphs over death in a divine comedy which has a gloriously happy ending. Sparkling with Greeley's vivacious and effervescent humor, the novels almost invariably end, as all good comedies should, with the marriage of lovers.

A consummate satirist and an eminent moralist who never preaches but rather illustrates the evils he attacks, often with caustic wit, Greeley permits the reader to draw the conclusion that although there is much wrong with society and the Church, there is tremendous hope for renewal. Always striving to reprove and correct those who most need it and are most apt to avoid the challenge of change, Greeley delineates the sin, weakness, inadequacy, ineptitude, and incompetence of the various types of men and women in our society. The greatest evils that he uncovers are angrily scrutinized, denounced, and often jeered in derision and laughed to scorn in his blistering satire. Among the many aspects of society that are satirized are the media, academia, the legal system and law enforcement, the Mafia, militant feminism, and the Catholic Church. It must be made very clear that Greeley never attacks Catholic doctrine—he is strictly orthodox when it comes to faith. What he satirizes is the style of ecclesiastical administration; theologians who abandon basic Christian teaching, such as belief in the resurrection of Christ; priests and nuns who confuse temporal and contingent political goals with the transcendent and the absolute in religious revelation; power-hungry Vatican bureaucrats; financial scandals; and the abundance of sociopaths who have made it through the seminaries and have risen even to becoming members of the hierarchy, among other similar things. At times the satire is black and caustic as the novels hold up to ridicule individual, institutional, and societal failings. Although the novels are excellent portraits of society, both secular and clerical, and the people who inhabit it, as one would expect from an eminent and distinguished sociologist, Greeley the priest is also ever present in his fiction, in which the workings of the human soul are laid bare and probed. Only a well-experienced priest who is skilled in the cure of souls could create such fiction in which the human psyche is so well analyzed and portrayed. Very astutely Greeley draws on the great learning and wisdom which he has acquired through years of research as a social scientist and as a priest to depict society and individuals as they really are. He knows the human heart with all its vagaries, meanderings, deceitfulness, and capacity for evil, as well as its hunger and thirst for life and heroic virtue. Greeley's unique blending of social science and religion makes his stories timeless and universal in appeal.

In the "comedies of grace," as Greeley refers to his stories, God is the great comedian and always the main character who writes straight with crooked lines, bringing a happy ending with her "cosmic joke" to each story in which life triumphs over death, love over hatred and joy and good humor drive out despair and depression.

Among the themes that recur in Greeley's stories, note the following. Greeley consistently uses the metaphor of human love in all its dimensions, including sexual, to demonstrate what the love of God is like, showing that human passion is a sacrament and an instrument of divine passion. In employing the theme of the search for the Holy Grail, Greeley demonstrates that man finds God when he finds his grail, his woman, who is almost invariably a very strong determined lady. When the man finds his grail and God after a long search, he learns that they have been pursuing him, even more vigorously that he sought them. By means of the love they experience, the male protagonists all learn to love and find the tender God dwelling within their hearts

Another recurring theme in Greeley's fiction is that of having a person in middle life, most often a male, usually disillusioned, often agnostic having lost faith, returning to the neighborhood that was home many years in the past. In returning, the character encounters many problems and usually a mystery that must be solved before happiness can be found. And happiness is found as the character succeeds in finding his holy grail, which is another way of saying the character finds a mate and God, the two being inseparably bound together. The Church helps to smooth out the difficulties the lovers experience through the ministry of people who are correlatives for the Church.

Greeley's stories tend to center around Christmas and Easter. Christmas is very important to Greeley because it tells us of the God who loves us like a mother and of the Mother of Jesus who is the transparency through which we see God and who is a metaphor for God's love. In these stories Greeley extrapolates on his religious theories on the androgyny of God, which he expounds in *The Mary Myth on the Femininity of God*. Greeley postulates a corollary to Mary's being a metaphor for God by saying that all women should be metaphors of God for the men who love them. This is especially illustrated in the story of Eileen and Red Kane, *Patience of a Saint*.

Since most of Greeley's characters are resurrection people it is fitting that many of his stories cluster around Easter and the Feast of the Resurrection. The characters rise from the ruins they have made of their lives to new hope, new faith, and new love, as do, for example, the Farrells in the Passover trilogy.

Almost all Greeley's novels contain an exciting mystery that the characters must solve in order to find peace with themselves and with God. The adventures that occur in regard to the mystery often take on mythic proportions as the male protagonist fights gallantly for the woman he loves.

One of the fine qualities of Greeley's fiction is that he uses literary genres in innovative and highly creative ways. Even in his speculative fiction, his characters develop. They are not the same at the end of the story as they were at the beginning. This is contrary to the usual practice in speculative fiction where the characters are flat, undeveloped, unchanging throughout the entire book in which emphasis is put on the story line. In his speculative fiction, Greeley makes ample use of the various techniques employed by the masters of the genre. In all his fiction he demonstrates an awareness of literary techniques, devices, and conventions. His use of symbolism and metaphor make for a rich and polysemous narrative. His ability to write equally well in a variety of genres is displayed in his legends, myths, romances, novels, science fiction, fantasy, *roman fleuve*, mystery and detective stories, poetry, and operatic librettos. He has even created a new genre that of the sociological apocalyptic novel, based on the idea of the sociological model. *White Smoke* is not a sociological model per se; the book does not contain the empirical data to support it as a model. It is rather a simulation.

Finally, Greeley's prose is rich and varied with his language colorful and humorous. He can fall into Irish dialect and sprinkle the story with colloquialism of the Irish, including their scatological vocabulary. The language of teens flows often through his pages. Some of the funniest dialogue is that which takes place between a member of the Mafia and one of Greeley's protagonists. He is also able to talk the language of the Vatican. Some of his sentences are truly picturesque with his phrases creating striking pictures in the reader's imagination. Memorable characters emerge with just a single sentence or two depicting a caricature that the reader cannot forget.

With his characters reappearing in one novel after another, much in the same way Balzac's do in *La comédie humaine*, Greeley has created an entire society, as Balzac did. But instead of being called simply a human comedy, Greeley's comedy must be described as the divine and human comedy of Andrew Greeley, since our author is both social scientist and priest.

Selected Bibliography

Balzac, Honoré de. *La comédie humaine.* Paris: Gallimard, 1952.
——. *Correspondence of Honoré de Balzac.* Trans. C. Lamb Kenney. 2 vols. London: Richard Bentley, 1878.
Bellemin-Noël, Jean. "Dès formes fantastiques aux thèmes fantasmatiques." *Littérature* 2 (1971): 103–18.
——. "Notes sur le fantastique (Textes de Théophile Gautier)." *Littérature* 8 (1972): 3–23.
Bernstein, Carl and Marco Politi. *His Holiness: John Paul II and the Hidden History of Our Time.* New York: Doubleday, 1996.
Bertault, Philippe. *Balzac and the Human Comedy.* Trans. Richard Monges. New York: New York UP, 1963.
Dante, Alighieri. *Dante's Convivio.* Trans. William W. Jackson. Oxford: Clarendon, 1909.
——. *A Translation of Dante's Eleven Letters.* Trans. C. S. Latham. London: Riverside, 1891.
Fletcher, Angus. *Allegory: The Theory of a Symbolic Mode.* Ithaca: Cornell UP, 1964.
Frye, Northrop *Anatomy of Criticism: Four Essays.* Princeton: Princeton UP, 1957.
——. *The Secular Scripture: A Study of the Structure of Romance,* Cambridge: Harvard UP, 1976.
Gougaud, Dom Louis. Les chrétientés celtiques. Paris: Gabalda, 1911.
Greeley, Andrew M. *Angel Fire.* New York: Warner, 1988.
——. *All about Women.* New York: TOR, 1990.
——. *Angel Light.* New York: Tom Doherty, 1995.
——. *The Angels of September.* New York: Warner, 1986.
——. *Ascent into Hell.* New York: Warner, 1983.
——. *The Cardinal Sins.* New York: Warner, 1981.
——. *The Cardinal Virtues.* New York: Warner, 1990.

————. *The Catholic Myth: The Behavior and Beliefs of American Catholics*. New York: Scribner's, 1990.

————. *Christmas Wedding*. New York: Tom Doherty, 2000

————. *Confessions of a Parish Priest: An Autobiography*. New York: Simon and Schuster, 1986.

————. *Contract with an Angel*. New York: Tom Doherty, 1998.

————. *Death and Beyond*. Chicago: Thomas More Press, 1976.

————. *Death in April*. New York: McGraw-Hill, 1980.

————. *Everything You Wanted to Know about the Catholic Church but Were Too Pious to Ask*. Chicago: Thomas More, 1978.

————. *Faithful Attraction: Discovering Intimacy, Love, and Fidelity in American Marriage*. New York: Tom Doherty Associates, 1991.

————. *Fall from Grace*. New York: Putnam, 1993.

————. *The Final Planet*. New York: Warner, 1987.

————. *God Game*. New York: Warner, 1986.

————. *God in Popular Culture*. Chicago: Thomas More, 1988.

————. *Lord of the Dance*. Boston: G. K. Hall, 1985.

————. *Love Affair: A Prayer Journal*. New York: Crossroad, 1992.

————. *Love Song*. New York: Warner, 1989.

————. *The Magic Cup: An Irish Legend*. New York: McGraw-Hill, 1979.

————. *Making of the Popes 1978: The Politics of Intrigue in the Vatican*. Kansas City: Andrews and McMeel, 1978.

————. *The Myths of Religion*. New York: Warner, 1989.

————. *A Midwinter's Tale*. New York: Tom Doherty, 1998.

————. *The Myths of Religion*. New York: Warner, 1989.

————. *An Occasion of Sin*. New York: Putnam, 1988.

————. *The Patience of a Saint*. New York: Warner, 1987.

————. *A Piece of My Mind on Just about Everything*. Garden City: Doubleday, 1983.

————. *Religion as Poetry*. New Brunswick: Transaction, 1996.

————. *Rite of Spring*. New York: Warner, 1987.

————. *Saint Valentine's Night*. New York: Warner, 1989.

————. *The Search for Maggie Ward*. New York: Warner, 1991.

————. *Sexual Intimacy: Love and Play*. Chicago: Thomas More, 1973. 1975. New York: Warner, 1988.

————. *Star Bright! A Christmas Story*. New York: Doherty, 1997.

————. *Summer at the Lake*. New York: Forge, 1997.

————. *Thy Brother's Wife*. New York: Warner, 1982.

————. *Virgin and Martyr*. New York: Warner, 1985.

————. *Wages of Sin*. New York: Putnam's, 1992.

————. *When Life Hurts*. New York: Doubleday, 1989.

————. *White Smoke*. New York: Tom Doherty, 1994.

————. *Year of Grace: A Spiritual Journey*. Chicago: Thomas More, 1990.

————. *Younger than Springtime*. New York: Tom Doherty, 1999.

————. and Mary G. Durkin. *A Church to Come Home To*. Chicago: Thomas More, 1982.

————. and Jacob Neusner. *The Bible and Us: A Priest and a Rabbi Read the Scripture Together*. New York: Warner, 1990.

Immerwahr, Raymond. "Romantic Irony and Romantic Arabesque Prior to Romanticism."

German Quarterly 42 1969: 665–685.

The Jerusalem Bible. Garden City: Doubleday, 1966.

John Paul II. *Ut Unum Sint*. *<http://vatican.va/holy_father/john_paul_ii/encyclicals>* May 25, 1995.

Kayser, Wolfgang. *The Grotesque in Art and Literature*. Trans. Ulrich Weisstein. Bloomington: Indiana UP, 1963.

Kierkegaard, Søren. *The Concept of Irony with Constant Reference to Socrates*. Trans. Lee. M. Capel. London: Collins, 1966.

Le Roux, Françoise. *Les Druides*. Paris: Presses Universitaires, 1961.

Lussky, Alfred Edwin. *Tieck's Romantic Irony*. Chapel Hill: U of North Carolina P, 1932.

Markdale, Jean. *Celtic Civilization*. London: Gordon and Cremonesi, 1978

Marx, Karl and Engels, Friedrich. *Literature and Art: Selections from their Writings*. New York, 1947.

Pasquariello, Ronald D., Ed. *Conversations with Andrew Greeley*. Boston: Quinlan, 1988.

Rabkin, Eric S. *The Fantastic in Literature*. Princeton: Princeton UP, 1976.

Randal, John Herman, Jr. *The Career of Philosophy from the German Enlightenment to the Age of Darwin*. New York: Columbia UP, 1965.

Richter, Jean Paul Friedrich. "Vorschule der Aesthetik," in *Werke*. Ed. Norbert Miller. Munich: Hanser, 1963.

Schlegel, Friedrich. *Kritische Schriften*. Munich: Hanser, 1964. (Translation mine).

Schlobin, Roger C. *The Literature of Fantasy: A Comprehensive, Annotated Bibliography of Modern Fantasy Fiction*. New York: Garland, 1979.

Scott, Sir Walter. "On the Supernatural in Fictitious Composition," in *Essays on Chivalry, Romance, and the Drama*. London: Frederick Warne and Co, 1887.

Shafer, Ingrid. Ed. *Andrew Greeley's World: An Anthology of Critical Essays*, 1986–1988. New York: Warner, 1989: 111–118.

Sprague, John, ed. *An Andrew Greeley Reader*. Vol 1. Chicago: Thomas More, 1987.

Todorov, Tzetvan. *Introduction à la littérature fantastique*. Paris: Editions du Seuil, 1970.

Urquhart, Gordon. *The Pope's Armada*. London: Corgi, 1996.

Walzel, Oskar. *German Romanticism*. Trans. Alma Elise Lussky. New York: Putnam's 1932

Wellek, René. *Confrontations: Studies in the Intellectual and Literary Relations between Germany, England, and the United States during the Nineteenth Century*. Princeton: Princeton UP, 1965.

———. *A History of Modern Criticism, 1750–1950*. Vol. 2. New Haven: Yale UP, 1955.

Wilcoxson, Kirby. "The Sociologist as Storyteller: Science and Fiction in the Novels of Andrew Greeley." *Andrew Greeley's World: An Anthology of Critical Essays, 1986–1988*. Ed. Ingrid Shafer. New York: Warner, 1989. 111–18.

Index

About the Author

ALLIENNE R. BECKER is Professor Emerita of the Department of Foreign Languages at Lock Haven University of Pennsylvania where she taught Comparative Literature courses. Her previous books include *The Lost Worlds Romance* (1992) and *Visions of the Fantastic* (1996), both available from Greenwood Press.